CCCC STUDIES IN WRITING & RHETORIC
Edited by Victor Villanueva, Washington State University

The aim of the CCCC Studies in Writing & Rhetoric (SWR) Series is to influence how we think about language in action and especially how writing gets taught at the college level. The methods of studies vary from the critical to historical to linguistic to ethnographic, and their authors draw on work in various fields that inform composition—including rhetoric, communication, education, discourse analysis, psychology, cultural studies, and literature. Their focuses are similarly diverse—ranging from individual writers and teachers, to work on classrooms and communities and curricula, to analyses of the social, political, and material contexts of writing and its teaching.

SWR was one of the first scholarly book series to focus on the teaching of writing. It was established in 1980 by the Conference on College Composition and Communication (CCCC) in order to promote research in the emerging field of writing studies. As our field has grown, the research sponsored by SWR has continued to articulate the commitment of CCCC to supporting the work of writing teachers as reflective practitioners and intellectuals.

We are eager to identify influential work in writing and rhetoric as it emerges. We thus ask authors to send us project proposals that clearly situate their work in the field and show how they aim to redirect our ongoing conversations about writing and its teaching. Proposals should include an overview of the project, a brief annotated table of contents, and a sample chapter. They should not exceed 10,000 words.

To submit a proposal, please register as an author at www.editorialmanager.com/nctebp. Once registered, follow the steps to submit a proposal (be sure to choose SWR Book Proposal from the drop-down list of article submission types).

SWR Editorial Advisory Board

Victor Villanueva, SWR Editor, Washington State University
Anna Plemons, Associate Editor, Washington State University
Frances Condon, University of Waterloo
Ellen Cushman, Northeastern University
Deborah Holdstein, Columbia College Chicago
Asao Inoue, University of Washington Tacoma
Jay Jordan, University of Utah
Min-Zhan Lu, University of Louisville
Paula Mathieu, Boston College
Nedra Reynolds, University of Rhode Island
Jacqueline Rhodes, Michigan State University
Eileen Schell, Syracuse University
Jody Shipka, University of Maryland, Baltimore County
Vershawn Ashanti Young, University of Waterloo

Reframing the Relational

A Pedagogical Ethic for Cross-Curricular Literacy Work

Sandra L. Tarabochia
University of Oklahoma

Conference on College Composition and Communication

National Council of Teachers of English

Staff Editor: Bonny Graham
Series Editor: Victor Villanueva
Interior Design: Mary Rohrer
Cover Design: Mary Rohrer and Lynn Weckhorst

NCTE Stock Number: 39783; eStock Number: 39790
ISBN 978-0-8141-3978-3; eISBN 978-0-8141-3979-0

Copyright © 2017 by the Conference on College Composition and Communication of the National Council of Teachers of English.

All rights reserved. No part of this publication may be reproduced or transmitted in any form or by any means, electronic or mechanical, including photocopy, or any information storage and retrieval system, without permission from the copyright holder. Printed in the United States of America.

It is the policy of NCTE in its journals and other publications to provide a forum for the open discussion of ideas concerning the content and the teaching of English and the language arts. Publicity accorded to any particular point of view does not imply endorsement by the Executive Committee, the Board of Directors, or the membership at large, except in announcements of policy, where such endorsement is clearly specified.

NCTE provides equal employment opportunity (EEO) to all staff members and applicants for employment without regard to race, color, religion, sex, national origin, age, physical, mental or perceived handicap/disability, sexual orientation including gender identity or expression, ancestry, genetic information, marital status, military status, unfavorable discharge from military service, pregnancy, citizenship status, personal appearance, matriculation or political affiliation, or any other protected status under applicable federal, state, and local laws.

Every effort has been made to provide current URLs and email addresses, but because of the rapidly changing nature of the Web, some sites and addresses may no longer be accessible.

Library of Congress Cataloging-in-Publication Data

Names: Tarabochia, Sandra, author.
Title: Reframing the relational : a pedagogical ethic for cross-curricular literacy work / Dr. Sandra Tarabochia, University of Oklahoma, Conference on College Composition and Communication.
Description: Urbana, IL : National Council of Teachers of English, 2017 | Series: Studies in writing & rhetoric | Includes bibliographical references and index.
Identifiers: LCCN 2017023504 (print) | LCCN 2017041297 (ebook) | ISBN 9780814139790 | ISBN 9780814139783 (pbk.)
Subjects: LCSH: English language—Composition and exercises—Study and teaching (Higher)—United States. | English language—Rhetoric—Study and teaching (Higher)—United States. | Interdisciplinary approach in education—United States.
Classification: LCC PE1405.U6 (ebook) | LCC PE1405.U6 T33 2017 (print) | DDC 808/.042071173—dc23
LC record available at https://lccn.loc.gov/2017023504

*For Craig
and
for Gabe
who sustain me*

CONTENTS

Acknowledgments ix

1. Cross-Curricular Literacy Work as Pedagogical Activity 1
2. Exploding the Dilemma of Expertise 29
3. Change as Transformative Learning 69
4. Possibility of Play: Teaching and Learning in Liminal Spaces 108
5. A Guiding Ethic for Cross-Curricular Literacy Work 145

Appendixes : Discursive Moves for Enacting Principles of a Pedagogical Ethic for CCL Work 175

Notes 179

References 181

Index 201

Author 209

ACKNOWLEDGMENTS

THIS BOOK IS ABOUT TEACHING AND LEARNING. I am profoundly grateful to the many people who have joined me in these mutual activities.

At the heart of this book are the eleven participants who so generously agreed to let me in on their conversations and reflect openly about their experiences as writers, teachers, learners, scholars, and conversation partners. You've taught me so much.

During my time at the University of Nebraska–Lincoln, Amy Goodburn, Shari Stenberg, Margaret Latta, and Chris Gallagher encouraged my curiosity, reflection, and inquiry—and reminded me when it was time to start making sense of things. My gratitude goes also to those who were there from the beginning: Eric Duncan Turley, Alison Friedow, Mike Kelly, Lesley Bartlett, Jessica Rivera-Mueller, and especially Whitney Douglas, who came through with last minute Skype visits, Idaho hikes, and collaborative dinking when it mattered most.

Thanks to Christiane Donahue and the distinguished facilitators of the 2013 Dartmouth Summer Seminar for Composition Research, especially Charles Bazerman, Chris Anson, and Neal Lerner, who patiently guided me to find the research story I had to tell.

And special thanks to members of my Dartmouth cohort, Rachael Cayley, Talinn Phillips, and Megan Titus, who have painstakingly responded to many versions of each chapter and to vague ideas before they became chapters.

Angela, Julie, and Kristy, the amazing women of the Friday morning run/write group, inspire me to reach for ambitious goals on the trail and on the page. Your camaraderie makes all the difference.

I am grateful to my former and current colleagues in the Composition, Rhetoric, and Literacy program at the University of Oklahoma; thanks to Chris Carter, Catherine Hobbs, Susan Kates, Roxanne Mountford, Kathleen Welch, Bill Endres, Will Kurlinkus, and Gabi Rios for their faith, support, and intellectual community.

Thanks, too, to Shannon Madden and Jerry Stinnett. In our long conversations about writing curriculum and pedagogy, you modeled genuine commitment to teaching and learning.

My deepest gratitude to Michele Eodice, who convinced me from the beginning to be bold and brave. Your enthusiasm for the project propelled me through moments of doubt, and your big-picture thinking (still) reminds me that the work is worth doing.

The research at the heart of this book was supported by travel grants and summer fellowships from the University of Oklahoma College of Arts and Sciences.

I am grateful to CCCC Studies in Writing & Rhetoric reviewers, including Rebecca Nowacek, who offered provocative feedback that inspired and challenged me, and to Victor Villanueva whose sustained commitment to the book inspired me to persist. Sincere thanks, as well, to Bonny Graham in the NCTE Books Program and copy editor Josh Rosenberg.

And most of all, thanks to my family—the Doughtys and the Tarabochias. The spring break visits and grandma camps made this book possible. My parents, Linda and Tony, offered sympathetic arms and ears, and loving support for my career in "hooey." Thanks to my brother, Marty, for your quiet, playful presence. And to my sister, Robin, in solidarity. Our morning conversations helped me keep perspective and take life in stride. And finally, my heartfelt love and gratitude to Craig and Gabe, the source of my energy and spirit and hope, for forcing me to dance in the kitchen. You make me a better researcher, writer, teacher, and person.

1

Cross-Curricular Literacy Work as Pedagogical Activity

TALK ABOUT WRITING AMONG FACULTY FROM DIFFERENT disciplines is the cornerstone of Writing Across the Curriculum (WAC)/Writing in the Disciplines (WID) initiatives (Bazerman et al., 2005; Russell, 2002). While WAC/WID efforts today take many forms—writing-intensive (WI) requirements; peer review of teaching projects; writing fellows programs; co-teaching opportunities; departmental curriculum mapping, assessment, and design; first-year writing seminars—cross-disciplinary interactions among faculty remain central. Indeed, relationships between writing specialists and faculty in other disciplines continue to be recognized as an essential component of cross-curricular literacy (CCL) work (Condon & Rutz, 2012; Jablonski, 2006; Jacobs, 2007; Kuriloff, 1992, p. 94; Paretti, McNair, Belanger, & George, 2009).[1] At the same time, the challenge of initiating and sustaining interdisciplinary relationships in CCL contexts is well documented (Kaufer & Young, 1993; Lillis & Rai, 2011; McCarthy & Walvoord, 1988; McConlogue, Mitchell, & Peake, 2012; Paretti & Powell, 2009; Soliday, 2011). Meeting these challenges matters now more than ever as trends toward globalization and internationalization in higher education and the professional world (Gustafsson et al., 2011) reinforce the need for college graduates to communicate across disciplinary lines. While stakeholders recognize the need for writing instruction across the curriculum (Addison & McGee, 2010; Thaiss & Porter, 2010), the current climate of higher education tests commitments to cross-curricular writing initiatives. If postsecondary educators are to recruit and retain students and help them develop complex literacies to navigate a multidisciplinary world, we must cultivate what Myra Strober (2011) calls interdisciplinary "habits of thought"—ways of "thinking, presenting, interacting, and questioning" and relationship building across disciplinary lines (p. 37). Toward that end, this book is about how faculty from different disciplines can engage more productively in conversations about (teaching) writing.

Such conversations take place in the context of increasingly diverse CCL initiatives that involve a range of consultation dynamics. Foundational WAC/WID faculty development models such as the workshop (Fulwiler, 1981; Magnotto & Stout, 1992), collaborative research (McCarthy & Walvoord, 1988), collaborative teaching (Kuriloff, 1992), and embedded writing fellows (Haring-Smith, 1992; Hughes & Hall, 2008; Mullin, 2001) remain valuable. More recently, Michael Carter (2003) developed an outcomes-based approach in which writing specialists work with groups of disciplinary faculty to make explicit their goals for student learning and recognize their expertise in (teaching) writing in their disciplines (p. 5), an approach that inspired the University of Minnesota's well-known Writing Enriched Curriculum Program ("University of Minnesota WEC Home Page," n.d.). In a similar vein, Anson and Dannels (2009) describe the collaborative process of composing "program profiles" by conducting individual and group consultations focused on formative assessment of Communication Across the Curriculum (CAC) initiatives within departments. Paul Anderson's work with small groups of faculty in learning communities at Miami of Ohio (Rutz, 2004), the many approaches to working with faculty writers in Geller and Eodice's (2013) recent collection, and the "distributed consultancy model" involving writing specialists, disciplinary faculty, and librarians (Harrington, MacKenzie, & DeSanto, 2016) further evidence the breadth of CCL consultation dynamics. Condon, Iverson, Manduca, Rutz, and Willett (2016) illustrate how a rich blend of formal and self-directed writing-focused faculty development efforts—including writing portfolio assessment (see also Rutz & Grawe, 2009), teaching workshops, summer course development grant programs, and campuswide initiatives on topics such as critical thinking and quantitative inquiry—have implications for faculty as well as student learning. As these examples suggest, configurations of CCL consultations vary across efforts and contexts, each dynamic sharing commonalities with the others and creating unique challenges and opportunities for cross-disciplinary communication.

A rich body of WAC/WID scholarship contributes to these efforts in important ways but rarely addresses day-to-day interactions among writing specialists and faculty in other disciplines. Research rooted in genre theory (Soliday, 2011) and textual analysis of writing assignments (Melzer, 2014) speaks to pressing programmatic and curricular issues. Studies draw on surveys, retrospective narrative accounts, and interviews with faculty to create useful portraits of challenges and benefits of cross-disciplinary collaborations, the forces enabling and constraining relationships, and various approaches experienced practitioners take to their work (Kaufer & Young, 1993; McCarthy & Walvoord, 1988; Walvoord, Hunt, Dowling, & McMahon, 1997). While researchers usefully identify forces impacting cross-disciplinary relations (Jacobs, 2007; Paretti et al., 2009) and attempt to codify writing specialists' tacit expertise (Jablonski, 2006), few attend to face-to-face exchanges so vital for cultivating productive cross-disciplinary relationships. As a result, practitioners find little guidance in *how* to engage productively in cross-disciplinary conversations about (teaching) writing.

Traditional approaches to WAC/WID consultations emerge implicitly in the history and professional discourse of the field and tend to be associated with stages of the WAC movement. Jablonski (2006) maps a rather linear progression of stages across time, each perspective and corresponding interactional practices responding to needs of writing specialists and disciplinary faculty in particular historical moments and addressing shortcomings of the previous stage. For example, stage one is associated with missionary models in which writing specialists seek to convert "content area" instructors to student-centered, expressivist practices with "messianic zeal" (Jablonski, 2006, p. 183). While the approach may have been valuable, even necessary, for launching a fledgling WAC movement, second-stage efforts sought ways to grow and sustain vulnerable programs (McLeod, 1989). Born out of social constructionism, stage two perspectives criticized writing specialists for "colonizing" colleagues, urging instead an anthropological stance in which disciplinary rhetorical conventions are studied in order to socialize students into disciplinary discourse communities (Bazerman, 1991; Jablonski, 2006, p. 186; Waldo, 1996). In turn, stage three critical approaches, exemplified by Mahala and Swilky (1994), LeCourt (1996), Malinowitz (1998), and Villanueva (2001), bemoaned the "conservative tendencies of both WAC and WID" and suggested writing specialists have a responsibility to take on the role of cultural critic advocating for students' agency and educational access (Jablonski, 2006, p. 184). For his part, Jablonski forwards a "more professional" fourth stage model in which writing specialists "foregroun[d] our role as rhetoricians . . . who assume an ideological and ethical responsibility for teaching others the value of rhetorical knowledgeability" (p. 189, 190). Although the stages do not represent static, inflexible models, especially in practice, Bergmann (1998) and Jablonski (2006) argue they can become "reified into fixed, prescriptive categories," the maintenance of which "bears little resemblance to the work of CCL specialists" (Jablonski, 2006, p. 187). They lack a coherent underlying philosophy, rooted in empirical understanding of professional practice, that resonates with the "ontology" or "way of being" characterizing faculty interactions in CCL contexts (Paretti, 2011). As a result, existing models may fail to help writing specialists adapt to shifting, unpredictable circumstances.

As Condon and Rutz (2012) point out, and the many types of consulting outlined above illustrate, "WAC as a phenomenon does not possess a single, identifiable structure; instead, it varies in its development and its manifestation from campus to campus" (p. 358). As a grassroots movement, WAC treasures local variety, but variation can be difficult to navigate when professional literature does not reflect the rich, messy materiality of CCL work. Jablonski (2006) observes, "[O]ur professional discourse socializes us to accept [the] competing positions" represented in "paradigm wars" (p. 185). Various approaches become "subject positions demarcating identity and professional values" leaving (particularly new) writing specialists hopping between "camps" in order to respond to the complex situations we find in the field (p. 185). A study that helps us better understand the dynamics of cross-disciplinary talk is needed to help writing specialists more effectively adjust their strategies for building relationships and revising writing curricula in ever-shifting circumstances.

In that spirit, I suggest we break the linear progression of stages and models of CCL work and seek out a more dynamic and flexible vision to guide our practice. The nature of CCL work calls for a guiding ethic, a spirit, habit of mind, or set of philosophical principles that is coherent enough to be useful and malleable enough to address the complexity of our daily work. A guiding ethic is apt given the unique challenges CCL interactions present. For one thing, the impetus for conversations—often top-down administrative mandates or faculty frustration with student writing—can generate conflicting attitudes and expectations. Further, institutional and departmental politics can complicate relational dynamics among conversation partners. Various epistemological assumptions undergirding disciplinary ideologies can make it difficult to find common ground (Gere, Swofford, Silver, & Pugh, 2015). Moreover, faculty conversations in WAC/WID contexts often exist at the intersection of several types of professional practice including professional development, university service, interdisciplinary collaborative research, faculty learning communities, and teacher development. Each practice involves different assumptions, challenges, and opportunities participants must navigate.

Under these unique circumstances, conversations among writing specialists and disciplinary faculty constitute what Karen Tracy (1997) calls "dilemmatic situation[s]—communicative occasion[s] involving tensions and contradiction" (p. 4). Acknowledging the dilemmatic nature of CCL conversations can make challenges seem less "diffuse and hard to articulate," make the inner workings of conversations more "sensible," and make the moral and/or practical intentions behind communicative action seem less obscure (Tracy, 1997, p. 5). The dilemmatic nature of CCL conversations reinforces the need for a guiding ethic that responds to recurring tensions faculty face in conversations about (teaching) writing and provides creative discursive practices to address key communication challenges. The purpose of this book is to flesh out an ethic for faculty interactions in CCL contexts that resonates with and expands our understanding of the ontology of CCL work. A guiding ethic will help writing specialists adjust communication strategies to foster productive conversations with faculty in other disciplines, build sustainable relationships, and revise writing curricula amid complicated, ever-changing dynamics.

METHODOLOGY

A guiding ethic must be rooted in the conversational realities of practitioners. In the spirit of sociolinguistic approaches that study how talk constructs relationships among people, disciplines, and institutions (Black, 1998, p. 20), I examine recorded spoken exchanges among writing specialists and disciplinary content experts to capture discursive strategies of interaction. I ask: What challenges to cross-disciplinary communication do faculty face in CCL contexts? How do dilemmas manifest discursively through interaction? How do participants discursively respond to the challenges they face? How might studying discursive practices of faculty in CCL contexts help others approach cross-disciplinary conversations more productively?

My methodology is inspired by Karen Tracy's (1995, 2005) action-implicative discourse analysis theory (AIDA), a blend of interpretive and critical approaches to inquiry, "melding the goal of constructing a rich understanding of how a practice operates (interpretive) with the goal of aiding a practice's participants in reflecting about how they might act more wisely (critical)" (Tracy, 2008, p. 150). Embracing this dual purpose, I identify the discursive moves that characterize faculty interactions in CCL contexts, not to determine best practices, but to stimulate reflection about how we conceptualize and engage in cross-disciplinary interactions. In focusing on writing-related talk, I join a rich tradition in composition studies of using discourse-based methods to study interpersonal exchanges around writing (Mortensen, 1992). I take a slightly different tack in that I do not focus on talk that "assumes *writing* as its primary object" (Mortensen, 1992, p. 116) because I am not interested in discerning relationships among reading, writing, speaking, and listening practices in relation to written texts. Instead, I focus on conversations about (teaching) writing in CCL contexts as a form of professional practice that is increasingly prevalent and uniquely challenging. My goal is to enhance this practice by identifying the communicative intentions, strategies, and implications of the discursive moves faculty use to interact with one another.

Theoretical Framework
Examination of conversations among writing specialists and disciplinary faculty demands what Karen Tracy (1997), citing Gary Bateson, calls a "situational frame" or "set of expectations about the nature of an occasion, the social meaning of a unit of interaction" (p. 6). As Tracy (1997) points out, the choice of frame is not trivial. How we conceptualize professional practices impacts how we understand the difficulties communicators face and the extent to which we can generate communication strategies that respond to the nature of the practice (Tracy, 1997). I use pedagogy as an interpretive frame for understanding CCL conversations among faculty, defining pedagogy as an inquiry-based process of collaborative meaning-making undertaken by teacher-learners (Gallagher, 2002; Kameen, 2000; Lee, 2000; Qualley, 1997; Stenberg, 2005). As opposed to traditional orientations that view pedagogy as a hierarchical, hegemonic, classroom-bound, one-directional transaction from teacher to student, I understand pedagogy as "ongoing learning, study, and development" by individuals-in-collaboration in a range of contexts (Stenberg, 2005, p. xviii). Inspired by Gallagher's (2002) descriptions of pedagogy-centered alliances, Brian Lord's (1994) notion of "critical colleagueship," and Anne Ellen Geller's (2009) call to approach "WAC work through the lens of Peter Elbow's 'methodological believing'" (p. 28), my framework treats CCL conversations as pedagogical opportunities for faculty to inhabit one another's beliefs, to listen more deliberately. In

choosing pedagogy as a frame, I take seriously calls for compositionists to "make pedagogy a central disciplined activity" (Stenberg, 2005, p. xviii; Gallagher, 2002; Gallagher, Gray, & Stenberg, 2002) and extend the call to writing specialists in CCL contexts. In her introduction to *Professing and Pedagogy*, Shari Stenberg (2005) outlines several characteristics of a sophisticated view of pedagogy that anchor my analytical framework: Pedagogy recognizes the interplay of theory and practice; pedagogy is ongoing, requiring a sustained commitment to reflexivity; and pedagogy is made and remade with each encounter among teacher-learners who are changing constantly (xviii). In other words, pedagogy is epistemic, reflexive, and relational. I will briefly elaborate on each dimension and explain how it works as a lens for understanding faculty interactions in CCL contexts.

Pedagogy Is Epistemic

Pedagogy, as I conceptualize it, is not a matter of transmitting or translating knowledge; rather I embrace a "complex understanding of pedagogy as shared knowledge building" (Gallagher, 2002, p. xvi). Individuals participate in pedagogical relationships when they focus less on what they know and more on what meanings they can generate by putting their own experiences and partial understandings in conversation with others'. As Gallagher (2002) puts it: "pedagogy is what happens when people seek to produce knowledge together" (p. xvi). Applying a pedagogical view to CCL conversations, then, anticipates collaborative meaning-making rather than transmission of knowledge. It perceives writing specialists and content experts as both teachers and learners, resists expert/novice designations, and expects cooperative knowledge building. It does not presume participants will merely tolerate or uncritically celebrate alternative disciplinary discourses, but that participants will "*engage* those other discourses, making them a central part of [their] evolving work" (Gallagher, 2002, p. 165).

Highlighting the epistemic dimension of pedagogy (Berlin, 1987) acknowledges that "subject matter" is not incidental but actively shapes and is shaped by interactions among learners (Gallagher, 2002). Emphasizing the Deweyian spirit of this relationship, Gallagher (2002) holds that "the subject matter *matters* only to the extent that teachers and learners can engage it, use, and ultimately reconstruct it" (p. xvii). He goes so far as to claim that "pedagogy *produces* disciplinary knowledge," as "teachers and learners collaborate in the construction of their objects of study" (Gallagher, 2002, p. xvii). In this view, writing specialists and faculty in other disciplines are not deliverers or receivers of the subject matter at the heart of CCL work but co-creators of it. Disciplinary knowledge from one field is not transmitted and applied to another. Rather, the disciplinary knowledge writing specialists and content experts bring to CCL conversations is developed, altered, created, and revised as participants collaboratively construct new subject matter across disciplines—subject matter that didn't exist before in quite the same way. Embracing the epistemic facet of a pedagogical frame for CCL work leads me to ask: (How) do participants make meaning together? For what purpose? Which discursive moves enable or constrain shared knowledge building?

Pedagogy Is Reflexive
Shared meaning-making calls for reflexive practice, "the act of turning back to discover, examine, and critique one's claims and assumptions in response to an encounter with another idea, text, person, or culture" (Qualley, 1997, p. 3). According to Gallagher (2002), reflexive inquiry brings a critical-reflective dimension to knowledge production; it involves teachers and learners taking "stock together of *how* they construct knowledge, *how* they make meaning" (p. xvii, emphasis added). In CCL contexts, "dialectical engagement" in the form of talk about (teaching) writing might inspire writing specialists and content expertise to be reflexive (Qualley, 1997, p. 11). The sense of "betweenness" that comes from engaging disciplinary difference creates opportunities for reflexive practice because "in the process of trying to understand an other, [individual] beliefs and assumptions are disclosed, and . . . can become objects of examination and critique" (Qualley, 1997, p. 11). The reflexive dimension of a pedagogical frame for faculty conversations in CCL contexts

draws attention to how writing specialists and content experts engage this process—approach and experience teaching and learning in conversation—and if/how they "ear[n] their insights" through critical questioning, exploration, and connection making (Qualley, 1997, pp. 35–37; Stenberg, 2005, pp. 74–75).

More than mere reflection, reflexivity is about understanding more deeply how one's own subjectivities are in dialogue with others. To understand reflexivity in CCL contexts, I ask if/how conversations support a "bidirectional process of education, one that allows [faculty] to continually reexamine [their] thinking from the perspective of [their] present encounters" (Qualley, 1997, p. 149). Because reflexivity is recursive, that process can happen moment-to-moment as well as over time. Qualley (1997) explains: "[R]eflexivity is a process that we engage in by degrees, like peeling the layers from an onion" (p. 121). It involves recursively nudging (and being nudged) "out of stasis," as well as "com[ing] to a new balance," making different sense of subjects and selves and temporarily "restor[ing] a center of gravity" (Qualley, 1997, p. 159). Thus, reflexivity as part of a pedagogical frame for CCL work respects the often excruciatingly slow pace of faculty learning and change and the nuanced sensibilities writing specialists and content experts employ to determine when to "nudge" or be nudged from comfortable "ready-made and coherent perspective[s]" and when to embrace reorientation and momentary stasis (Qualley, 1997, p. 159). In short, I "understand pedagogy as *the reflexive inquiry that teachers and learners undertake together*" and explore the potential of writing specialists and content experts' discursive strategies for supporting such inquiry during conversations about (teaching) writing (Gallagher, 2002, p. xvi).

Pedagogy Is Relational
A pedagogical framework calls for attunement to the relational—to the interplay among teacher-learners, context, and subject matter because "pedagogy is always a form of collective action" that is made and remade among particular people in particular contexts (Gallagher, 2002, p. xvii; Stenberg, 2005, p. xviii). There is no ped-

agogy without relation (Bingham & Sidorkin, 2004). Relational attunement precludes clean models for teaching and learning because "pedagogy cannot be finished" (Stenberg, 2005, p. xviii; Lee, 2000, p. 89); it is a "vision that can never be enacted the same way twice because any 'version' will evolve out of local practice" (Gallagher, 2002, p. 155). To identify templates for pedagogical activity, Amy Lee (2000) explains, "would require that the conditions we teach within remain stagnant, and that our instructional praxes somehow produce universal and guaranteed results" (p. 89). Such is not the case with CCL work. Thus, a relational lens compels me to treat writing specialists and content experts "as complex subjects always in process" and to "attend to the impact and fluctuation of the conditions [they] work within" (p. 89). Applying a pedagogical frame to conversations in CCL contexts not only highlights the importance of faculty relationships but also allows previously unrecognized or unexamined types of relationality to emerge.

I look for ways writing specialists and disciplinary faculty use discursive strategies to establish trust, build camaraderie, and pursue enjoyment, as well as to navigate conflict and address communicative challenges. I look for ways communication practices are loosely associated across participant groups but also differ according to the uniqueness of individual participants. The relational dimension of my pedagogical frame allows for variance in the discursive techniques used in CCL interactions because it recognizes that meaning does not evolve from the writing specialists' or content experts' "experiences, interests, or knowledge, but precisely from the meeting of these" (Gallagher, 2002, p. 156). A relational frame acknowledges *both* sides of what Paul Kameen (2000) calls "the transformative equation of pedagogy" (p. 32)—positioning participants simultaneously as teachers and learners.

A pedagogical frame that assumes interactions among writing specialists and faculty in other disciplines are epistemic, reflexive, and relational challenges the potentially rigid roles and expectations forwarded in traditional models. It usefully disrupts the linear progression of "stages" of WAC, each replacing and defining itself in relation to the last, but never fully capturing the richly complex nature of this work. A pedagogical frame generates new understandings of the communication challenges and opportunities that enable and constrain cross-disciplinary conversations about (teaching) writing, brings "fresh insights to reflection" about this unique communicative practice, and invites targeted conversations about "better and worse ways for [faculty] to conduct themselves as they juggle the multiple aims of [CCL] practice" (Tracy, 2008, pp. 158, 157). On this foundation, I construct a guiding ethic to help faculty realize the pedagogical potential of CCL interactions.

Methods

In order to root a guiding ethic for CCL work in faculty practice and experience, I collected data from five participant groups from four different postsecondary institutions. Snowball sampling was used to recruit writing specialists. I contacted several WAC/WID/CAC directors directly and posted a call on the WPA and WAC listservs. Because my goal is to map a range of communicative strategies used in CCL consultations, rather than cull "best practices" exclusively from high-profile experts, I did not establish rigid criteria for participation. I recruited folks who served as writing specialists in their institutional contexts and planned to meet in that capacity with a colleague from another discipline at least twice during the Fall 2012 semester to discuss teaching writing. As a result, writing specialists in the study represent a range of professional training, practical experience, and disciplinary knowledge.

Once writing specialists agreed to participate, they described the study for content experts at their institutions with whom they planned to meet, and I obtained consent from willing participants. Disciplinary content experts were faculty members or instructors from a field outside composition or writing studies who were teaching writing and planned to meet with a writing specialist to discuss strategies and experiences. With Jablonski (2006, p. 14), I acknowledge that terminology can be problematic—*content experts* can suggest that writing specialists' expertise does not have content; *disciplinary faculty* may imply writing studies is not a discipline;

further, the use of the term *faculty* may imply a tenured or tenure-track department member, although one graduate student writing instructor from an art education program participated in the study. While *faculty/instructor in other disciplines* seems most appropriate, it can be cumbersome to repeat. Therefore, I use these terms interchangeably.

Although I did not recruit nor accept/reject participants based on institution, the study does include a range of institutions in terms of enrollment, Carnegie Classification, and educational mission (see Table 1.1). One original participant group from a small, private, Catholic institution withdrew from the study before data collection began. Otherwise, all initial participants remained in the study. According to demographic information provided by nine of the eleven participants, all but one identified as white/Caucasian, heterosexual, and middle or upper-middle class. I did not collect information about language dialect, but one participant described her experience as an international, nonnative speaker, teacher, and writer. All four contexts were predominantly white institutions, which may explain why participants rarely discussed issues of difference in recorded conversations or interviews. As noted during the closing plenary of the 2016 International Writing Across the Curriculum (IWAC) conference, the field remains troublingly homogeneous in terms of race, class, and nationality. Indeed, scholarship points to the need for WAC/WID research, theory, and practice that attends to difference, including race (Poe, 2013), class (Villanueva, 2001), and gender (Tarabochia, 2016b). While I did not deliberately disregard these issues, because I recruited volunteers, participants and contexts reflect the homogeneity of the field. Future studies might deliberately target institutions and participants to shed light on elements of difference in CCL conversations. Nevertheless, varied sites and participants included in my study provide an appropriate basis for an initial "philosophical and pragmatic reconstruction of practice" (Tracy, 1997, p. 18).

Table 1.1. Information on Institutions Involved in the Study

Institution/ Region	Carnegie Classification	Student Population	Mission
University X Midwest	Public; doctoral universities: highest research activity	31,237; mostly in state; 14.4% students of color	Land grant
Private College Midwest	Private not-for-profit; baccalaureate colleges: arts & sciences focus	1,400; from rural areas	Liberal arts education
Public College Northeast	Public; master's colleges & universities: larger programs	9,260; 19% students of color	Comprehensive; accessible education for traditional and nontraditional students
State U. Midwest	Public; doctoral universities: highest research activity	55,014; 16.4% students of color	Public comprehensive research university

Participant Overview

Each participant group included at least one writing specialist and at least one disciplinary content expert. Writing specialists, three women and three men, represented institutional ranks from undergraduate writing fellow to tenured professor. One writing specialist earned tenure during the semester I conducted the study. Writing specialists performed different roles at their institutions, came from a variety of home disciplines, and had worked in WAC/WID for varying amounts of time. Each brought a different type of knowledge and experience to their roles as experts on campus. Disciplinary content experts, three women and two men, represented five disciplines and ranged in rank from executive level administrator to graduate teaching associate (see Tables 1.2–1.5). While all participant groups shared a common purpose—to talk about (teaching) writing in disciplinary courses—the impetus for the conversations varied across groups. Differences among participants and contexts illustrate the diversity and breadth of CCL efforts. They are a significant strength of the study, creating a rich data set from which to examine the complex communicative challenges of CCL work and the dynamic discursive practices faculty used to navigate them.

University X: Alicia and Ann
University X is a large research university in the Midwest with a land grant mission and well-established campus writing initiative. The campuswide writing program supports students and faculty in satisfying a two-part writing requirement that includes one writing-intensive course in any discipline and one upper-level writing-intensive course in the student's major. To support faculty as primary agents of the culture of writing at University X, the program hosts regular faculty writing retreats and workshops for faculty teaching writing-intensive courses. Alicia and Ann met at a contemplative writing retreat for faculty the summer before they participated in this study. While Ann had worked with the writing program as a new faculty member years ago and regularly taught a WI course on language disorders and children, prior to the retreat she'd had little contact with the program. At the time of the study, Alicia was an English education professor finishing her first year as director of the writing program, and Ann was a tenured associate professor in communication science and disorders, specializing in speech language pathology. The two met four times during the semester to discuss Ann's assignments and activities for Ann's WI course and changes she could make in the future.

Private College: Frank, Thomas, and Chuck
Private College is a tiny, private liberal arts college in the Midwest, serving students from surrounding rural communities. In an effort to smooth the transition to college-level reading and writing, all new students are required to take a first-year seminar (FYS) in

Table 1.2. Overview of Participants from University X

University X	Gender	Rank	Role	Discipline	Years Doing CCL Work
Writing Specialist: Alicia	W	Tenure track, assistant prof.	Director, campus-wide writing program	English education	1–3
Disciplinary Content Expert: Ann	W	Tenured, associate prof.	Faculty instructor, writing-intensive course on speech lang. pathology	Comm. science and disorders/ speech language pathology	

the fall. While students can choose from a range of seminar topics, all FYS courses emphasize writing. Faculty from across the college teach in the program and score student writing portfolios as part of their institutional service. At the time of the study, Frank, Thomas, and Chuck were all teaching FYS courses. Frank was a tenured faculty member in rhetoric completing his twenty-seventh year at Private College. He began his career as an adjunct instructor at the college before he spontaneously applied for an administrative position in the writing center. At the time of the study, Frank was director of the writing center, coordinator of the WAC program, and considered *the* writing person at Private College. In that role Frank invited Thomas and Chuck to have conversations about their FYSs.

Thomas, a tenured professor in chemistry and associate dean of faculty, hadn't taught an FYS since the program had undergone significant changes in structure and philosophy. Thomas's seminar, "Water and Place," emerged from his scientific interest in water, but he tried to keep the course as unscientific and "squishy" as possible in order to break out of his "chemist" mindset when it came to teaching and grading writing. While Frank and Thomas were long-time friends, they'd "never really talked very much about, specifically, writing issues." The FYS was also unfamiliar territory for Chuck, an assistant professor in computer science, beginning his second year at Private College and his first faculty position out of graduate school. According to Chuck, his FYS on 1980s music and culture was related to personal rather than disciplinary interests. Chuck was conflicted about teaching writing because he felt less than confident about his own writing abilities, but Frank found him to have a "really strong interest in pedagogical issues" and exploring new ways to teach. Frank met with Chuck and with Thomas separately three times each over the course of the semester, sometimes discussing particular assignments or classroom experiences, but more often exploring larger questions about teaching and learning through an experiential lens.

Table 1.3. Overview of Participants from Private College

Private College	Gender	Rank	Role	Discipline	Years Doing CCL Work
Writing Specialist: Frank	M	Tenured prof.	Writing center director/ WAC coordinator	Rhetoric	26
Disciplinary Content Expert: Thomas	M	Tenured prof./ associate dean of faculty	Faculty instructor, first-year seminar on water and place	Chemistry	
Disciplinary Content Expert: Chuck	M	Tenure-track assistant prof.	Faculty instructor, first-year seminar on 1980s music culture	Computer science	

Public College: Bill and Lena
Public College is a small institution serving approximately nine thousand undergraduates, including many first-generation or nontraditional students. Beyond the first-year writing program, which is housed in the English department and consists of mostly adjunct instructors, Public College has an unofficial WAC program, the main feature of which is an interdisciplinary Writing Board that sponsors faculty development around the teaching of writing. In addition, a summer seminar focused on teaching writing was offered for faculty. Bill, a faculty member in the English department and chair of the Writing Board who earned tenure during the course of my study, often co-facilitated the summer seminar. According to Bill, he "stumbled into . . . working with faculty on teaching writing" and did not claim background or training in WAC/WID work. Still, his research interests included literacy learning and development and he embraced his work with teachers.

Bill worked professionally with Lena for the first time during a summer seminar. Traditionally, facilitators had little contact with participants post-seminar as they worked to implement what they learned. However, at the time of my study, Bill had recently been named a teaching fellow for the teaching and learning center and decided to use his course release to follow up more directly and consistently with one or two seminar participants, including Lena, a tenured associate professor in political science, who despite her twenty years of teaching experience, was embroiled in a personal crisis around the work of teaching. Lena had become rather disillusioned with teaching and was motivated and excited by the ideas Bill introduced. The two met twice during the fall semester to discuss Lena's efforts to create and grade writing assignments in her courses including a political science course developed around election year politics.

State U: James, Liliana, Emily, and Kim
State U, a public research university serving more than fifty-five thousand undergraduates, is the largest institution in my study. The institution sponsors a range of writing initiatives including writing-

Table 1.4. Overview of Participants from Public College

Public College	Gender	Rank	Role	Discipline	Years Doing CCL Work
Writing Specialist: Bill	M	Tenure-track to tenured	Writing board chair and teaching fellow	English education, composition	4–6
Disciplinary Content Expert: Lena	W	Tenured associate prof.	Faculty summer seminar participant; incorporating writing in political science course	Political science	

based research projects, a minor in professional writing, the writing center, various outreach efforts, and a WAC program that supports instructors teaching writing outside of English and composition courses as part of a three-tiered system of general education writing courses. At the time of my study, the WAC program piloted a Writing Fellows Program that paired trained undergraduate writing associates (WAs) with instructors teaching writing in discipline-based courses. As coordinator of the WAC program, a non-tenure-track administrative position, James spearheaded the Writing Fellows Program. He saw himself as a "nexus of knowledge" determined to "bring [State U's] best teachers in conversation with each other about writing." Liliana, assistant coordinator of the WA program and graduate student in art education, brought a multifaceted perspective to the pilot based on her unique combination of experiences as a graduate student, a writing associate, and a writing instructor. Emily was a senior English major and first time WA, who had taken classes in writing consulting and observed writing center consultants working with student writers. She was assigned to support Kim, an international graduate student in art education, and students in her second-level general education writing course. Hard at work on her dissertation, Kim contributed a valuable perspective as an international student, writer, and first-time writing teacher. Kim was the only participant who preferred not to be interviewed for the study. During four semester meetings, James and Liliana worked to establish a productive relationship between Emily and Kim, address logistical issues, encourage reflection, and troubleshoot challenges. The only group to bring more than two people into conversation about (teaching) writing, the four demonstrated a unique interactional dynamic.

Table 1.5. Overview of Participants from State U.

State U.	Gender	Rank	Role	Discipline	Years Doing CCL Work
Writing Specialist: James	M	Non-tenure-track, PhD	WAC program coordinator; WA program pilot director	Medieval studies	7–10
Writing Specialist: Emily	W	Undergraduate student	Writing associate	English	1–3
Writing Specialist: Liliana	W	Graduate student and teaching associate	Assistant coordinator of WA program	Art education	4–6
Disciplinary Content Expert: Kim	W	International graduate student and teaching associate	Instructor, second year general education writing course	Art education	

Data Collection

Over a ten-month period, I collected several types of data from the five groups.

- I used a written survey to gather general information about participants and their experiences with CCL relationships on their campuses. With permission, I adapted the survey used by Paretti et al. (2009), hoping to situate my participants and their institutions in relation to the picture of cross-campus partnerships the authors paint. However, the survey mostly provides background information in the analysis presented here.
- A second survey was used to collect demographic information.
- I collected audio and video recordings of at least two meetings from each group (approximately thirteen hours and 352 pages of conversation transcripts total).
- I conducted at least two interviews (over the phone or through Skype) with each participant. Interviews took place soon after each recorded meeting and I drew on my initial analysis of recordings to develop semi-structured interview questions.
- I conducted a follow-up interview with each participant during the spring semester with semi-structured interview questions based on ongoing analysis of recordings and transcripts of earlier interviews (approximately thirty hours and 624 pages of interview transcripts total).

The range of materials collected allowed me to build a rich description of CCL work as a professional practice. By recording spoken exchanges among participants, a method used in studies of interdisciplinary and writing-related talk in other contexts (Black, 1998; Godbee, 2011, 2012; Nowacek, 2005, 2007, 2011)1998; Godbee, 2011, 2012, Nowacek, 2005, 2007, 2011 but underutilized in CCL research, I was able to access potentially unconscious rhetorical and discursive strategies participants didn't always recall during interviews. Interviews were an important complement to recordings, and I treated them as "metadiscourse about interactive occasion[s]" (Tracy, 1997, p. 16). I used them to probe participants' experiences and encourage "constructive reflection" by reminding faculty of particular exchanges (Yancey qtd. in Jablonski, 2006, p. 47).

Data Analysis
Interpretive data analysis took place iteratively over two years and adapted methods from action-implicative discourse analysis (AIDA), rooted in practical grounded theory (PGT) (Craig & Tracy, 1995; Tracy, 1997, 2005, 2008). Consistent with AIDA/PGT, my analytical goal was to reconstruct communicative practices in CCL contexts on three levels by: articulating "the web of . . . dilemmas that confront practitioners," teasing out a range of "conversational moves and discursive techniques used to manage problems," and specifying a philosophical "rationale" for interacting in this unique communicative situation (Tracy, 1997, pp. 11–12). To begin, I screened, loosely transcribed, and annotated recorded meetings as I received them, using initial impressions to compose semi-structured interview questions. Interviews and conversations were then fully transcribed for further analysis. I used line-by-line coding to analyze at least one meeting transcript from each group and at least one interview from each participant, noting discursive moves such as minimal response, question posing, changing one's mind, tempering advice, shifting expectations, and referencing faculty allies. Drawing on my own previous research and experience as a writing specialist (Tarabochia, 2013), and using pedagogy as a situational frame, I grouped codes into categories that seemed to indicate key communicative activities and/or instances of pedagogical potential: negotiating expertise, openness to change, willingness to play, reflexive practice, and relationship building. Through constant comparison of interview and conversation data within and across participant groups and recursive memoing, I deepened my understanding of each category and identified illustrative examples of each.

In the spirit of AIDA/PGT, my goal was not to quantify qualitative data but to build a "rational reconstruction of practice" (Craig

& Tracy, 1995). Therefore, I did not segment language units or force one-to-one correspondence between discursive moves and descriptive codes. For example, transcript excerpts coded as "storytelling" were varying lengths and sometimes associated with more than one category, such as embracing play and relationship building. Rather than make claims about the frequency of discursive moves and functions (by counting how many times writing specialists negotiated expertise by referring to fellow faculty, for instance), I gathered multiple examples of moves and functions within and across participant groups and used scholarship in composition studies, rhetorical theory, and education to consider their pedagogical potential. I departed from AIDA methodology in that I did not systemically gather or analyze data to determine "situated ideals" based on "patterns of praise and blame" in participant "talk about the speech occasion" (Tracy, 1995, p. 211). However, the theory I build, based on my own practice-based research and experience and reading widely across disciplines, is "defensible" and implicative for action insofar as it prompts "thought about how a practice ought to be conducted and cultivated" (Tracy, 1995, p. 211).

As Tracy (2005) explains, discourse moments should be carefully selected for their salience in revealing communicative problems, responses, and action-implicative philosophies of interaction. In that vein, I chose to focus my analysis on three discursive activities— negotiating expertise, navigating change, and embracing play—because they fit the criteria for "useful problem framing" (Tracy, 1995, p. 210). That is, they are specific enough to manifest in particular interactions and abstract enough to resonate in related situations; they capture the complexity of practice while simplifying it enough to generate useful insights; they provide opportunities to "mak[e] visible tacit beliefs and concerns of the communicative practice and the tensions that exist among them"; and they are "helpful in fostering reflection about how to act" in CCL contexts (Tracy, 1995, p. 210). These activities make good problem frames because analysis of conversational exchanges and interview comments in these realms reveals dilemmatic tensions at the heart of CCL work as well as opportunities for pedagogical engagement. I will briefly describe each discursive activity and explain how I associated pieces of interview and conversation transcripts as well as particular discursive moves within each category.

Activity 1: Negotiating Expertise
Negotiating expertise—putting one's knowledge and experience in conversation with others' differently situated knowledge and experience—creates unique communication challenges for writing specialists and disciplinary faculty in CCL contexts. The activity is relational, rhetorical, and bound up in often-complicated power dynamics (Hartelius, 2011). If and how individuals negotiate expertise depends on existing relationships, knowledge about the subject matter or topic at hand, and the goal of the exchange among other factors. Negotiating expertise can be especially challenging in cross-disciplinary conversations where individuals' disciplinary expertise can be vastly different, rooted in complicated institutional histories, and enmeshed in individuals' sense of identity, motivation, and professional self-worth (Strober, 2011; Thompson, 2009). Cross-curricular literacy work further complicates the negotiation of expertise because of historically vexed relationships between composition and more established academic disciplines and because of composition's ongoing struggle with issues of disciplinarity. At the same time, the communicative act of negotiating expertise has pedagogical potential (Tarabochia, 2013). Calling forth, valuing, and integrating individuals' expertise can support collaborative inquiry and sense making, sponsor reflexivity, and forge relationships around teaching and learning.

I categorized as "negotiating expertise" moves or exchanges from conversation data in which a speaker treated her own knowledge or understanding as tentative, partial, or open for examination *or* in which a speaker sought out knowledge or experience of the other as a source of exploring perspectives and/or possibilities (as opposed to a source of definitive knowledge to be employed). Examples include: "naming or recognizing another speaker's expertise"; "referring to experts outside the conversation"; and "using facets of own expertise to confirm the other speaker's idea or practice." When analyzing interview transcripts, I categorized excerpts as "negotiating expertise" when they helped me understand the communicative challenge and how participants oriented to it. I then returned to all data in this category and parsed out distinct communicative "moves" that accomplished (to varying degrees) the negotiation of expertise, including "drawing on institutional knowledge," "acknowledging limited expertise," "modeling," "inviting reflection," and "offering multiple options." In Chapter 2, I explore the *pedagogical* potential of these moves by considering how they might support collaborative meaning-making, reflexivity, and relationship building.

Activity 2: Orienting to Change
Faculty members' attempts to navigate change during conversations about (teaching) writing—how they identify who or what should change, encourage or inspire change in others, and/or embrace change themselves—reveal a second site of communicative challenge and opportunity. Varied, vague, or conflicting perceptions or assumptions about change can create challenges for productive communication in CCL contexts. Divergent expectations can make it difficult for writing specialists and disciplinary experts to identify shared objectives and discursively orient to change in ways the other finds satisfying. Despite inherent challenges, the process of navigating change presents opportunity for deep, meaningful teaching and learning at the heart of pedagogical activity. "To teach is to change," says Paul Kameen (2000) in his introduction to part I of *Writing/Teaching: Essays Toward a Rhetoric of Pedagogy*. "Or at least to try to," he adds, signaling the complexity of the role of change in pedagogical relationships; but "who is supposed to be changed, in what ways, and how much, through our work?" (p. 3). As I will show throughout the book, particularly in Chapter 3, a pedagogical frame throws these questions into relief, treating cross-disciplinary dialogues about teaching and writing as "junctures of circumstance" that "demand some accounting" for how we understand and pursue change (Kameen, 2000, p. 3).

From a pedagogical perspective, change is not an individual accomplishment, but a collaborative, interactive phenomenon, grounded in a sustained commitment to openness. When populating this category, I specifically looked for discursive moves or exchanges wherein participants demonstrated openness to change (Qualley, 1997). I coded as "openness to change" any instance in which a speaker indicated an inclination to change assumptions, beliefs, behaviors, practices, or expectations. Examples include instances when a speaker "indicated practices had changed over time"; "suggested she would apply a practice in the future"; or "indicated that she would not make a change after carefully considering and explaining why the change was not appropriate." To make sense of the data in this category, I identify and analyze excerpts that depict various states of deep learning, strategies for embracing those experiences, and/or techniques for supporting fellow learners.

Activity 3: Embracing Play
Play initially materialized in my study as curious, seemingly pleasurable conversational exchanges that at first glance seemed "off topic" or frivolous. Intrigued, I turned to play theorists, who describe play as an attitude or phenomenon that is engrossing, unselfconscious, improvisational, and challenging (Brown & Vaughan, 2009; Csikszentmihalyi, 1979, 1990, 1996). Play can be fun, spontaneous, silly, goofy, imaginative and relational (Tanis, 2012); it can function as "a medium for teaching and learning" (Latta, 2013, p. 2) as "the abilities to make new patterns, find the unusual among the common, and spark curiosity and alert observation are all fostered by being in a state of play" (Brown & Vaughan, 2009, p. 128). Play resonates with my pedagogical framework because it can encourage collaborative meaning-making, sponsor reflexive practice, and foster relational attunement. Despite rich conversations about play among writing center scholars and curriculum theorists, I found that play is not often the focus of WAC/WID theory and practice, perhaps because it poses interesting communication challenges. Because play is often defined in opposition to work, it can be difficult to appreciate the potential for play in environments we consider

professional or serious. In CCL contexts, participants' expectations are also influenced by the no-nonsense transactional attitudes at the heart of service and consultancy models of WAC/WID that can foreclose opportunities for play. To respond to the discursive challenge (and realize the potential benefits) of enacting play, we need a better understanding of how play can look and function in CCL contexts.

Toward that end, I used "embracing play" to name moments when a speaker allowed for (or embraced) uncertainty, disorder, lack of clear purpose or direction, including instances in which a speaker "followed a line of thinking without a clear tie to writing or teaching writing"; "demonstrated openness to following the conversation where it led"; "made intuitive connections that resonated with a fellow learner"; or "acted silly or spontaneously" among others. I noticed relatively few instances of play in my data, and the majority seemed to be associated with one participant group. Still, the challenge and pedagogical potential of these instances made it a worthy problem frame. Drawing on play theorists and adult learning scholars, I analyze data in this category to distinguish forms of play and begin to understand their discursive and pedagogical impact on CCL interactions.

As Karen Tracy (1995) explains, the rigor of interpretive research such as AIDA is not determined by validity or reliability in an empiricist sense, but according to usefulness for guiding future practice. That is, analyses should: be "plausible and persuasive" by "direct[ing] attention to things that would normally go unnoticed," by "bring[ing] clarity to confusion, mak[ing] visible what is hidden or inappropriately ignored, and generat[ing] a sense of insight and deepened understanding" (p. 209); "advance[e] a coherent central claim" that ties discursive techniques to "situated problems" (p. 210); and be implicative for action within the community of scholar-practitioners (p. 211). In accomplishing these ends, the study at the heart of this book makes a unique contribution to CCL scholarship and practice. Using pedagogy as a frame for analyzing discursive moves in relation to key communicative activities sheds new light on the dilemmas of CCL work, illuminates the pedagogical potential of particular exchanges, and identifies communication strategies for making conversations and relationships more pedagogical. In the following chapters, I draw on current work in rhetorical theory and learning theory to conceptualize the nature of the communication challenges and opportunities study participants faced. I then "theorize out" of particular conversational exchanges among writing specialists and disciplinary content experts, analyzing excerpts from interview and conversation transcripts to construct a guiding ethic for CCL work and suggest how it can be "enacted, critiqued, expanded, and revised" (Lee, 2000, p. 11, 10).

2

Exploding the Dilemma of Expertise

NEGOTIATING EXPERTISE IS PERHAPS ONE OF the most pressing communication challenges writing specialists and disciplinary content experts face in WAC/WID contexts (Fulwiler, 1981; Jablonski, 2006; Jones & Comprone, 1993; Mahala & Swilky, 1994; Norgaard, 1999; Soliday, 2011, p. 17). In fact, questions of expertise drive a major paradox at the heart of WAC/WID work: How do writing specialists claim and validate our writing-related expertise and also urge disciplinary colleagues to recognize their own writing expertise and take responsibility for teaching writing in their disciplines? Billig et al.'s (1988) notion of ideological dilemma is useful for understanding the paradox of expertise in cross-curricular literacy contexts. Billig (1988) and his colleagues explain: "Ideologically produced dilemmatic thinking arises when two valued themes of an ideology conflict, and these dilemmatic elements can spill over into a full-scale dilemma, when a choice has to be made" (p. 66). In the case of WAC/WID contexts, two valued themes of WAC/WID ideology consistently conflict for writing specialists—the need to have writing expertise acknowledged and respected and the need to encourage disciplinary colleagues to share responsibility for teaching writing. In conversations with disciplinary faculty, writing specialists constantly make decisions about how to perform expertise and engage the expertise of colleagues, thus the "dilemmatic elements [regularly] spill over into a full-scale dilemma."

I use a rhetorical theory of expertise (Hartelius, 2011) to categorize particular discursive moves writing specialists use to address the first dilemmatic element of the paradox (claiming expertise) and to explain from a rhetorical perspective why it can be so difficult to pursue the second dilemmatic element (sharing expertise) while still attending to the first. I argue that distinguishing among types of expertise allows writing specialists to preserve specialized, disciplinary knowledge about (teaching) writing; better articulate and grow the unique knowledge and experience they bring as designated writing specialists in their particular contexts; and support colleagues in integrating what they know as writers and teachers in their disciplines with new knowledge and/or understandings built through CCL interactions. I layer a pedagogical view of expertise with Hartelius's (2011) rhetorical one to illuminate the epistemological, reflexive, and relational potential of the strategies writing specialists use to negotiate expertise in response to our unique paradox. Based on those observations, I tease out initial insights for building a cohesive guiding ethic for CCL work.

CLAIMING EXPERTISE: A RHETORICAL VIEW

E. Johanna Hartelius's (2011) rhetorical view of expertise provides a useful heuristic for understanding how and why writing specialists respond to the persuasive exigency inherent in the first part of the dilemma of expertise. According to Hartelius (2011), expertise is "grounded in a fierce struggle over ownership and legitimacy" (p. 1). "To be an expert," she continues, "is to rhetorically gain sanctioned rights to a specific topic or mode of knowledge" to "claim a piece of the world, to define yourself in relation to certain insights into human experience" (p. 1). These goals resonate with writing specialists' need to claim and legitimize our expertise. Because of the historically vexed relationship between composition/writing studies and academic disciplines in the modern research university, writing specialists are justifiably determined to have our expertise recognized and valued by disciplinary colleagues, to claim our piece of the world. A rhetorical model of expertise highlights how certain communicative strategies accomplish this persuasive purpose.

Based on an analysis of rhetorical patterns demonstrated by experts across four spheres of public discourse, Hartelius (2011) identifies "rhetorical congruencies" in performances of expertise, including: associating with expert networks, establishing expert techne, teaching expertise, asking for deference or participation, constructing a rhetorical situation for which expertise is the most fitting response, and orienting to "everyday life" (pp. 18–29). Writing specialists in my study employed these rhetorical strategies in different ways and to different degrees in response to the ideological dilemma of expertise. I will focus first on the congruencies that have a clear persuasive purpose—expert networks, expert techne, fitting response, and everyday life—illuminating the pedagogical potential of discursive strategies in these areas. Then I will examine congruencies that involve decisions about how to teach expertise and whether to seek deference to expert knowledge or invite participation in expert practice. Using a pedagogical framework to analyze communicative strategies related to these rhetorical activities, I suggest how they might set the stage for collaborative meaning-making, reflexive practice, and relationship building.

Associating with Expert Networks

According to Hartelius (2011), one rhetorical congruency among experts is the tendency to associate with "expert networks," including other individuals and areas of knowledge. The communicative move aims to garner cultural capital and position individuals in relation to other experts—to show how their expertise fits within a larger network (p. 18). Writing specialists in my study associated with expert networks by drawing on localized knowledge and experience. For example, Frank drew on knowledge of shared institutional context early in his conversation with Thomas, a faculty member in chemistry. The chemistry department previously offered their introductory course as an FYS to attract strong students and recruit majors. However, when the program was revised faculty could no longer designate catalog courses as FYSs. Frank knew chemistry faculty resisted the change and now had reservations about teaching FYS courses. Frank sensed if not "bitterness" then "lack of enthusiasm" from chemistry faculty, including Thomas. Because Frank had been a writing specialist at Private College for over two decades, he was able to draw on his institutional knowledge and awareness of recent changes to the FYS program and invite Thomas to share his feelings about the change, acknowledging that he "managed to escape for ten or twelve years and how things are different now." Thomas recalled teaching the course over a decade ago, admitting he felt "disillusioned" by the experience. With gentle teasing Frank created a nonthreatening space for Thomas to explore his feelings and reflect on how teaching the seminar might be different this time.[1]

> FRANK: And, and I sense still a certain bitterness here.
> THOMAS: Well, yeah.
> FRANK: And, and kind of anger with . . .
> THOMAS: Yeah. Deep seated.
> FRANK: Mm-hmm.
> THOMAS: Do you want me to talk about that?
> [laughter]
> FRANK: Yeah, well . . .
> THOMAS: My feelings?
> [laughter]
> FRANK: Yeah, we'll turn this into a counseling session.
> THOMAS: Yeah, that's fine.
> [laughter]
> THOMAS: It's cheap.
> [laughter]
> THOMAS: That works. Um, but that course had a structure superimposed on it.
> FRANK: Yes.
> THOMAS: I mean, because I was covering the nature of atoms and stoichiometry and all this stuff and the first-year seminar-ness of it was secondary.
> FRANK: Yes.

Frank openly acknowledged Thomas's past experience, inviting him to share any lingering "anger" or "bitterness" while at the same time softening the potentially tense exchange with humor. Thomas responded good-naturedly; he jokingly confirmed his anger was "deep seated" and seemed to enjoy the idea of turning their conversation into a "cheap counseling session." Despite the humor (or perhaps because of it), Thomas had room to articulate the differences between FYS courses in chemistry before and after the change before describing his current approach to the course. By drawing on his knowledge of institutional and programmatic history to frame his conversation with Thomas, Frank associated with the network of faculty who'd undergone programmatic change and lived with the resulting tensions. He performed his association so as to acknowledge the complicated feelings likely undergirding Thomas's approach to teaching writing and used humor to make visible those feelings without communicating judgment. The laughter and mutual banter suggest Thomas appreciated Frank's move to ground himself in the local context and acknowledge Thomas's past experiences.

In addition to drawing on institutional history, writing specialists who'd been in their positions for several years associated with expert networks by foregrounding lessons learned from working with faculty in other disciplines. James, for example, described himself as a "nexus for local knowledge" whose expertise was rooted in institutional awareness based on conversations with faculty.

> I think simply having the opportunity to talk with a wide range of instructors and faculty throughout the university and learning a lot about what the contexts of teaching are in different departments, and what particular strategies that different instructors do. In some ways, I think I'm like a local WAC Clearinghouse. [laughter] I've had an opportunity to talk with a lot of people and hear a lot of approaches, seen people try out new things. Part of what I see myself as is somebody who can bring all of that knowledge to other people, to bring [State University's] best teachers in conversation with each other about writing. In some ways, my knowledge of writing theory and writing research, that helps me put all of that into context, but what's really important is me being a nexus for that local knowledge.

As this excerpt suggests, James utilized the knowledge and experience developed through conversations about teaching with faculty across disciplines. Based on those conversations he had a better sense of the range of possibilities and made suggestions about what strategies might work in which contexts and why, based on a range of faculty experiences. As with the experts Hartelius (2011) studied, referencing expert networks has persuasive potential in CCL contexts; it can make writing specialists' knowledge of theory and practice in the discipline appear more relevant.

While James and Frank utilized their experience as writing specialists, Emily, the undergraduate writing associate, drew on expert networks by referring to what she'd seen experienced peer tutors do during writing center consultations. For example, in the following exchange, Emily mentions writing center observations in response to Kim's concern that students might try to use the WA to undermine her authority.

> KIM: I was a little like worried since I'm an international TA here teaching American culture and teaching writing. I was a little worried about how I maintain the control of the class. And I went far beyond and was thinking, what if my student got [her] grade and [she's] not satisfied with her grade and [goes] to a writing associate and [shows her] work and [complains that her] instructor gave this grade and this comment. I don't agree with her comment and her grade, what do you think? What if the writing associate [responds] that I agree with you?
> JAMES: Yeah. Yeah. That's . . . We will . . .
> LILIANA: [Emily], this a question for you really. [laughter]
> JAMES: Yeah, how would you respond to that kind of situation?
> LILIANA: How would you respond? [laughing]
> EMILY: Well, I actually did see that situation occasionally when observing in a writing center when the student would come in insisting that the writing center changed

the grade. And so, yeah, basically, I just have to tell the students that they have to respect their instructors' decisions. And if I really do think that the student might have a point, I'd still explain to them that they respect your decision, and then, I can talk with you about it privately if I think it's an issue.

Perhaps because James is the senior writing specialist in the discussion, outranking Emily and Liliana in terms of institutional position and experience, he makes the first move to respond to Kim's concern. Liliana quickly steps in, however, and redirects the question to Emily. Because Emily is an undergraduate student serving as a WA for the first time, she cannot draw on experience the same way James and Liliana can. Instead, she refers to a larger expert network of experienced peer writing consultants to frame her answer. Like Frank's reference to the experience of chemistry faculty, Emily's move appears to have persuasive potential by relying on an established community of experts to lend credence to her knowledge.

Associating with expert networks also has pedagogical potential. It is epistemic in a Berlinian (1987) sense: It reflects knowledge writing specialists constructed in local contexts in collaboration with differently positioned experts. Moreover, James, Frank, and Emily had to be reflexive to integrate their own disciplinary knowledge with on-the-ground experience interacting with expert networks to decide when and how to share that understanding in new situations. Teaching and learning is dependent upon participants respecting and trusting one another's expertise. They must be interested in what the other knows and see the potential relevance of others' knowledge to their own understandings and endeavors. As a communicative strategy, then, association appears to be one way to lay the relational foundation for pedagogical activity.

Establishing Expert Techne
A second rhetorical congruency writing specialists demonstrated is the move to establish expert *techne*. Hartelius (2011) explains:

All experts in some way explicate their epistemologies and methodologies. They state what they know, how they know it, and how they practice or implement what they know. Because the notion of expertise is so closely related both to knowledge and to the practice of a craft, references to epistemology and methodology are a key rhetorical strategy. Indeed, they are persuasive indicators of an expert techne. (p. 20)

That is, expertise, to be acknowledged as such, must consist of theoretical knowledge as well as skilled practice. Writing specialists in my study made visible those strands by representing teaching writing as "productive activity" grounded in "rational principles" (Hartelius, 2011, p. 22).

Sharing examples from their own teaching is one way writing specialists communicated methodology, presenting teaching writing as a productive activity. Alicia explained to Ann how she used "learning letters" to encourage students to reflect on their growth as writers and give her insight into their learning; Bill detailed how he used the affordances of computer classrooms to organize workshop days; James shared lessons he'd learned about the complexity of constructing feedback from his experience responding to his wife's book manuscript. In these examples, writing specialists made visible the methodological dimension of their expertise—the craft-ful practice of teaching writing. At the same time, writing specialists communicated the epistemology, the rational principles, undergirding expert practice by drawing on theoretical expertise from their home disciplines (writing studies, education, rhetoric, etc.). For instance, Bill used research-based knowledge strategically to persuade skeptical faculty. He discovered that psychology professors at his institution tended to be persuaded to try "best practices" when he used George Hillocks's meta-analysis as evidence for those practices. Once Bill discovered that "*meta-analysis* is a word that the psychology professors like to hear," he built Hillocks into his faculty writing seminars as a way to highlight the epistemology behind the methods he suggested for teaching writing.

Bill's example emphasizes the importance of both the epistemological and methodological dimensions of expert techne. Methodology alone may not only be unconvincing but might also support a skewed sense of the substance of writing expertise. According to Bill, even though he was at a teaching-focused institution, faculty had trouble taking him seriously as a scholar because of his investment (and his field's investment) in teaching. Perhaps motivated by this skepticism, writing specialists in my study were committed to gently and strategically showing that writing studies expertise is built on more than teaching methods. James explained: "Part of that is simply to let people know that such research exists because they're more apt to understand what the context is—that we're not making [it] up on the spot. Just to give a background." Hartelius (2011) reinforces the sentiment; experts work so hard to "creat[e] the impression of a techne" because "it suggests to an audience that expertise exists, and that the expert is authentic and genuine. It indicates that the expertise is real" (p. 22).

Perhaps one of the most creative and useful ways writing specialists established expert techne was to illuminate connections *between* methodological strategies and epistemological principles. For example, in the following excerpt, Alicia responds to Ann's concern about making grading "fair" with multiple graders. She begins with the methodological, suggesting a way Ann might adjust her process of norming graduate TAs.

> ALICIA: Maybe a way to set that, because what you're doing, I wouldn't necessarily quit doing that. 'Cause I think that if I was your TA that would be very helpful, if I saw examples of, the kinds of comments, the things you're looking at. But it would probably be helpful at that beginning, especially since they won't both have gone through a recent TA workshop. But to take one of the papers first time around and all three of you read it. Score it. Compare what did you give. And then, I think it will help them then to understand more why you may have certain things you're looking for, and to understand what it is those things are.
>
> ANN: Mm-hm.

ALICIA: That doesn't take very long,
ANN: OK.
ALICIA: Even if it's just one paper you're all looking at together and comparing.

After establishing the methodology of grade norming, Alicia goes on to suggest that Ann talk with students about different ways to understand the purpose and value of grading writing. She urges Ann to consider and guide her students to consider how having multiple graders simulates writing feedback "in the real world."

ALICIA: And then, what I would think about, too, is in talking with students about this. And I'm just brainstorming here so this may not make sense. But you're giving your students in many ways, a very real world experience when there are multiple people, multiple audience members reading one of their papers. And to understand that when they're writing for people it's going to be not just a one-member audience. They're going to get different kinds feedback, they're going to get different viewpoints. That's part of, "Welcome to the world of writing." You know?
ANN: Yeah.
ALICIA: When they get out into their job. They'll have different supervisors . . .
ANN: Totally.
ALICIA: Different audience members of what they're writing. So to start to see how it's not necessarily a matter of fairness. It's a matter of, "We are different in the way we read and interpret things."

Alicia doesn't just stop with methodology. She emphasizes the epistemological principles behind the general consensus among writing researchers that "it's really very helpful to get multiple kinds of feedback," that writers should learn to make decisions about revision based on different, even conflicting, responses from readers. In an effort to make the principles convincing to Ann, Alicia framed them in terms of Ann's likely experience as a faculty writer:

For instance, when we send off articles to get hopefully published and we get reviewers' comments. Those reviewers' comments are usually going to be very different. They may have some common things they'll notice, but they're going to notice different things. And the advantage of having multiple reviewers is that you get that multiple feedback. And same thing then as in their writing, they're just going to learn more by having multiple graders. Because you'll notice this, one certain aspect of their writing, but the different, the TAs may notice other things. It just gives them overall more feedback.

Alicia incorporated both epistemological expertise and methodological expertise to persuade Ann to shift from a focus on grading "fairly" to a focus on helping students understand the rhetorical nature of writing and the complex reality of multiple audiences.

Viewed through my particular interpretative framework, interweaving methodologies and epistemologies—creating an expert techne—and convincingly highlighting its logic and relevance in the context of disciplinary faculty members' lives has pedagogical promise. The act of entwining the two, as Alicia's example shows, takes careful reflection on connections between disciplinary theory and practice, an act made reflexive through consideration of how writing specialists' praxis relates to the lived realities (scholarly and classroom-based) of colleagues in other disciplines. Arguably, synthesizing knowledge and practice, as Alicia did when she suggested Ann both norm her TA graders and reframe the value of variable feedback for students, is epistemic, a form of meaning-making. Moreover, Alicia's decision to situate her argument about multiple forms of feedback in the scholarly publishing experiences she and Ann shared reaches toward the relational, a key dimension of pedagogical activity.

Because creating and communicating an expert techne requires knowledge of disciplinary methodologies and epistemologies, persuasive strategies for negotiating expertise will be differently available for writing specialists according to their institutional status and experience. For example, while Emily had taken a course theorizing peer writing consultations and observed experienced consultants, she was not immersed in the field in the same way Frank, Bill, Alicia, and James were and thus could not communicate expert techne as they did. Nevertheless, examining "associating with expert networks" and "creating an expert techne" as communicative moves in CCL contexts suggests that discursive techniques that may initially seem to serve persuasive ends, particularly when it comes to expertise, might actually have underacknowledged pedagogical potential as well.

A Most Fitting Response

Like the experts Hartelius (2011) analyzed, writing specialists worked to persuade disciplinary content experts that writing expertise was appropriate and relevant for their needs. "All experts identify or construct a rhetorical situation," says Hartelius (2011), "in which their expertise is the most fitting response" (p. 25). Drawing on Lloyd Bitzer's definition of exigence, Hartelius explains how experts "present themselves as uniquely capable" and their expertise as a solution, response, or answer to "a thing which is other than it should be" (Bitzer qtd. in Hartelius, 2011, p. 25). By arguing that they will successfully respond to an urgent need where others have failed or provide a needed alternative to traditional response, many experts appeal to *eunoia* by framing their interest in terms of upholding the greater good, constructing a "critical argument for legitimacy and purpose in the rhetoric of expertise" (pp. 26–27). Creating a most fitting response in CCL contexts may seem like a matter of *kairos*—of identifying the right time and place to make an argument about teaching writing. However, given misconceptions about writing, writers, and writing expertise, for writing specialists, persuasively crafting a fitting response might often mean shifting what faculty consider exigencies for writing expertise as well as how they judge the relevance and success of writing expertise applied to the exigencies they identify. Thus, framing writing expertise as the most fitting response is not merely a matter of timing but of teaching (and rhetorically convincing) faculty what counts as writing expertise and how, when, and why it can be valuable.

Exigencies for teaching writing proliferate. They range from laments about the most recent "literacy crisis," to administrative mandates to teach writing, to professors' personal frustration with poor student writing. However, it can be challenging to construct expertise as the most fitting response to these existing exigencies because, absent sophisticated understanding of how teaching and learning writing works, they can set up false expectations about what meaningful response should look like or about how (and who) will determine if responses are effective. For instance, a faculty member who seeks out a writing specialist because of frustration with poor student writing in her classroom may judge the value of disciplinary writing instruction as the "solution" to the problem (and by extension the value of the writing specialists' expertise) based on whether student grades on writing assignments improve. If grades don't improve, she might reject the value of writing expertise and disciplinary writing instruction as a response to her problem. To frame writing expertise as a fitting response to disciplinary needs, writing specialists must both rhetorically tap into existing exigencies and sometimes, in a more pedagogical sense, gently alter misleading expectations about writing expertise based on those exigencies. Rather than a precondition for negotiating expertise, then, making writing expertise a fitting response can require negotiation strategies including referencing expert networks and establishing expert techne.

Rhetorically framing a sophisticated version of writing expertise as the most fitting response requires understanding what content experts hope to accomplish and what challenges they face as teachers. For example, Alicia explained the peer review process by emphasizing the benefits of the activity in relation to Ann's learning goals for students and tempering aspects Ann might perceive as drawbacks. In a similar vein, other writing specialists framed a fitting response by recognizing when faculty members' practices already demonstrated "rational principles" valued in WAC/WID. Doing so emphasized how valuable writing specialists' epistemological expertise could be for disciplinary content experts, tied theoretical knowledge to methodology, and framed their own expert techne as relevant for tangible, appropriate exigencies. For example, during their second conversation, Chuck described for Frank a conversation in which a senior colleague implied that one of Chuck's writing assignments was "too broad." Frank listened to Chuck work through his experience of the conversation and then used the situation to both affirm Chuck and draw a connection between Chuck's practice and "rational principles" underlying writing instructors' decisions to teach different kinds of research papers.

> FRANK: Other faculty, particularly with regard to first-year students and first-year experience [want writing that is focused and thesis driven], where you are much more interested in kind of fundamental processes. You want the students to explore, to discover some things on their own. And, you're not too worried about a thesis-driven, argument-driven paper. So it's OK that it strikes out broad and then may be talking about alcohol use but that happens then to lead to counterculture in the 1960s and how that still shows up in the 1980s and it ends with an interview on Mick Jagger and The Rolling Stones. [laughter]
> CHUCK: Yeah.
> FRANK: You know what I mean?
> CHUCK: Yeah.
> [. . .]
> FRANK: You wanted people to mess around. Kind of like in a sandbox.
> CHUCK: Yeah.
> FRANK: And . . .
> CHUCK: That's true.
> FRANK: . . . let's see what we come up with.
> CHUCK: You have a nice way of making me feel better.

Frank described Chuck's assignment in detail—what it was after, what it allowed students to do and teachers to see—and emphasized why it might be appropriate for a first-year writing seminar. He intuited goals that Chuck may not have articulated for himself

—like wanting students to "mess around in a sandbox"—and introduced ways of thinking about assignments that Chuck may not have been conscious of before. Frank blended his methodological and epistemological expertise to affirm and surface the strengths of Chuck's practice; he also generated a new, richer understanding of the principles of solid writing pedagogy it enacted. Simultaneously nurturing Chuck's self-efficacy and framing writing expertise in relation to Chuck's circumstances was not only persuasive, but potentially pedagogical. It began to put knowledge and experience in conversation and establish the attunement at the heart of epistemic and relational dimensions of pedagogical activity.

In a similar vein, James often "pitched" the value of teaching writing in both rhetorically persuasive and pedagogical ways. James explains:

> Now that I think about it, I do try to pitch it in what I think I understand is their professional practice. To a scientist, the journal model might be familiar with them but I also might talk about applying for grants, articulate it in that way to appeal to that. One of the things that I want instructors to think about is the relationship between their disciplinary values about knowledge production and how that's connected to the activity of writing because that's, I think, a way that we can make that connection clearer. If they've got this sense that writing is this something different that I can't spend time in class [on], how do we help them understand how writing is tied up into these ways of thinking and knowing and writing, to go to Michael Carter's article, and get them talking about that? One, that helps them make the connection and, in the end, I think it also can help them make the case for their students as well.

As his comments suggest, James creates an appropriate exigency for writing expertise by showing faculty how closely "the activity of writing" is tied to disciplinary values and knowledge production in their fields. He rhetorically shifts the exigency from "we have to teach writing because students can't write" to "we should teach writing because it is inherent to our disciplinary work," ideally altering content experts' fundamental understanding of those activities. He nudges faculty toward developing a more nuanced sense of their needs, a more accurate view of *how* writing expertise is a fitting response, and more realistic standards for judging what can be gained by drawing on writing expertise in their context.

Orienting to "Everyday Life"

One last set of persuasive strategies writing specialists used to validate writing expertise involves orienting to daily life. According to Hartelius (2011), experts "must orient themselves and their subject matter relative to 'everyday life'" (p. 27). In other words, "it is imperative" that experts, "situate and embed their expertise deeply" in the "day-to-day preoccupations" of others (Hartelius, 2011, pp. 27–28). All "experts face the task of persuading the audience that their daily lives depend on expertise" and many do so by "formulat[ing] their awareness of everyday experiences," routines, habits, and shared needs and wants, "as an appeal to identification" (p. 28). Various experts Hartelius (2011) studied did this by mentioning dirty dishes, dust, and unopened mail, or by conjuring shared values like order and fairness (pp. 28–29). Similarly, writing specialists in my study made their expertise "relevant and accessible" (Hartelius, 2011, p. 28) for disciplinary content experts by communicating an understanding of their daily lives as faculty, instructors, scholars, and/or human beings. Some made it a point to position themselves as fellow professors rather than administrators with no sense of the lived realities of faculty life. For example, Alicia told me that her experience teaching writing-intensive courses before she became director of the campuswide writing program helped her connect with faculty.

> Well, certainly there's that empathy factor of being able to say to someone that you kinda get where they're coming from even though you can in no way know everything that they're experiencing or questions/concerns they would have . . . I realized what was so important was that I had taught writing-intensive courses for so many years. I'd gone through the pro-

posal approval process. I've gone through having to have the coordinators call me and remind me twenty times. [laughter] Having gone through thinking about a course, turning it into . . . being a writing-intensive course and meeting the guidelines . . . I try to let the faculty know that I'm coming at this, not as some outside administrator, but as a fellow faculty member who is also invested in the program as an instructor, teacher, or professor.

By drawing on shared experience, Alicia could demonstrate she understood faculty members' situations firsthand, which reinforced the relevance of her expertise. Likewise, Frank talked about his commitment to teaching first-year seminars as long as he was coordinating the program:

If you've got a program that's so important to the college, which is our first-year seminars, people who are administering that should really have a passion for it and should certainly be teaching every year. You can't have somebody administering this without actually [being] in the trenches. [. . .] If I'm talking with Chuck, and maybe there are going to be times when I may make suggestions of things he would want to think about, that should come out of speaking as though I'm in the trench with him. He's fighting on the front lines and I'm sitting back in the Pentagon with a nice desk and air conditioning and so forth.

As in Alicia's case, Frank strove to narrow the gap sometimes perceived between writing program administrators and disciplinary faculty teaching writing.

Their institutional positions in relation to content experts' shaped how writing specialists oriented to daily life. For example, Liliana, a graduate student administrator who had not yet experienced faculty life, explained how she strove to recognize more generally the lived realities of her colleagues as beings who exist outside of professional contexts. Acknowledging that instructors have different levels of emotional attachment to teaching and their disciplinary work and various demands on their time and energy influenced how Liliana thought of the boundaries of her expertise and what she felt she could realistically suggest:

> I recognize that people have different levels of attachment, detachment from their teaching work, but it can be very time and sort of emotionally intense. I think that's important to take into consideration because it affects how feasible suggestions are because I'm not gonna suggest to someone that they should devote every weekend to providing comments on brief in-class writing assignments that are all scaffolded toward the final paper or what have you, or that they should do a bimodal distribution of papers . . . because if that's not realistic then it's just incredibly arrogant to even suggest that somebody should give up even more of their time to do something. So, I think that's where I guess my personal life comes in.

Taking a holistic view of colleagues allowed Liliana to shape her expertise realistically, making her suggestions more applicable and manageable.

Emily, the only undergraduate writing specialist in my study, didn't try to orient to Kim's daily life as a graduate student, writing teacher, or individual outside academic contexts, perhaps because Emily believed her role as a WA was to share expertise with student writers rather than with Kim. According to Emily it was a shift for her to realize that she could have a relationship with Kim at all:

> I had thought mostly about what role am I going to have with the students. I think that [hearing Kim's concerns about students disrespecting her authority] really helped me realize how I could really also be having a relationship with her, not just with the students. I think that helped. It really encouraged me to communicate with her more, especially whenever the students will bring up issues with their interactions with her. It kind of helps me better see what role I can have in that relationship.

Differences like this one highlight how institutional position and status can enable or constrain opportunities for rhetorically negotiating expertise in CCL contexts. Ultimately, though, orienting to daily life has pedagogical potential as a strategy geared toward making connections, acknowledging common ground, highlighting shared experiences, and generally foregrounding the mutual humanity of individuals in relation. Put differently, orienting strategies have the potential to enact what Nel Noddings (2004) calls a philosophy of relational pedagogy by "accept[ing] an internal theory of motivation, one that locates motive energy within the [learner] and his or her interests and purposes" (p. vii). Accepting that disciplinary faculty have widely varying interests, experiences, comfort levels, and intentions when it comes to (teaching) writing, and acknowledging that writing specialists bring different types of expertise based on their disciplinary knowledge and practical experience, might empower writing specialists to "continue to learn and to share [our] learning in response to the expressed needs" of colleagues in other disciplines (p. viii).

The rhetorical strategies for constructing expertise explored thus far—associating with expert networks, establishing expert techne, framing expertise as most fitting response, and orienting to daily life—have focused on persuading disciplinary colleagues that writing expertise is legitimate, relevant, vital, and realistic. These moves represent ways to address one side of the ideological dilemma of expertise in CCL work—the need to validate writing expertise—and create opportunities to embrace the pedagogical potential of conversations about (teaching) writing. In the following section, I turn to two rhetorical congruencies that speak more directly to the other side of the dilemma—the need to share writing expertise.

SHARING EXPERTISE: URGING ACQUIESCENCE AND INVITING PARTICIPATION

The remaining two rhetorical congruencies Hartelius (2011) identifies involve decisions about teaching either the object of expertise or the process of enacting it and, relatedly, about whether to ask for deference to expert knowledge or invite participation in expert practice. According to Hartelius (2011) many "experts teach the public *what* they know, few teach the public about the ways in which they put their expertise into practice. And even fewer are willing to share *how* they know what they know" (p. 23). For example, the historians Hartelius (2011) studied shared the object of their expertise by explicating the factors that led to the 9/11 attacks (p. 23). They didn't teach the general public how to determine those factors for themselves, didn't expect everyday citizens to become social historians. Most laypersons are happy to defer to historians' expertise, and few would argue they could or should learn the inquiry methods of social historians, a perception that is "a product of the rhetoric of expertise" (Hartelius, 2011, p. 23). Other experts, however, must teach processes of engagement because they need audiences to participate. For example, Hartelius (2011) argues that "blurring of the traditional distinction between experts and laypersons is *Wikipedia's* defining characteristic" (p. 25). The site needs public participation to survive and grow. As Hartelius (2011) points out, the "distinction between teaching a product and teaching a process or practice is inextricably linked to the nature of experts' expectations for the audience's response" (p. 23). Experts who teach products, such as the historians, use rhetorical strategies to encourage audiences to defer to their expertise, while experts who teach processes, as in the Wikipedia example, use rhetorical strategies to convince users to engage.

Because respect for specialized expertise often hinges on how exclusively it is associated with particular experts, teaching a product and expecting deference can reinforce expertise, while teaching a process and inviting participation can threaten it. Writing specialists must walk this precarious line, for we need disciplinary faculty to both respect writing expertise as specialized and legitimate and participate in expert practice by teaching writing in their courses. Indeed, writing specialists in my study both (1) taught products—asked colleagues to defer to their expertise—and (2) taught processes—invited colleagues to participate in expert practice. By analyzing discursive moves used to enact these two activities, I highlight the rhetorical and communicative challenges involved in navigating the dilemma of expertise and surface the pedagogical potential of their responses. My pedagogical interpretation of these activities challenges Hartelius's dichotomies and reveals more options for writing specialists navigating the dilemma of expertise.

Teaching Product: Urging Acquiescence

In Hartelius's (2011) analysis, a psychiatrist is the epitome of an expert who teaches the object or product of his expertise, who "divulges what he knows but not how he knows it" (p. 23). The specialist she studied published a book reporting the results of scientific research and clinical experiments about depression. The book does not teach readers how to replicate disciplinary "ways of knowing" or "the procedures of medical expertise" (p. 23). Instead, it reinforces the rarity and urgency of the psychiatrist's specialized expertise by asking readers to acquiesce to it. In a similar vein, writing specialists in my study identified certain instances when they felt compelled to urge acquiescence to their expertise. When faced with questions about programmatic policies and procedures, for example, writing specialists pressed disciplinary faculty to defer to their expertise, which often took the form of research-based guidelines about best practices. In these instances, expertise was not up for discussion or even explication. Alicia explains:

> Certainly, when people are just getting started on proposing a course, we're first hearing what their ideas are for the course and their goals for the course. Then, we're providing information and the guidelines of, "these will be the things that you'll want to make sure your course does." That [may] come across as very directive, which is probably exactly what Ann would have gotten when she first started here. You need to have this many pages, it needs to cover this amount of revision. Again, this is [a well established] program, and we have people who have been doing this for a really long time, and so they are now at that point of really fine-tuning things, saying, "I've been doing this assignment, and I'm going to tweak it this way." It's a wonderful, I guess, evolution to see that in people's teaching.

Alicia alludes to the difference between seeking deference to guidelines and policy and staying open to adaptation and revision once disciplinary faculty have some experience and are ready to "tweak" their assignments. Deciding among these options calls for reflexive practice and relational attunement, reading the situation and mediating potentially conflicting goals.

Writing specialists also sought deference when dealing with research-based values or principles at the heart of WAC/WID, what Bill called "big T truths." An example of such a principle might be the idea that marking every single sentence-level error does not effectively facilitate student learning or improve writing over the long term. Writing specialists spoke of such principles as "messages" they tried to deliver to disciplinary faculty. In addition to policy and foundational principles, writing specialists also sought deference to expertise when they felt ethically bound to promote a particular position. For Bill, his views on plagiarism-detection software were nonnegotiable. As one of the only writing specialists on campus, he felt obligated to make his views visible and to explicitly challenge what he saw as colleagues' problematic thinking:

> They're wrong. If you believe in making your students pass their papers through plagiarism-protection software, and nine and a half out of ten people at this school believe that that's an OK practice, I stand up and say it's ethically wrong for you to do that. I also want to challenge them, because I think, especially when it comes to writing, I'm one of the only people around here saying certain things about writing. How do I decide what to share? It's strategic. It really is strategic. In some instances I want them to know I'm on their side. "I'm with you. I get it, too. I hate the testing thing. I'm with you." In other instances, I want them to know, "I disagree with you. I think there's a different way of looking at that, and that you should consider it."

Bill highlights the fact that his choice to take a stand is strategic. He does not take those decisions lightly, nor shrink away from saying what he believes.

Frank insisted on deference when it came to how faculty treated undergraduate writing fellows. He described an instance in which a writing fellow was concerned about the role she was playing in a disciplinary course. Frank called the instructor who explained that someone from his department suggested the best way to use the writing fellow. Frank patiently tried twice to explain why the suggested practice was, in fact, not a productive use of the writing fellow. When the instructor once again refused to consider Frank's suggestion, Frank became angry and demanded the instructor acquiesce to his expertise:

> I didn't feel like he was listening to what I said, and so I said, finally, "Listen. You're getting terrible advice, terrible advice. The advice that was given to you by the person in your department is wrong. It is just dead wrong. In this case, you do need to realize that I know more about writing fellows than that person that you were talking to in your department. I don't know who it was. I don't want to know who it was. It was stupid advice. That person does not know what they're doing, and I would appreciate it in the future, if you have questions about how to use the writing fellow, why don't you contact the person who set the program up, and who is responsible for the writing fellows? And I've been using writing fellows for over ten years. I have extensive experience. It doesn't mean that everything I say is right. I make mistakes all the time, but in this case, I can tell you explicitly (do you understand this?) that the advice that you received from the person in your department is wrong advice. It is not productive. It's not the best way to use the writing fellow." Then I apologized for getting mad, because my voice was a little sharper than what it is in this conversation now.

Frank was more direct with this instructor, in his advice and in his tone of voice, than he was in other conversations with faculty colleagues. He used words like "terrible advice," "dead wrong," and "stupid." He explicitly outlined his years of experience and asked the instructor to defer to his advice. As Frank explained, the decision to be forceful and overt was rooted in the fact that the faculty member was using a service provided by the writing center, participating in a program-sponsored initiative. Frank also clearly felt an ethical obligation to protect the time and energy of the undergraduate writing fellow as well as the students in the class. His substantial experience with writing fellows and his felt responsibility motivated him to strongly urge acquiescence to the product of his expertise.

When writing specialists urged disciplinary colleagues to defer to the product of their expertise they sought "a kind of special appointment," implicitly asking to be "deputized as well-suited agents, judges, and decision-makers" (Hartelius, 2011, p. 24). Writing specialists didn't urge acquiescence often; when they did, they needed content experts to trust and respect them enough to defer. This suggests that more typical efforts to temper expertise using strategies described in the previous section might be necessary for establishing a relationship that makes attempts to urge acquiescence more persuasive. Making strategic decisions about when to use more measured discursive techniques and when to urge acquiescence demands pedagogical thinking, because it calls for writing specialists to reflect on the teaching and learning needs of colleagues in any given moment and decide if/when demanding deference is the most appropriate choice. Although it may not initially seem so, when done strategically, urging acquiescence can lay the groundwork for pedagogical relationships by communicating personal values and commitments, the desire to act ethically, and trust in colleagues to respond in good faith.

Teaching Process: Inviting Participation
Writing specialists can't only communicate the products of writing expertise and ask faculty in other disciplines to defer. To forward foundational goals of the WAC/WID movement, writing specialists must teach expert practices; we must invite disciplinary experts to share responsibility for literacy education by teaching writing in their disciplines. Therefore, to some degree at least, we need disciplinary colleagues to understand how we know what we know and how (and why) we put it into practice. This desire creates a rhetorical challenge for, as Hartelius (2011) explains, "widespread participation threatens the material and symbolic value of . . . expertise" (p. 25). That is, experts like the psychiatrist who merely expect audiences to acquiesce to their expertise become more pow-

erful, whereas those who encourage involvement, such as writing specialists, risk diminished views of their expertise, as it appears less specialized. The question becomes: How do writing specialists teach expert processes and practices while maintaining respect for specialized writing expertise?

I use Collins and Evans's (2007) realist theory of expertise to investigate this question. It holds that expertise is not only relational, or rhetorical, but also "the real and substantive possession of groups of experts" (p. 2). That is, expertise is not just a matter of rhetorical persuasion and social attribution; it involves acquisition and maintenance through sustained "socialization into the practices of an expert group" (p. 3). Writing specialists know something about writing—as process, product, and subject of study. Through disciplinary and/or professional training and through ongoing interaction with communities of writing specialists, we have substantive knowledge about writing development and writing pedagogy. Of course, not all writing specialists possess the same expertise. As my study shows, individuals are deemed writing specialists at their institutions based on various criteria, thus the substance of their expertise is different. Alicia has a degree in English education and experience teaching disciplinary WI courses; Bill earned degrees in education and comp/rhet and collaborated with his center for teaching and learning; Frank and James acquired experience and became actively involved in the field through institutional appointments; Liliana's expertise was rooted in her experience teaching writing; and Emily was invited to join a fledgling WA program because of her undergraduate coursework and success as a student. Likewise, disciplinary faculty bring and need/want to develop different types of writing expertise based on various past experiences and current goals. A realist theory sheds light on the dilemma of writing expertise by "taking into account the many different ways of being an expert, the distribution of differing expertises among different groups, and the relations between those groups" (p. 4).

To visualize the integration of rhetorical and realist theories of expertise and understand implications for sharing writing expertise in CCL contexts, imagine a grid with x and y axes. Level of expertise in (teaching) writing moves from novice to expert along the x-axis and writing knowledge moves along the y-axis from broad practitioner knowledge needed to teach writing at the top to specialized scholarly knowledge needed to conduct writing studies research at the bottom. This process resonates with Michael Carter's (1990) notion of "pluralistic expertise" in which writers acquire general knowledge as well as more local or specific knowledge as defined by a particular expert community. As Qualley (2016, p. 97) illustrates, the process is applicable not only for writers but teachers of writing as well. Writing specialists, depending on their home discipline and practical experience, likely begin somewhere to the right of the y-axis. A writing specialist without disciplinary training or active research agenda in writing studies, who has well-developed expertise in teaching writing and facilitating WAC/WID initiatives would be in the upper right quadrant (see Figure 2.1, A), while a writing specialist who conducts research in a focused subdiscipline of writing studies (writing center, writing program administration, workplace literacy, etc.) would be in the lower right quadrant (see Figure 2.1, B). Those in the lower right quadrant possess "contributory expertise" or knowledge of theories, epistemologies, inquiry practices, research methods, knowledge making, and sharing conventions specific to writing studies that allow them to "contribute" to the field (Collins & Evans, 2007; Qualley, 2016). A writing specialist who has both kinds of expertise might have a point in the upper quadrant and a point in the lower quadrant connected by a straight line that shifts according to how the points move from left to right as expertise develops in each area.

Content experts involved in CCL efforts might begin anywhere along the x-axis (see Figure 2.1, C). They could be expert writers in their fields, but have little conscious knowledge about how writing works or how to teach writing in disciplinary courses. As they participate in CCL initiatives (and experience the complex of forces shown to impact professional development and learning), they move diagonally from left to right across the top two quadrants, developing expertise in the practice of teaching writing. In Collins and Evans's (2007) terms, they develop "interactional expertise," or "expertise in the language of a specialism" absent the expertise needed to fully contribute to the knowledge domain (p. 28). As

Donna Qualley (2016) explains, "teaching in all forms would be considered a form of interactional expertise," for while content experts "contribute" to the practice of teaching writing, most don't contribute to "the practice of being a rhetoric and composition scholar" (p. 97). Perhaps with the exception of faculty involved in writing-focused scholarship of teaching and learning (SoTL), who might dip below the x-axis to develop more specialized knowledge in rhetoric and composition or writing studies, content experts probably need only learn enough about writing to teach it, assess it, and build disciplinary writing curriculum. As studies of GTA writing instructors have shown, this process is slow, multidimensional, and developmental (Adler-Kassner & Estrem, 2015; Estrem & Reid, 2012b; Qualley, 2016; Reid, Estrem, & Belcheir, 2012). Plotting it across an imaginary grid acknowledges that faculty may have different end goals and respects the expertise they contribute from any location. Considering how writing specialists and content experts are located in relation to each other on the grid, as well as determining where each needs/wants to go, can inform decisions

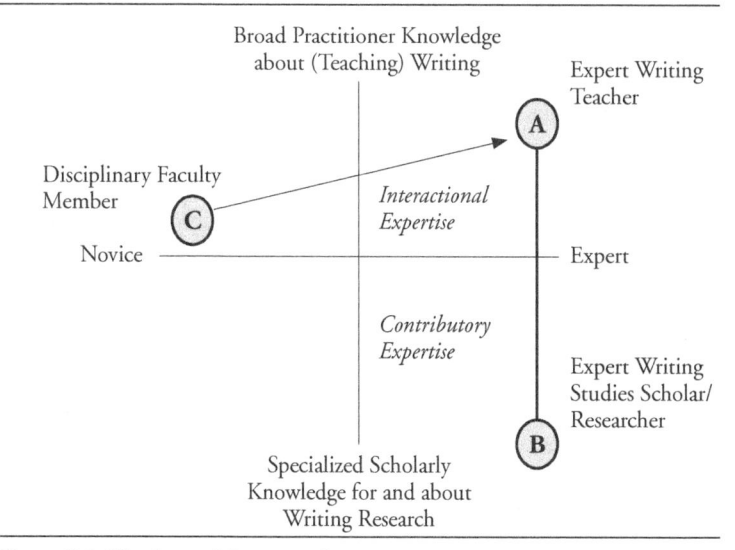

Figure 2.1. Plotting writing expertise.
Grid inspired by IWAC 2016 presentation (Adler-Kassner, Estrem, & Brennan, 2016).

about when and how to share certain types of expert processes as well as when and how to invite participation in expert practice.

Writing specialists hoping to move disciplinary faculty toward the upper right quadrant might begin by plotting their initial position. Collins and Evans (2007) offer a classification system that can help differentiate the kinds of "expertise" about writing content experts bring with them to CCL conversations and reveal how strategies used by writing specialists in my study might move them across the grid. What Collins and Evans (2007) call *popular understanding* and *primary source knowledge* can be types of expertise content experts bring with them or initially acquire upon entering conversations about teaching writing. Popular understanding involves knowledge gained from "mass media or popular books" (Collins & Evans, 2007, p. 19). Disciplinary faculty might have views of writing based on the "literacy crisis" as reported in popular media and/or romantic images of writing and teaching from film, for instance. What Wardle and Downs (2014) call "the traditional story about writing" is another form of popular understanding in which writing is considered an innate "grammatical skill of transcribing speech into print" based on universal rules (p. 2). Popular understandings such as these can be problematic when they gloss over nuance and ignore alternatives. They can trap content experts in the left quadrant of the grid just above the x-axis by predisposing them toward mistaken perceptions of the value or nature of teaching writing and inappropriate expectations for WAC/WID projects. For example, James worked with a political science lecturer who believed "coddling" students by allowing revision or making time for peer review lacked rigor and led to poor writing skills. The lecturer's view was likely rooted in his own experiences as a developing writer and informed by "the traditional story about writing." In this case, popular understanding was problematic. In order to move the lecturer across the grid, James had to shift his (mis)conceptions. He did so by framing writing pedagogy as professionalization, a process that connotes rigorous development, rather than coddling. James urged his colleague diagonally along the x and y axes from more novice assumptions about (teaching) writing to more expert understandings. This example suggests that recognizing, building on, and sometimes shifting faculty members' popular understandings might be one way writing specialists can help them develop writing expertise and invite them to participate in the informed practice of teaching writing.

Another form of expertise writing specialists can recognize and address in disciplinary colleagues is *primary source knowledge*, or expertise gained by reading literature from the domain of expertise without necessarily socially engaging with contributory experts from the domain (Collins & Evans, 2007, pp. 22–23). This type of expertise may develop when disciplinary faculty attend isolated workshops or events sponsored by writing programs in which they read an article or two or study WAC/WID websites without sustaining conversations with writing specialists. According to Collins and Evans (2007), primary source knowledge can lead to "false impression[s]" about the nature of the subject matter" (p. 22). For example, Ann drew on primary source knowledge when she prefaced a description of a "writing tip of the day" she had designed for speech pathology students with "I know this is probably going to drive you [Alicia] crazy. One of our tips is that passive voice is not always a bad thing when you're report writing." When I asked Ann why she framed her tip that way she explained:

> It's common knowledge that in English 101 classes, they teach students not to use the passive voice because it eliminates information. So, when I've attended the writing-intensive workshops in the past, that's been something that has sort of been highlighted tangentially—that students can learn to write more clearly and effectively when they write in the active voice and so I felt like I was sort of directly speaking to her program.

Ann's understanding of what the writing program, and by extension Alicia, believed about passive voice was based on primary source knowledge, attending a workshop, and perhaps reading writing program material. While Ann had experience teaching writing and demonstrated many innovative practices, her problematic primary source knowledge may have kept her from moving across the grid toward a well-informed disciplinary writing pedagogy.

Alicia responded by challenging Ann's primary source knowledge. She praised Ann's choice to begin with a note about passive voice because it connected to what students may have learned in other classes, emphasizing the ways different conventions are embraced by different disciplines.

> ALICIA: That is great. And you know I think the active/passive is a wonderful one to begin with, because most of them have—that's one thing they may be familiar with when it comes to grammar. They probably had English teachers that say, "Use active voice."
>
> ANN: Yeah.
>
> ALICIA: But one of the things that I definitely learned when we work with writers across campus is that there are some forms in, especially in the sciences and report writing like that, that passive voice is expected and needed. Students need to know how to be able to move back and forth.

Alicia carefully nuanced Ann's assumption about the writing program's "stance" on passive voice by tying her own complex understanding of the value of passive voice to her work with writers across campus, "especially in the sciences." The move "reconstituted" the primary source knowledge Ann had developed, and "gradually thickened and layered [it] with more nuance" (Qualley, 2016, p. 98).

While popular understandings and primary source knowledge can contribute to problematic versions of writing expertise, content experts can also bring promising practices to CCL contexts. Recognizing when disciplinary faculty teach writing in ways that align with expert practices in the field, when they are located farther along the x and y axes, can encourage ongoing participation by helping them feel part of a community of practice. For example, Alicia drew attention to specialized disciplinary language as one way to name a writing practice or activity, leaving open the possibility that others may engage in a similar practice and call it something different. During her conversations with Ann, Alicia qualified the names she gave to particular activities (such as learning letters or writing conferences) by saying "at least that's what I call it" or "that's the name I've given it." Alicia explained her strategy this way:

> I realize that these things do go by lots of different names. So just to help people realize I'm not calling something one thing doesn't mean then . . . they may do learning letters themselves and they call it something different. I guess just to keep our thinking open to, "Oh! I do do that but I call it such and such!"

Alicia immersed Ann in the language of writing expertise by using terminology like "learning letter" associated with that discourse community. At the same time, she invited and encouraged cross-disciplinary connections by "keep[ing] thinking open." Alicia's attention to language demonstrates one way to share the product of writing expertise (learning letters) while also encouraging consideration of that product in relation to contextualized practice. Alicia resisted being "too programmatic and prescriptive" to make room for discussion of the processes and theories underlying the product, giving Ann the opportunity to integrate writing expertise with her own in ways that ideally informed and inspired practice in her unique classroom context.

These examples suggest that identifying types of expertise content experts bring with them might allow writing specialists to recognize when certain (problematic or promising) understandings are at play and more strategically negotiate their expertise in ways that productively move disciplinary faculty horizontally and vertically across the grid from novice assumptions or unexamined practices, toward more informed understandings that support their participation in teaching writing as an expert practice.

Writing specialists also invited participation by widening, rather than narrowing, a community of expert practitioners. Unlike Hartelius's (2011) psychiatrist for whom "expert status has material and symbolic value—a value that decreases as more people are inducted into expert cohorts," writing specialists seemed not to buy into "the diminishing value calculus" (p. 24). They treated expertise more like the activists Hartelius (2011) describes, whose success depended on encouraging and facilitating participation rather than establishing exclusivity. In many cases, writing specialists negotiated expertise in learning-centered ways, gesturing toward different sources and locations of expertise. Returning to the image of the grid, they acknowledged valuable points of expertise all across the quadrants instead of relegating it to the far right. I will discuss several discursive practices they used to "enliven possibilities for shifting sites of expertise" (Toohey & Waterstone, 2004, p. 307).

One way writing specialists shifted the locus of expertise was by using collective or mixed pronouns to disrupt the I/expert versus you/novice dichotomy. In the following excerpt, Frank responds to a question Chuck asked about fairness and grading by emphasizing the community-building aspect of the portfolio assessment process embedded in the first-year seminar program at their university (emphasis added in following excerpt). Faculty who teach the first-year seminars grade and respond to student portfolios composed in other sections.

> *I try* not to get too hung up about [laughs] the fairness in grades in one sense because I recognize that just the way in which *we grade*, it's inevitable that it's going to be so imperfect. *I just can't obsess* about, "Oh, my God, it's not perfect." Well, it's just impossible to have even anything remotely close to a perfect system. On the other hand, *I think* there are things that *we can do* so that *we can feel* comfortable that whatever grades *we're coming up* with . . . and *for me,* it's important with regard to sort of community standards, sort of a sense of how *I'm treating the student* is not too far off from how some other people would be evaluating that work. That's why the portfolio assignment in first-year seminar, for example, has really been important *for me personally* [because] every year *I kind of have this way of checking* to see exactly the same text being read by other faculty. What do *they see*? How do *they evaluate* it? What do *I see* and how do *I evaluate* it? How do *I respond* to

that student writing? [. . .] Overall, *you get confirmation.* On the other hand, there certainly are times when either somebody sees something and, "oh, my gosh, that's right." [laughs] *I just didn't [think]* about that angle at all. Or certainly other instances where people are upset or they point out something that *I'm thinking,* well, no, *I'd never think of . . .* identifying that as an important characteristic of this student's writing.

Frank uses *I, we, they, me,* and *you* throughout his comments on the value of portfolio assessment to address the challenge of grading. The "I" refers to his thinking about the process or his personal grading experiences. The "we" references teachers who grade writing—not necessarily just Chuck and Frank, though the "we" does include Chuck in a potentially welcoming way, as a new member of the group of teachers teaching first-year seminars. Frank emphasizes "I" with "for me personally," explaining what he values, as a fellow teacher, about the process of portfolio grading, which is different from describing what is valuable about it from a programmatic or administrative perspective. When Frank mentions getting confirmation from fellow faculty graders he shifts to "you" ("you get confirmation"), linguistically urging Chuck to imagine himself as a part of the community of practice getting confirmation from fellow community members. When Frank allows for possible lack of confirmation or differing opinions in grading he shifts back to "I," effectively distancing Chuck from that potentially threatening possibility and emphasizing that he personally appreciated those experiences even as a seasoned teacher. Through the blending of pronouns, Frank discursively invites participation by including Chuck in a community of first-year seminar teachers ("we") and framing grading as something with which they all wrestle.

Alicia articulates how the pronouns "I" and "we" do different rhetorical work:

> When I'm using that first person reference to "I" just singular there . . . I think about my own teaching or my own interpretation of something. I notice, I've caught myself a lot using "we." Because again, this isn't my program. I recognize very

much that I identify with what I do with a whole group of people. The board and its "we" is meaning the faculty that drive this program, the staff that help run this program. . . .

Alicia's institutional situation is unique in that her writing program was initiated by faculty from across the university. The program features an interdisciplinary writing board, which makes decisions about policies and procedures related to writing research and teaching, and has roots in a campuswide culture of writing that includes and particularly values Alicia's expertise as a writing specialist but goes beyond it as well. Alicia thinks it important to remind faculty about the wider community of writers and writing teachers.

> I guess I would hope and I would expect that when it is the plural big group of us, it does help communicate then that yes, this is bigger than just one class. It's bigger than just two people talking about the teaching of writing, but it is definitely part of a long-standing program in place here. And yet then, when I'm talking about my own experiences then again, it's communicating that this is—I'm sharing with them from my own experience, not just what somebody told me to say. Yes, this is what I've found has been helpful. So . . .

While the writing program is the core and driver of a larger culture of writing at University X, it cannot be the only locus. Pronoun use can invite participation by reminding faculty about the larger community featuring multiple dimensions and locations of writing expertise—various plots on the grid.

In a similar vein, writing specialists shifted the locus of expertise by referring disciplinary content experts to other faculty with relevant writing expertise, a move Alicia called "matchmaking." She explains:

> I was talking to a woman from Women's and Gender Studies, and then there was this nursing faculty member who was already doing the kind of assignment that this other . . . [laughs] I said, "OK, you two need to meet. You need to ask

L. this question because she has a whole semester's worth of ideas to tap into." That's what I'm learning, is huge, is being able to just know, OK, this person has this question. Well, here's a great resource in another faculty member.

Alicia put the matchmaking technique into practice when Ann described experimenting in her speech pathology course with what she called "Writing Tip of the Day." Ann began most classes with a disciplinary-specific "writing tip" (such as when to use passive voice) to help students with writing they were doing in the course. The first time Ann described the writing tips, Alicia immediately mentioned a faculty member from human development doing something similar. When writing tips came up again in a later conversation, Alicia mentioned she shared Ann's practice with the faculty member from human development, reminding Ann of the connection. When the writing tips came up in a third conversation, Alicia explained in more detail how the writing tips worked in the human development professor's course. Ann seemed impressed with how the faculty member's approach might make grading more efficient, and Alicia embraced the opportunity to emphasize how something like a writing tip could function as more than a handbook when teachers help students make connections between the tips and their own writing.

> ALICIA: Now, what [human development faculty member] then does is to number them, so like, you know, [Writing] Tip One, [Writing] Tip Two, [Writing] Tip Three, and then when she's commenting on student writing, she can say, "See [Writing] Tip Two, or see [Writing] Tip Three," you know . . .
> ANN: Wow!
> ALICIA: . . . so that way for a greater explanation behind her comments she directs them right . . .
> ANN: Oh I love that idea.
> ALICIA: . . . to those tips.
> ANN: Yeah. That would be so, and it would be so much faster when we're grading to just reference that.

ALICIA: And it would help them, also, you know, almost—it's you are creating your own handbook for writing, but you are also then putting in, through the instruction, ways for them to use that information, 'cause you know students can be surrounded by that content, but, we know it's hard, for us even, at times to make use of that content, to know how to go back to it, but, by doing that it can, perhaps make that connection better for them.
ANN: Yeah. Yeah. That's a good idea.

Alicia negotiated expertise by using her knowledge of how another faculty member (who we might plot close to Ann on our grid) used Writing Tips to both acknowledge and affirm Ann's expertise, to extend the scope of what the Writing Tips could do, and to emphasize writing studies values—teaching students writing conventions in rhetorically specific ways grounded in their own writing.

Toward the end of their last conversation, Alicia extended possibilities for matchmaking by suggesting the expertise Ann and the faculty member from human development were building would be useful for other faculty as well. She invited Ann to form a panel with the faculty member from human development to share their approach at a future campus writing program workshop. The move reiterated, once again, that Ann had valuable expertise in teaching writing; it decentered Alicia's expertise without discounting it and drew connections across types of expertise located at various points across the grid. Like pronoun use, matchmaking worked particularly well in Alicia and Ann's context because University X has an established writing program long focused on peer learning among faculty. Other writing specialists in the study didn't use this particular move (though they drew out and valued the expertise of disciplinary faculty in other ways) because they didn't have the structures in place to sustain it. Ultimately, the move suggests writing specialists can make different use of the sources and contexts available to them to invite participation by relocating writing expertise.

Writing specialists also shifted the locus of expertise by repositioning themselves as experts, creating moments when they could learn from disciplinary faculty. This move draws attention to the situated experience of individual writing specialists and how CCL conversations can foster movement and growth for writing experts as well. For example, James shifted the flow of expertise by valuing the unique perspective Kim brought to their collaboration as an international writer and teacher of writing. He asked Kim what had helped her, as an international writer and international scholar, to develop her writing. The evocation of Kim's expertise invited her to articulate and explore the "irony" of writing center pedagogy she experienced as a writer firsthand. While she understood the writing center's tendency to resist proofreading and acknowledged that copyediting wouldn't help her develop her writing skills, she explained that often she just needed proofreading. She supported the claim by describing several specific episodes. During his interview, James explained how Kim facilitated his learning by sharing her experience:

> It was good to hear what her experiences were as an international student working with the writing center and saying that that policy [against proofreading], while she understands it, is something that she doesn't find helpful in a lot of situations. That led us to an interesting conversation in, how can we position [Emily, the WA] so that she's doing the kind of work that tutors should be doing.

By acknowledging and drawing on Kim's unique perspective, rather than stating a writing program policy and moving on, James invited her to "share equitably in owning and producing knowledge" (Toohey & Waterstone, 2004, p. 292). The result was a pedagogical one—a new understanding produced collaboratively through the exchange that shaped how James thought of his work and perhaps informing his development as an expert.

Taken together, these strategies for sharing expertise—responding to existing knowledge and practices, strategic pronoun use, matchmaking, and relocating expertise—highlight the "recursive and mutually constitutive relation" among learners and the expert communities of practice they come to join (Beach, 1999, p. 111; Qualley, 2016, p. 98). That is, as novices move from "ubiquitous expertise" (Collins & Evans, 2007) to more specialized forms of (interactional) expertise, and then as they move back and forth between CCL contexts and teaching writing in disciplinary contexts, they help develop knowledge and practice around teaching writing. The strategies explored in this chapter suggest that, like the physics team Jacoby and Gonzales (1991) studied, writing specialists can create situations in which "expertise is shifting and the relationships between newcomers and novices and old-timers and experts are neither linear nor static," where "expert knowledge is assumed by different persons temporarily in ongoing interaction" (Toohey & Waterstone, 2004, p. 293).

Visualizing this process of negotiating expertise as movement across a grid illustrates how teaching writing expertise need not mean diluting its "material or symbolic value" (Hartelius, 2011, p. 24). Much CCL work takes place in the upper two quadrants of the grid—writing specialists help faculty move diagonally upward from the x-axis on the left, across the y-axis, and into the upper right quadrant as they join a diverse community of expert writing teachers. At the same time, particular types of writing expertise, such as research methodologies and specialized theories or concepts pertaining to writing-related subdisciplines, remain the purview of writing specialists located in the bottom right quadrant of the grid—a related but separate, developmental continuum exists below the x-axis for specialists acquiring general and local knowledge in the field of writing studies. Plotting expertise in (teaching) writing dynamically across the grid acknowledges various types of expertise disciplinary faculty and writing specialists possess and graphically illustrates how "differently situated" experts can "talk back to, create, and modify their own and others' theories and knowledge" (Toohey & Waterstone, 2004, p. 291) through interaction. As I have shown, it also draws attention to the epistemic, reflexive, and relational potential of strategies used to negotiate expertise—the pedagogical dimension.

Taking a pedagogical view explodes the dilemma of expertise by disrupting the product/process and defer/participate dichotomies. Writing specialists in my study did not subscribe to a zero sum mentality that would have them doggedly protect the exclusivity of their expertise; nor did they completely relinquish claim to specialized, substantive writing expertise. Instead, they embraced a pedagogical process of negotiating expertise by: (1) persuading content experts writing expertise is valid; (2) teaching the products and processes of writing expertise in ways that encouraged and supported participation in the expert practice of teaching writing; (3) maintaining the material and symbolic value of specialized writing expertise as it emerges from a disciplined field of study; *and* (4) remaining open to learning themselves. Their communicative practices have the pedagogical potential to "allow relationships to be more fluid, rather than becoming static or fixed in one position or another," and "increase the possibilities for diverse participants to share equitably in owning and producing knowledge" (Toohey & Waterstone, 2004, p. 292).

CONCLUSION

Teasing out the pedagogical promise of communicative practices used to negotiate expertise generates initial insights toward a guiding ethic for CCL work. For example, strategies for shifting problematic assumptions based on primary source knowledge or popular understandings highlight the role of reflexive practice. Writing specialists were attuned to the (often hidden) logics informing faculty perspectives, as well as the effects of local institutional histories and situations, and found ways to surface and gently shift them to establish appropriate exigencies for writing expertise and means of determining its value. Strategies for sharing products and processes of expertise, such as pointedly urging acquiescence and inviting participation through pronoun use, matchmaking, and repositioning expertise, illuminate the centrality of collaborative meaning-making and suggest that a guiding ethic for negotiating expertise might involve both teaching and learning dimensions. Orienting moves such as respecting lived realities and acknowledging shared humanity tap into the relational aspect of pedagogical relationship building, while the sheer number of possible communicative options indicates the need for guiding principles that help writing specialists make deliberate, informed, pedagogical decisions about how to communicate across disciplines in CCL contexts.

I continue to elaborate and nuance these tentative insights in the chapters that follow, slowly building toward a cohesive ethic for CCL work. Toward that end, Chapter 3 investigates pedagogical aspects of faculty interactions through the lens of an important trope in WAC/WID theory and practice: change. What can/should change look like when we assume CCL interactions involve the intersection of various types of expertise and the generation of new knowledge? Who should change? Why? When? For what purpose? How can writing specialists both facilitate and embrace meaningful learning and change?

3

Change as Transformative Learning

LIKE THE CONCEPT OF EXPERTISE, CHANGE IS CENTRAL TO CCL efforts—change in how students and teachers understand writing, teaching, and learning; change in curriculum; change in disciplinary writing pedagogy; change in institutional structures and ideologies that devalue writing; change in funding and assessment procedures, and so on. Viewing faculty interactions in CCL contexts as pedagogical activity reveals how notions of change embodied in common approaches to CCL work and popular methods for measuring change don't necessarily support collaborative meaning-making, reflexive practice, or pedagogical relationship building. In this chapter, I use transformative learning theory as an alternative lens for interpreting how faculty perceive and pursue change in ways that attend more carefully to the pedagogical. Drawing once again on conversation and interview transcripts from faculty members in my study, I identify the pedagogical potential of discursive strategies writing specialists use in day-to-day conversations with content experts as well as forces that constrain that potential. From there, I extrapolate further insights that contribute to an overarching ethic for CCL work.

While the objects, agents, and goals for change vary across stages of the WAC movement, a largely limited, one-directional view of change remains constant. For instance, the "evangelical zeal" that characterized the "so called missionary stance" of stage one approaches to WAC (Jablonski, 2006, p. 20) might encourage single-minded pursuit of transformations in disciplinary colleagues rather than the social, collaborative, and multidirectional change that marks pedagogical exchanges. Missionaries "wish to enlighten the unenlightened, convert the heathen, save the damned," Susan

McLeod (1995) explains. "They certainly do not wish to have a dialogue with or to learn from the foreign culture—only to teach their views as the correct ones" (p. 111). Of course few writing specialists approach our work with disciplinary colleagues from such an extreme colonizing perspective, and the field has problematized missionary approaches to WAC/WID work (see, for example, Bazerman, 1991; Bergmann, 1998; Jablonski, 2006). Nevertheless, assumptions underlying this approach, rooted in prominent "conversion" narratives from faculty transformed by WAC experiences, are not uncommon and continue to underlie many prominent metaphors for and approaches to WAC/WID work (McLeod, 1995, p. 111).

Stage two models that emerged in response to critiques of missionary models can also perpetuate one-dimensional change. According to Mahala and Swilky (1994):

> The problem with second-stage calls to base WAC in discipline-specific research is that they usually emphasize . . . the strategic expediency of muting criticism of disciplinary rhetoric and accommodating disciplinary conventions and dominant ways of knowing in order to achieve "permanence" for WAC. (p. 48)

In other words, efforts to make WAC feasible and sustainable can lead to over-willingness to change on the part of writing specialists. By way of example, Mahala and Swilky cite Jones and Comprone's (1993) call to accommodate disciplinary practices by grounding WAC theory in knowledge of disciplinary discourses, methods, and conventions, along with Christine Farris's (1992) decision not to critique troubling uses of writing in disciplinary courses she observed. The problem with this view of change is that in our haste to transcend missionary models, writing specialists can de-emphasize and devalue (to a fault) our own disciplinary expertise (Jablonski, 2006, p. 21). The desire to accommodate disciplines can lead writing specialists to reinforce potentially problematic disciplinary practices and swallow criticisms of writing in the disciplines *because* they are rooted in our own disciplinary values and understandings

(LeCourt, 1996; Mahala & Swilky, 1994). When we are the only ones changing, writing specialists limit opportunities for meaningful, multidirectional change.

Taking a different tack, stage three writing specialists become cultural analysts who examine disciplinary discourses, conventions, pedagogies, and faculty members, advocating for writing assignments and classroom practices that encourage "critical consciousness" of ostensibly oppressive disciplinary structures and conventions. Like the critical pedagogical philosophy it seeks to enact, this conceptualization of change can be troubled on the grounds that it fails to recognize its own politics, that it stops at critique without offering viable options for pursuing material change, and that the single-minded pursuit of others' transformation can be as disempowering as missionary mentalities. Jablonski's fourth stage of WAC seems to have more obvious pedagogical potential, particularly in his suggestion that writing specialists learn to translate our expertise in ways that make sense and prove meaningful to disciplinary colleagues. For that matter, I can imagine particular manifestations of each of the approaches I have outlined here that might support pedagogical change in the form of collaborative, reflexive inquiry (see, for example, McCarthy & Fishman, 1991; McCarthy & Walvoord, 1988). Nevertheless, the view of change implied by traditional approaches tends to move in one direction only, rarely emphasizing multidirectional learning and change.

Similarly troubling assumptions about change are evident in the way faculty engagement in CCL initiatives is commonly assessed, as Walvoord et al.'s (1997) survey of WAC assessment methods reveals. For example, match-to-sample studies rely on faculty self-reports to measure change defined as satisfactory implementation of WAC strategies post-workshop as determined by the researcher (p. 13). Open-ended interview questions capture faculty beliefs about "change and improvement" as a result of WAC, but can be so broad they fail to capture the complexity of faculty's lives and classrooms, whereas case studies tend to adhere to the genre conventions of conversion narratives, once again determining success (or resistance) according to the researcher's definition (p. 13). In short, traditional approaches to measuring change in CCL contexts often obscure the messy, long-term struggle, strife, and delight that constitute faculty experiences of change.

In contrast, Walvoord et al.'s (1997) longitudinal, multi-institutional study treated faculty as learners by seeking to "understand WAC's role in teacher-directed, multifaceted, career-long development, driven by the teacher's struggle to define a self, to balance constraints, to maintain control, and to realize educational objectives in ways consonant with that teacher's own personal vision and wisdom of practice" (p. 16). Not surprisingly, they came to more nuanced conclusions about the nature of change in CCL contexts. For example, they realized faculty development cannot be completely predicted or controlled because faculty members, like all learners, construct meaning by integrating new and existing knowledge. Their study concludes that "the atmosphere, the kind of community" created through cross-disciplinary exchanges has a lasting effect on faculty and a significant impact on their learning (p. 140). Writing specialists are encouraged to "stimulate, not evangelize" and be more deliberate about the environments we foster and relationships we facilitate (p. 140). Condon et al. (2016) have recently contributed to this nuanced picture of faculty learning. They report on a mixed methods study that used a holistic, systems perspective to examine the effect of faculty development on student learning. Findings revealed how programs "can interact with other sites of faculty learning" and draw strategically and meaningfully on local institutional cultures, contexts, and structures to cultivate a "generative culture of teaching and learning [that] provides the crucial environment for ongoing faculty learning" (Huber, 2016, p. x; Condon et al., 2016, p. 6).

My effort to view CCL work as pedagogical activity continues in this vein, shifting the conversation about change from a one-directional focus on outcomes to an investigation of the process of change as an experience of learning. From a pedagogical perspective, change is not the object of missionary zeal, a concession in the name of sustainability, the result of cultural critique, or the goal of rhetorical translation; rather it is a matter of learning through collaborative meaning-making, reflexive practice, and relationship building. In this chapter, I use the notion of liminal learning from transformational learning theory to better understand how writing specialists and content experts experience change-as-learning and to determine how we can better support one another in a mutual pedagogical endeavor. I identify particular discursive moves writing specialists and content experts in my study used to recognize, sponsor, reject, and embrace change-as-learning in order to generate insights that continue to build toward a guiding ethic for CCL work.

FACULTY AS LEARNERS: UNDERSTANDING THE EXPERIENCE OF TRANSFORMATION

If we treat faculty as learners in CCL contexts, it makes sense to consider change in their perspectives and practices in terms of transformative learning. Drawing on the field of adult learning, I define transformative learning as "learning that change[s] . . . meaning perspectives or basic ways of looking at the world" (Mezirow, 1991, p. xvii). According to adult learning theorist Jack Mezirow (1991), meaning perspectives, or sets of "habitual expectation . . . (created by ideologies, learning styles, neurotic self-deceptions) constitute codes that govern the activities of perceiving, comprehending, and remembering" (p. 4). These expectations govern how people see the world and how we understand our experiences within it. Expectations also shape how we behave in the world. Meaning perspectives are made up of "meaning schemes . . . the particular [sets of] knowledge, beliefs, value judgments, and feelings that become articulated in interpretation" and "guide our actions" (Mezirow, 1991, p. 44). We build meaning perspectives and schemes throughout our lives, often absorbing them uncritically from the people, institutions, and environments surrounding us. Inevitably, ideas or events will challenge established meaning-making frameworks. When we respond to such disruptions by critically reflecting on and revising our "habitual expectations" in order to act from a new point of view, we engage in transformative learning.

According to Patricia Cranton (2006), several key features associate transformative learning with adult learning and make it distinct (though not completely unique) from other types of learning; these include the voluntary, self-directed (often collaborative) nature; association with practical needs; relevance of self-concept; attention to experience; and emphasis on individual learning styles (p. 17). Cranton (1996), one of the first to apply transformative learning theory to educators as learners, provides a useful example of transformation in terms of meaning perspectives and meaning schemes: "If an educator holds a perspective on the role of educators as powerful figures of authority and expertise, he or she might then hold a set of interrelated beliefs about what an educator should do, such as determining the agenda, presenting the information, and evaluating the learning" (p. 96). In this instance, the particular understanding of the role of educators is a meaning perspective and the actions taken "are evidence of specific meaning schemes" based on that understanding (p. 96). Taken together, "meaning schemes and meaning perspectives constitute our 'boundary structures' for perceiving and comprehending" (Mezirow, 1991, pp. 4–5). A learning experience is transformative when a person becomes aware of "an invalid, underdeveloped, or distorted meaning scheme or perspective," revises that scheme or perspective, and "acts on the revised belief" (Cranton, 1996, p. 113). With clear ties to the perspective transformation Qualley (1997) describes as central to reflexive inquiry (p. 13), this learning process is different in key ways from how children learn: "*formative* [emphasis added] learning of childhood becomes *transformative* [emphasis added] learning in adulthood" (Mezirow, 1991, p. 3). Because transformative learning theory offers insight into "the dynamics of the way adults learn," it provides a useful framework for writing specialists working with faculty in CCL contexts (Mezirow, 1991, p. 3; see also Vrchota, 2015).

While Mezirow's (1978) mostly cognitive transition process, which Cranton (2006) summarizes to include experience of disorienting incident, critical assessment, exploring options, planning action, and applying and assessing new actions, among other elements, has since been elaborated upon, the underlying theory remains: Transformative learning is defined as the process by which people examine "problematic frames of reference . . . to make them more inclusive, discriminating, open, reflective, and emotionally able to change" (Mezirow qtd. in Cranton, 2006, p. 23). The nature and purpose of transformation have also been extended in various directions (Cranton, 2006, pp. 39–56; E. W. Taylor, 2000)—including a focus on liberatory goals; attention to developmental dimensions (K. Taylor, 2000); attention to the role of individual difference (Cranton, 2000); and exploration of spiritual aspects of transformation (Tisdell, 2003). No matter the scholarly angle, however, "discourse is central to the process" of transformative learning, for "we need to engage in conversation with others in order to better consider alternative perspectives and determine their validity" (Cranton, 2006, p. 36). The role of discourse in transformative learning experiences makes conversations between writing specialists and content experts ideal sites for investigating the phenomenon in CCL contexts.

My study of the nature of transformative learning in CCL interactions is aligned with scholars who attend carefully to unequal power dynamics and connected ways of knowing and learning (Belenky & Stanton, 2000; Gilly, 2004). Through the lens of transformative learning, faculty change is a recursive process of reflection and revision where action "is not only behavior, the effect of a cause, but rather 'praxis,' the creative implementation of a purpose" (Mezirow, 1991, p. 12). This creative, relational view of change shifts away from a view of change as simple cause and effect and troubles the notion that meaningful, lasting change should manifest in observable or reportable behaviors. Instead of determining how to inspire conversion (stage 1 WAC models), accommodate disciplinary needs (stage 2 WAC models), convince faculty to accept (or join us in) critique of disciplinary discourses (stage 3 WAC models), or translate writing expertise (stage 4 WAC models), writing specialists might ask: How can we sponsor "creative implementation of purpose"? How can we build pedagogical relationships that sponsor transformative learning? How can transformative learning lead to meaningful change in individual perspectives and behaviors, as well as the generation of new knowledge and understanding? To answer these questions, we need a richer understanding of the *experience* of transformation through learning.

THRESHOLD THEORY AND STAGES OF LIMINALITY

I find threshold theories useful for making faculty learning visible. Indeed, Land, Meyer, and Baillie (2010) note "a number of resonances" between a thresholds approach to learning and transformative learning theory (p. xii). For example, behaviors exhibited by learners during threshold experiences largely align with Mezirow's phases of perspective transformation. Just as transformational learning theory has evolved to consider noncognitive dimensions, threshold researchers explore the role of affective processes on transformational experiences (Land et al., 2010, pp. xii–xiii). For the purposes of this chapter, threshold theory offers a window into the experience of transformative learning by drawing attention to the messiness of the process and acknowledging the difficulties learners endure. Because transformational learning is inherently integrative, troublesome, and irreversible, the experience is often fraught with anxiety and "stuckness." To make better sense of that stuckness, Land, Meyer, and Baillie (2010) understand the experience of transformational learning in relation to features of threshold concepts (TCs), which they describe as:

> certain concepts, or certain learning experiences, which resemble passing through a portal, from which a new perspective opens up, allowing things formerly not perceived to come into view. This permits a new and previously inaccessible way of thinking about something. It represents a transformed way of understanding, or interpreting, or viewing something, without which the learner cannot progress, and results in a reformulation of the learners' frame of meaning. (p. ix)

Teachers and researchers across fields have found the idea of threshold concepts useful for theorizing, investigating, and scaffolding transformative learning. Recently, the field of composition and rhetoric has begun to articulate writing studies threshold concepts (Adler-Kassner & Wardle, 2015b), to use threshold theory to understand the role of transfer in the development of writers and teachers of writing (Adler-Kassner & Estrem, 2015; Adler-Kassner, Majewski, & Koshnick, 2012; Clark & Hernandez, 2011; Moore,

2012); and to explore how threshold concepts might work their way into WAC/WID efforts (Anson, 2015).

Despite the energy around threshold theory, it might initially seem incompatible with the pedagogical framework I use here, rooted in constructivist values such as collaborative meaning-making, reflexive practice, and relational attunement. Notwithstanding an emphasis on recursive movement and liminality, threshold implies crossing over from novice to expert; "irreversible" threshold concepts are presumably determined by a community of experts who help facilitate newcomers' engagement with them through a socio-cognitive process of acculturation. However, it is important to remember that threshold concepts are not static or stable. They are messy, morphing ideas that can grow and change over time. David Perkins (2010) celebrates "the fecundity of threshold concepts, the evolutionary proclivity of the idea toward adventurous and fruitful mutation" (p. xliii), and Adler-Kassner and Wardle (2015b) refer to writing studies threshold concepts "as 'final-for-now' definitions of some of what our field knows" (Land, 2015, p. xiii). Meyer and Land's original characterization of threshold concepts as "discursive in nature" and "subject to the endless play of signification" actually resonates with a pedagogical framework that seeks to understand the work teacher-learners undertake together (Land, 2015, p. xiii). Throughout this chapter, I will note places where faculty in my study seemed to be wrestling with writing studies threshold concepts as they are currently articulated. However, for the purpose of this project, I'm less concerned with threshold concepts as objects of study and more interested in threshold theory, broadly conceived, as a lens for making learning visible. For me, the notion of learning thresholds draws attention to learners' experiences of troublesomeness and "stuckness," opening those experiences up for inquiry and investigation.

More specifically, Land et al. (2010) treat transformative learning as a recursive journey through various states—preliminal, liminal, postliminal, and subliminal—a perspective that highlights for closer study key moments in which learners' experiences seem to have shared characteristics. In the preliminal state, the transformational journey is initiated by troublesome or provocative knowledge that "unsettles prior understanding rendering it fluid" (Land et al., 2010, p. xi). The key feature of this state, the encounter with troublesome knowledge, or what Mezirow (1978; 1991) would call the "the disorienting dilemma," has an "instigative" effect that propels learners into a liminal state (Land et al., 2010, p. xi). Learners begin "a reconfiguring of . . . prior conceptual schema and a letting go or discarding of any earlier conceptual stance" (Land et al., 2010, p. xi). Important shifts (ontological, epistemological, identity-based) begin to build toward new understanding, which carries learners across "conceptual boundaries" to a new space wherein "both learning and the learner are transformed" (p. xi). At this point the learner has entered a postliminal state; an "irreversible transformation" has taken place in which the learner will never see herself, the subject matter, or the world around her the way she previously did (p. xi). Land, Meyer, and Baillie (2010) reiterate the recursiveness of this journey; learners tend to "oscillate" among states rather than progress sequentially through them. The transformational process also involves a "subliminal mode" in which the "underlying game" or "ways of thinking and practicing that are often left tacit come to be recognized, grappled with and gradually understood" (p. xi). While researchers have mapped student learning across these states in various disciplinary contexts (see, for example, Land, Meyer, & Smith, 2008; Meyer & Land, 2006), we've yet to investigate if, when, and how disciplinary faculty experience those stages in CCL contexts. Doing so can enhance our understanding of change as transformative learning in CCL contexts and reveal communicative practices for embracing and scaffolding the journey.

Understanding the Pre/Liminal State: Constructivist Responses to Troublesomeness
The preliminal state, in which provocative knowledge troubles previous understandings or views of the world, is characterized by discomfort. Perhaps this is not surprising; teachers know that uneasiness or disquiet has the potential to make space for learning. Chuck, the computer science faculty member in my study, put it this way:

If you reflected on your own behavior and you didn't have some negative feeling about it, you probably wouldn't change it, right? You wouldn't change. You wouldn't have a reason to. It's like it's no big deal. The whole reason that it is a big deal is what makes you change it, but it's also the thing, that as a side effect makes you feel kind of self-conscious about your actions.

Julie A. Timmermans (2010) reinforces Chuck's sentiment: "in order for transformation to occur" learners must experience dissonance, or find knowledge/phenomenon "troublesome" (p. 9). While troublesomeness is an inherent feature of threshold concepts, it is not arbitrary; in fact, it carries great promise. Land and Meyer (2010) elaborate: "Troublesomeness and disquietude is purposeful, as it is the provoker of change that cannot initially be assimilated, and hence is the instigator of new learning and new ontological possibility" (p. 63). Change can only happen when existing ways of knowing are disrupted; when new knowledge cannot be assimilated, different ways of knowing, doing, and seeing the world become possible.

The implicit promise of troublesomeness does not make it less painful, however. Drawing on Robert Kegan's (1982) interdisciplinary constructive-developmental theory, Timmermans (2010) explains transformative learning as the coordination between what we experience as subject—what we cannot see as separate from ourselves—and what we experience as object—that which we see, engage, reflect on, and control outside ourselves. Coordinating this duality, achieving "dynamic equilibrium," means seeing as object more of what we used to see as subject or self (Timmermans, 2010, p. 7). This dynamic process involves separation, disconnection, and loss, constituting "both a cognitive *and* a deeply emotional venture for learners" (Timmermans, 2010, p. 7). In other words, transformation is innately painful because it involves a giving up of self. In fact, as Timmermans points out, Boyd and Myers (1988) associate stages of grief with the transformative learning process. Acknowledging the role of troublesomeness in transformative learning highlights what writing specialists know as classroom teachers but may not always remember in our work with faculty colleagues: difficulty, discomfort, and unease are part of learning.

According to Land, Meyer, & Baillie (2010), the painful disequilibrium provoked in the preliminal stage lingers into the liminal stage as well. Liminality is characterized by "integration of new knowledge" and reconfiguration of existing meaning-making frameworks which "occasio[n] an ontological and an epistemic shift" as new understanding is achieved (p. xi). The reconfigurations and shifts unfold in a recursive process that involves starts and stops, dramatic change and periods of "conceptual stasis," as well as ongoing cognitive and emotional discomfort (Kinchin, 2010, p. 53). The more we can identify and understand factors shaping learners' experiences of liminality, the better we can encourage persistence in the face of the pain and uncertainty that characterize this aspect of transformational learning. David Perkins (2006) identifies five types of troublesome knowledge, each of which illuminates different reasons learners may experience "stuckness." Mapping these types across faculty learning in CCL contexts can help writing specialists better understand and support diverse and potentially painful experiences of pre/liminality.

Ritual Knowledge

The first type of troublesome knowledge Perkins (2006) distinguishes is ritual knowledge. Ritualized knowledge "has a routine or rather meaningless character" (p. 37), like memorizing dates in history or rotely applying a routinized mechanism for problem solving in mathematics. Comments from Ann suggest that the act of assigning writing initially constituted ritual knowledge for her.

> When I started as an assistant professor I really showed up to campus on the first day and the first thing I did was attend the writing-intensive workshop because I have been told that I was going [to] teach this course. And I hadn't finished my dissertation, I was going to finish it that semester, and I did and that was fine. It's just that the farthest thing from my mind was developing this course in which writing was going to be

a major component. And I didn't want to do it and I went to the course and it was fine . . . I taught the class, writing-intensive, and it was fine.

Ann's first experience teaching writing in a disciplinary course was a "fine," somewhat meaningless, surface-level practice. She went to her first WI workshop for instrumental reasons, so she could survive the WI course she'd been assigned to teach. As Ann's comments indicate, ritualizing the knowledge and practice of teaching writing was by necessity her goal the first time she worked with a writing specialist. She needed the practice to quickly become routine, to require little thought, because as a newly hired, tenure-track assistant professor still working on a dissertation, she simply could not prioritize teaching writing at that time.

> I really used the writing specialist in a very different way. I mean I needed her to show me how to structure this class, given what the content of the class was. And when at the end of that first semester my teaching evaluations weren't great, I needed her to show me changes that I could make that would not be overly time consuming because I was a stressed out assistant professor, that I could gradually start to incorporate and improve the quality of the course.

Ann appreciated ritual knowledge as a "stressed out assistant professor" because she had other demands on her time. Perkins (2006) acknowledges that learners might resort to ritual knowledge as a means of coping with less than ideal circumstances for learning. As a result, they learn enough to get by "without developing any real insider feel" (p. 37). Ann was probably not transformed by her learning in this instance.

However, Ann's circumstances were different when she began working with Alicia. She was a tenured professor who had enjoyed some success with the WI course she'd taught for some time. Those conditions created space for her to think more critically about ritualized knowledge and practice in teaching writing. Ann explained her situation this way:

I've never sat down and just talked to someone in recent years about how the writing-intensive class is going, and my experiences, and just get her feedback. Like I mentioned before, I had met with writing-intensive, or the writing center staff, when I first came here. That was in more of a crisis situation where I didn't feel like the class is going well and I needed some advice to sort of remedy the situation. [. . .] But this was really an opportunity to just talk about assignments that I had been giving over the years for a while and not because I necessarily needed to put something in place right away, but just an opportunity to kind of talk to somebody about how could I do this differently, how could I make it better? And so I found it really positive and so good for me, in terms of thinking through the course in a more critical way.

As Ann explained, she had been teaching the course the same way for a while and things were going fairly well. The lack of urgency to improve it and reduced pressure in other areas of her professional life created the conditions for Ann to dig into her practices more deeply and consider changing them from a more informed perspective.

During their conversations, Alicia took advantage of Ann's desire to critically consider her practices. Rather than rubber stamp practices that were working well or offer quick fixes for issues Ann described, Alicia helped prevent ritualized knowledge by making particular approaches to teaching writing meaningful for Ann as a learner. Alicia and Ann's exchange about the value of Ann's writing tips of the day described in the previous chapter is a perfect example. By situating her Writing Tips in disciplinary terms, Alicia showed how Ann's activity enacted a WAC/WID threshold concept—"writing is a way of enacting disciplinarity" (Lerner, 2015). In doing so, Alicia made what could have become a ritualized practice meaningful in the context of Ann's teaching and in the context of their conversation.

While contextualizing practice seems to be a useful strategy for making ritual knowledge meaningful, it is important to remember the role of timing in the process of change. Alicia's strategy worked because Ann was where she was in her life and career. Put differently, addressing this type of troublesome knowledge takes pedagogical tact (Van Manen, 1991, 2015). Writing specialists must learn to interpret the circumstances enabling and constraining learning in any given moment and make communicative decisions in response. Certain situations can encourage or even demand ritualized knowledge, which might be a good place to start working with someone new to teaching writing; other circumstances might call for disrupting ritualized knowledge to make it differently meaningful. Writing specialists need communicative strategies and habits of mind for encouraging transformative learning in the face of this type of troublesomeness.

Inert Knowledge
The second type of troublesome knowledge Perkins (2006) identifies is inert knowledge, or knowledge that "sits in the mind's attic," called forth only when directly prompted (p. 37). Knowledge becomes inactive or inert when learners don't see ways to make it immediately applicable to the world around them. Seemingly abstract biological concepts, irrelevant math formulas, and passive vocabulary are examples of inert knowledge (p. 37). Perkins (2006) identifies inert knowledge as a problem with learning transfer. As Elizabeth Wardle (2013) puts it, transfer involves "bringing prior knowledge to bear to solve problems" (p. 150). Sometimes, Wardle explains, the relationship between an existing problem to be solved and prior knowledge is clear and prior knowledge can be applied directly more or less in the current situation (near transfer). Other times, differences between an immediate situation and the context in which prior knowledge was learned is so different that one does not appear relevant to the other. In these situations, prior knowledge must be adapted or revised more substantially. As Wardle (2013) suggests, far transfer can call for "*repurposing*" (Prior and Shipka, 2003; Roozen, 2008), "*transformation*" (Wardle, 2012), or "*integration*" (Nowacek, 2011, p. 149). When learners do not see opportunities for transferring prior knowledge or integrating new knowledge, that knowledge is likely to become inert.

In the case of content experts in CCL situations, inert knowledge may take the form of achieving some understanding of a concept or principle and then losing that understanding because it cannot be immediately transferred. For example, near the end of Frank and Chuck's first conversation, Chuck worried that while his "mind [was] churning" in the moment, he would "probably forget" the insight he discovered if he did not "use it." Chuck's concern illuminates the reality that knowledge (especially partial understanding) can become inert due to lack of use. Alternatively, putting initial insights into practice immediately, grounding them in lived experience, is a good way to actualize learning, to keep partial knowledge active rather than inert, and encourage transfer. For instance, Alicia resisted inertia by making active use of an idea both in conversation and in Ann's teaching context.

During their first recorded conversation, Ann explained that students wrote a short diagnostic report early in the semester and then a more involved "research-based paper" later in the semester. Ann typically began focusing on the research paper after midterm, but based on students' feedback, she was "trying to figure out if it would be appropriate to really put the paper very early on." As the following excerpt shows, Alicia urged Ann to consider how moving the assignment would work with her carefully sequenced lesson plans.

>ALICIA: So, if you were to move that earlier, would that mess up the overall flow of what you think needs to happen and when, because . . .
>ANN: Yeah.
>ALICIA: . . . it looks [like] these things [daily lesson plans] are building up to that.
>ANN: I know, that's the problem. Well, I wondered if maybe we could introduce this early on, like in the second week of class. Give them the possible topics of . . .
>ALICIA: Mm-hmm, OK [simultaneously].
>ANN: . . . interesting things that they could work on, so that they could be thinking about it in advance, and you

know they'd have the assignment guidelines in advance, that's something else I usually give that to them after the midterm. So I could give them assignment guidelines, and then they could have an opportunity to start gathering . . .

ALICIA: Mm-hmm.

ANN: . . . articles

ALICIA: Mm-hmm.

ANN: . . . but not maybe making the arguments yet.

ALICIA: OK.

ANN: I don't know if that would make it too disjointed, to introduce it, then say: "But we're really going to work on this other, other thing for the next many weeks." So I need to think about this . . .

Ann suggested a possible solution to a practical problem—giving students enough time and support to engage in a major writing project without interfering with carefully structured lesson plans. At the same time, she worried that her solution—to introduce the research assignment early, then focus on the diagnostic report before coming back to the research assignment—might be too "disjointed." For her part, Alicia was an active listener, indicating her engagement and encouraging Ann to continue thinking/talking out loud (Mm-hmm; OK; It looks like . . .) without offering specific suggestions or advice.

Following the exchange above, Ann began to imagine how she could make more time in class for students to develop their thinking about the research project without disrupting her carefully sequenced schedule. She recalled how she used online lectures the previous year when traveling for a conference and wondered if incorporating the lectures this term would open up class time for students to work on their major writing project. The move demonstrates transfer in action. Ann drew on her past teaching experience to imagine a response to a different challenge she was facing. She brought prior knowledge to bear on the present, adapting it to solve a teaching problem. Alicia let her come to the solution on her own. She didn't immediately suggest that Ann "flip" her classroom, a practice we might align with what Adler-Kassner and Estrem (2015) call threshold concepts of constructivist teaching, which are often promoted as part of sound writing pedagogy. Such a move might have led to ritualized knowledge if Ann made the change without fully understanding it, or inert knowledge if she decided not to take the suggestion. Instead, Alicia listened and encouraged Ann's active problem solving. Only after Ann had come to her own sound solution for the teaching problem did Alicia interject by tying Ann's plan to inquiry-based writing pedagogy. She described the framework of KWL from education, which asks students to articulate what they Know, Wonder, and Learn, as a way to structure the brainstorming session Ann made time to build into her class. Ann expressed interest in Alicia's explanation of KWL perhaps because Alicia contextualized the concept in relation to Ann's plan for addressing her specific problem.

According to Perkins (2006), "engag[ing] learners in active problem solving with knowledge that makes connections to their world" is one way to keep knowledge from becoming inert (p. 38). In a similar vein, adult learning theorists (A. Y. Kolb & Kolb, 2010; D. A. Kolb, 2015; Mezirow, 1991, p. 200) cite the importance of emphasizing real world connection and experiential learning when working with adult learners. Gayle, Randall, Langley, and Preiss's (2013) study of faculty learning processes likewise found that "faculty members' confidence in their capabilities to explore and implement new ideas appeared to be related to their ability to bring theoretical and pedagogical knowledge to specific teaching and learning situations" (p. 82). Alicia scaffolded that process for Ann by introducing KWL in a way that subtly prompted Ann to engage in premise reflection—a type of reflection that involves reconsidering the nature of a problem and has the greatest potential to lead to transformative learning (Cranton, 2006; Mezirow, 1991; Mezirow & Associates, 1990). By making the connection to KWL, Alicia suggested that Ann's problem was about more than addressing students' discontent, it was also about making room for the collaborative inquiry process involved in undertaking a sophisticated writing project over time. That idea, which resonates with writing studies TCs such as "all writers have more to learn" (Rose, 2015), "failure can be an important part of writing development" (Brooke & Carr, 2015), "learning to write effectively requires different kinds of practice, time, and effort" (Yancey, 2015), and "revision is central to developing writing" (Downs, 2015), had the potential to be troublesome because it challenged coverage models of instruction and contradicted commonplaces about writing. Alicia and Ann's exchange, however, demonstrates how writing specialists might address possible troublesomeness in conversations with disciplinary faculty by contextualizing problems and solutions, encouraging active problem solving, and inspiring premise reflection.

Conceptually Difficult Knowledge

A third "sort of trouble" learners face, according to Perkins (2006), is conceptually difficult knowledge. Here "a mix of misimpressions from everyday experience, . . . reasonable but mistaken expectations, . . . and the strangeness and complexity of [disciplinary-specific] views of the matter . . . stand in the way" of learners' attempts to comprehend conceptually difficult knowledge (p. 38). In the context of CCL work, disciplinary experts faced with conceptually difficult or counterintuitive knowledge might accept WAC principles on a basic level without really understanding what they mean or the practices they necessitate; or faculty might embrace a WAC practice without achieving deep understanding of the principles behind the practice and consequently fail to communicate those principles to students. According to Perkins (2006), misimpressions or mistaken expectations can lead to a reliance on ritual knowledge—knowledge applied mechanically without deep comprehension (p. 37). Because the successful application of ritual knowledge can mask misunderstandings due to conceptual difficulty (Perkins, 2006, p. 38), to sponsor transformative learning, writing specialists need strategies for recognizing conceptually difficult knowledge and encouraging the patience and commitment necessary to work through the troublesomeness it creates.

The idea of writing as a conversation—rooted in writing studies TCs such as "writing is a social and rhetorical activity" (Roozen, 2015), "writing expresses and shares meaning to be reconstructed by the reader" (Bazerman, 2015), and "assessing writing shapes contexts and instruction" (Scott & Inoue, 2015)—was troublesome for Thomas, the chemistry professor. It was conceptually difficult knowledge because it disrupted the "traditional model" of teaching and learning in science he'd always embraced. His comments below suggest that Frank helped him wrestle with the troublesomeness by capturing his interest and prompting him to imagine a different type of student-teacher relationship at least in first-year seminars.

> I don't know that I've precisely come to grips with what [this whole idea of writing assignments as a conversation] means in terms of my assignment design, but I feel like at a higher level, it makes me think about, "Well, why am I doing writing in my classes?" Which, I think is important. [. . .] It changes my thinking about an assignment from, me in a position of authority, making certain demands upon the students to, perhaps, having us more on the level of peers and iterating something back and forth. I think that's a considerable change in perspective. When I give a chemistry exam, we don't have that much . . . [laughter] of "Oh, let's talk about how you solve this." There's "Oh, no you solved this problem incorrectly." [laughter] [. . .] Actually, I'm gonna be doing a first-year seminar again next year, and so I'm really thinking about those assignments, and there's more opportunity there for having that kind of conversation.

Frank's disciplinary-specific idea of writing as a conversation initially felt strange to Thomas. But Frank was able to plant a seed of change by introducing the concept in a nonthreatening way, speaking from his own experience, and offering concrete teaching practices that enacted the principle. He prompted Thomas to engage in premise reflection, to question what difference it made to see writing as a conversation. While Thomas's exchanges with Frank did not necessarily lead to immediate changes in his assignment design or teaching practices, they did encourage him to reflect "on a higher level" about his goals for students and the kinds of teacher-student relationships that would support those goals. Cases like Thomas's reinforce the value of treating disciplinary faculty as learners and conceptualizing change as the messy, recursive, uneven process of learning. Berger (2004) explains: "As [learners] feel supported and safe, it is easier for them to draw courage from their colleagues—and themselves—instead of from the false sense of certainty that pulls people away from the edge of their understanding" (p. 348). Frank sustained the potential for transformative learning by giving Thomas the space to grapple with conceptually difficult knowledge.

In a similar vein, Perkins (2006) suggests scaffolding conceptually difficult knowledge by inviting learners to (re)discover a principle for themselves under actual circumstances, to "confront the character of the phenomenon" directly and test it on their own terms (p. 39). The importance of trusting learners' processes of self-discovery is central to many theories of writing pedagogy. Learners need space "to consider what they want and need to know" and "devise variations and applications of received knowledge" (Bergmann, 2008, p. 524). "Without space, [learners] cannot come freshly to their experiences under their own volition. Without space, they cannot come authentically to their judgments, findings, observations, actions, and exchanges" (Barnett, 2007, pp. 149–50). Thus, to support transformative learning, writing specialists must give faculty the space they need to learn. After all, as Melamed (1985) observes, "we seem to do our best work when connected with others who trust us and make room for our mistakes" (p. 103).

Alicia brought to light the challenge and payoff of trusting faculty learners with space to explore conceptually difficult knowledge. She told me about her experience working with a nursing faculty member, who I will call Tess, who was looking for ways to analyze and assess student writing. Alicia shared with Tess a report she'd written on writing assessment for the National Writing Project (NWP), hoping it might pique her interest and inform their work together. However, Tess "latched onto" an aspect of the report about which Alicia felt conflicted, the Writing Project's analytical writing continuum based on Six Traits. "This [Six Traits] developed to be a language to talk about writing, and a way to share ideas with students and across—especially that K–12 world—to talk about writing," Alicia explained. "I'm fine with the Six Traits." She clarified, "that's one of those times where—if you're familiar with that from . . . OK. I do shudder when people latch onto that and it becomes their program and their end-all be-all to writing." Because Tess embraced a conceptually complex practice without really understanding it or the implications of using it, Alicia worried that the tool was shaping Tess's understanding of writing development and assessment in problematic ways.

As Alicia continued to meet with Tess, she wondered whether she should explicitly warn her colleague about the pitfalls of applying the traits wholesale and wrestled with feelings of guilt for perpetuating what she thought were misconceptions about writing assessment. At the same time, she put faith in her long-term relationship with Tess, trusting that ongoing conversations would support learning over time. "But we're continuing to work together," Alicia reasoned. "We'll see where that goes. If anything, actually, her students have been thrilled with this and have found it to be very helpful. They're nursing students, they are very lacking in their writing and confidence is nonexistent." While Tess's use of the Six Traits was troubling to Alicia, she was able to acknowledge the use in a particular disciplinary context. She also trusted that Tess's understanding of the traits in relation to writing assessment, clearly a form of conceptually difficult knowledge, would continue to evolve and grow over time. Indeed, as Berger (2004) points out, "the relationships [teachers] have with [learners]—over time—are often our most helpful transformative practice" (p. 347). Alicia's patience with Tess, her trust in Tess as a learner, and her gentle guidance over time opened the possibility of cultivating a long-term pedagogical relationship.

"Foreign" or "Alien" Knowledge
Unfamiliar or contradictory knowledge is a fourth type of troublesomeness that can make learning painful and transformation

difficult. Knowledge is "foreign" or "alien" when it "comes from a perspective that conflicts with our own" (Perkins, 2006, p. 39). Value systems and cultural understandings or mindsets might constitute "foreign" knowledge. For example, Perkins describes how history students often automatically apply present-day mindsets when judging decisions made in different historical eras (p. 39). The cultural and contextual mentalities of the past constitute "foreign" knowledge for these learners. Because CCL work involves interactions among faculty from different disciplinary communities of practice, "alien" knowledge can be a main source of troublesomeness. Mindsets grounded in particular disciplinary logics can understandably feel "foreign" to faculty outside the discipline.

Perhaps the best example of "foreign" knowledge as troublesome emerged in a story Bill told me about his interactions with a psychology professor during a summer workshop. Bill explained how the faculty member, who I will call Ted, rarely contributed to discussion and when he did his comments were "cryptic." Slowly, Bill began to connect Ted's reluctance to differences between his view of teaching and learning and the one implicit in the workshop.

> We learned as the week went on and he had this kind of vision, a very scientific vision, of the classroom where it was basically a bell curve . . . he explained to all of us, a third of the students [in any environment] don't really belong there, they're not gonna pass, a third are the average middle, and the third are the top. And he was explaining to us that this is not just true of his classroom, it's true of the whole college. This is just the way it works in any sort of group.

As Ted's "scientific vision" of the classroom emerged, Bill began to understand his skepticism differently. Ted's view conflicted significantly with the view Bill and his co-facilitator assumed throughout the workshop: Everyone can learn to write. Ted had trouble accepting much of what Bill had to offer because it was rooted in writing studies TCs such as "writing is not natural" (Dryer, 2015a), "all writers have more to learn" (Rose, 2015), and "failure can be an important part of writing development" (Brooke & Carr, 2015), with which he fundamentally disagreed.

> Once he shared [his] viewpoint, it kind of called into question the full enterprise, 'cause if you're saying that . . . the students that you teach are incapable and they're going to fail the day they step in the door, that's the exact opposite premise from the one we're working under which is that, "everybody can do this, the students, that we can all write. We can all have success." So, once he said that, it was like, wow, if that's his worldview, he must be really skeptical of what we're selling here, because that's not our worldview. Our premise is the antithesis of that. But he wasn't like slamming that down our throats or anything, it was just sort of this thing he was quietly holding and then it would come out every once in a while.

From Bill's description, it seems likely Ted (and Bill) were experiencing "foreign" knowledge as troublesome.

As I alluded to briefly in the previous chapter, Bill responded to the psychology faculty member's skepticism by supporting strategies for teaching writing with evidence based on a particular writing research methodology, meta-analysis, that resonated with disciplinary inquiry practices in psychology. "I've had to learn what they will accept as evidence," Bill told me. Because he discovered "meta-analysis is a word psychology professors like to hear," Bill now incorporates George Hillocks's "meta-analysis of what works [in] teaching writing" into writing pedagogy seminars. Instead of putting explicit pressure on Ted's view of teaching and learning or arguing for his own disciplinary mindset, Bill offered compelling evidence for the value of particular approaches to teaching writing. By offering evidence in a familiar form, he likely made his suggestions less "foreign" for Ted and his colleagues and perhaps even encouraged them to experiment with practices they may have originally dismissed.

Bill admitted that "the process of imagining [the] world[s]" of people from disciplines such as math, science, and finance was more difficult for him. The greater the distance between his own and other faculty members' philosophical perspectives, the more Bill relied on the faculty member to put in the effort to bridge the gap. Bill explained:

> I will defer more, I won't challenge as much, I won't question as much, if I challenge or question at all, because I just assume at a root level, there's a lot of things about what they do that I can't understand and don't understand. . . . My suggestions are hedged a bit more . . . I just try to be more respectful of what I don't know.

While Bill frames his hesitancy to engage foreign disciplinary worldviews as a matter of respect, the lack of engagement could have implications for how faculty learners are able to process "foreign" knowledge. At the same time, deferring may prevent writing specialists from learning about our own disciplinary expertise from and through other disciplinary perspectives. In short, writing specialists must learn to walk the line between respecting and failing to engage perspectives they don't understand.

Perkins (2006) suggests that actively exploring alternative perspectives can be a more direct response to learners struggling with "foreign" knowledge. "We can provoke compare-and-contrast discussions that map the perspectives in relation to one another," Perkins explains (pp. 39–40). Workshops like the one in which Bill and Ted interacted, where faculty from across disciplines work together over a week or more, provide a perfect opportunity for this type of comparative exploration. Faculty learners have the chance to engage "in dialogues and debates that require representing different points of view" (Perkins, 2006, p. 40). The variety of perspectives might defuse resistance to any one mindset and illuminate connections among them. Moreover, as writing specialists investigate disciplinary worldviews in workshops and other settings, they bring those perspectives into one-on-one conversations like the ones I observed for my study, and can potentially achieve the same effect as workshop dialogues and debates.

Tacit Knowledge

Tacit knowledge—that which we know but cannot tell (Polanyi, 1966), "knowledge we act upon . . . but are only peripherally aware or entirely unconscious of"—is an additional source of troublesomeness for learners (Meyer & Land, 2003; Perkins, 2006, p. 40). Perkins calls tacit knowledge "one of those good news bad news stories" (p. 40). We need implicit, commonplace understandings to act efficiently in practical or professional situations. It would not do us well if we had to stop and think deliberately each time we were called upon to drive a car or do simple multiplication. At the same time, a learner's tacit knowledge can get in the way of deeply understanding a new concept. Because tacit knowledge is buried in the subconscious, the learner cannot articulate or examine it, nor can a teacher identify or correct it, which can leave teachers and learners both baffled by misunderstandings. By the same token, the tacit knowledge a teacher holds, can "operate like a conceptual submarine that learners never manage to detect or track" (Perkins, 2006, p. 40). Teachers' unidentified tacit knowledge, when it remains invisible to learners, can make deep learning long and painstaking if not impossible. In short, teachers' and learners' tacit assumptions can unwittingly operate at cross-purposes and impede learning.

In CCL contexts, content experts bring tacit knowledge about writing and learning to write to their teaching and to conversations with writing specialists. As Perkins (2006) points out, "we often get the hang of enquiry in a discipline without having a clear reflective conception of what we are doing" (p. 40). This phenomenon is perhaps more common for writing than inquiry, because while disciplinary faculty may have received explicit instruction in the inquiry methods valued in their fields, they are less likely to have been taught directly how to write. As I suggested in Chapter 2, faculty members' tacit knowledge and unexamined assumptions about writing based on their own experiences shape how they teach writing as well as how they understand and interact with ideas writing specialists introduce. Their "tacit presumptions can miss the target by miles," as when faculty are determined to find and mark all grammatical mistakes in student writing because their own writing as students was similarly scrutinized (Perkins, 2006, p. 40). Alternatively, making tacit knowledge visible can lead faculty to make connections between their own experiences writing and learning to write and writing specialists' ideas and suggestions about teaching writing. Those connections can make seemingly troublesome knowledge appear less "foreign" and more personally relevant.

James, who directed the undergraduate Writing Associates Program at State U., put it this way:

> Suddenly when [content experts] make that connection, they come to their own conclusions about making that connection clearer. Suddenly, "I go through this process of drafting, and it's messy, and I do all of this informal writing to prepare for my research, and I really consult with my colleagues, so why don't I ask my students to do that?" [. . .] People make that connection more quickly, and more thoroughly, than if we had just sat down and say, "Here's what you're going to do to create a writing-intensive course. You must have a drafting. You must have these informal assignments." They end up doing that on their own, when they start making the connection between their own professional practice. As I read some of the older articles about the early writing across the curriculum workshops, say at Michigan Tech. That was always the fundamental place to begin.

As he explained, James helped content experts make explicit tacit knowledge by prompting them to reflect on their past experiences and current practices. As James also pointed out, writing specialists have long taken this approach, making faculty members' unexamined assumptions and experiences with teaching and learning writing the center of CCL workshops and conversations.

The approach is not unlike a constructive teaching strategy Perkins (2006) calls "surfacing and animating" (p. 40). The goal is to "get tacit presumptions out on the table at least for a while" so they can be examined "not just as objects of discursive analysis but as systems of activity to engage" (p. 40). In the case of disciplinary faculty, the aim is not to analyze and critique disciplinary perceptions of writing but to illuminate them and situate them in disciplinary communities. Those assumptions are then put in conversation with ways of thinking (about teaching and learning) from writing specialists' perspective so as to explore resonances and departures. Ideally, the result for all involved is a deeper understanding of how writing works and a richer sense of how teaching and learning writing happens in different contexts.

The following excerpt from a conversation between Frank and Thomas shows one way "surfacing and animating" can look in conversation. Thomas shared with Frank a realization about how his own day-to-day experiences with writing might help convince students that writing matters, even in the sciences. He started off describing his experience working collaboratively with colleagues to write a proposal. They had circulated a document, editing and commenting in the margins, highlighting changes in color. Thomas told Frank he was considering sharing the text with students as an example of collaboratively writing and revising a professional document. Thomas wanted to use his example to make a compelling case for the value of writing in science and to illustrate that writing, for anyone, is a process. He was tacitly engaging with TCs from writing studies: "writing is a way of enacting disciplinarity" (Lerner, 2015), and "writing is a social and rhetorical activity" (Roozen, 2015).

Thomas went on to tell Frank about a writing experience he has shared with students about revising a grant proposal three times in response to reviewer feedback. Eventually the proposal was accepted. Thomas used the story to convince students to invest in peer review. Once again, in conversation with Frank, Thomas reflected on connections he had already been making (and sharing with students) between his own writing experiences and the enterprise of teaching and learning writing, this time implicitly tapping into the writing studies TC "revision is central to developing writing" (Downs, 2015). The conversation gave Thomas the space to continue to make his understanding of writing explicit, rather than tacit, and help make disciplinary understandings of writing explicit for students as well. Frank encouraged and reinforced Thomas's insights. When Thomas admitted, "you know, in grad school, we didn't get trained to do that [write persuasively], we just kinda read the . . .", Frank capitalized on the ellipsis, interrupting to suggest Thomas create for students an experience, like the ones Thomas had writing collaboratively and processing feedback from reviewers, in which they could get feedback from peers in order to revise their writing. Frank's move transitions between surfacing and animating. Thomas had begun to surface his understanding of his own writing processes and how those might be useful for students to see. Frank guided him to animate those insights with particular teaching practices (in this case peer review). He encouraged Thomas to operationalize the connections he was making between his writing and his students' learning and to explicitly teach students to write in a way that he was never trained. This example illustrates how surfacing and animating might function as a useful strategy for addressing tacit knowledge as troublesome.

As writing specialists accrue more experiences talking with faculty about writing, they might learn to recognize the kinds of knowledge that tend to remain tacit for disciplinary faculty and more purposefully work to surface and animate those understandings. Writing specialists in my study did this with disciplinary writing practices, as I have shown, as well as with issues such as the tendency to reduce writing to surface-level features. But writing specialists must also be ready "to draw out preconceptions that are not predictable," and "to work with preconceptions so that [learners] build on them, challenge them, and when appropriate, replace them" (Bransford, Brown, & Cocking, 2000, p. 20). Ways of teaching writing should not be based on buried assumptions and unexamined internalized experiences but embraced deliberately because they resonate with teachers and learners in a given context.

Given the myriad manifestations of troublesomeness I have explored in this section—ritual knowledge, inert knowledge, conceptually difficult knowledge, "foreign" knowledge, and tacit knowledge—it is clear writing specialists need a range of strategies for supporting learners in liminal spaces. No matter what brings faculty learners to "the cliff" or how exactly they experience the "edge of understanding," they "need help to sustain the courage to stand at the edge and work to grow" (Barnett, 2007; Berger, 2004, p. 347). I have used Perkins's (2006) types of troublesome knowledge as a heuristic to pin down and investigate various experiences of liminality because I believe "understanding pieces of the transformative journey allows us [in this case writing specialists] to be more thoughtful, intentional guides" for faculty colleagues in the midst of that journey (Berger, 2004, p. 350). I have highlighted specific ways writing specialists in my study responded to and supported faculty learning, many of which resonate with Perkins's (2006) constructivist teaching practices, including: making knowledge meaningful by grounding it in disciplinary contexts; unearthing discrepancies in initial assumptions; comparing conflicting perspectives to capture the nuance of conceptually difficult or "foreign" knowledge; and surfacing and animating our own and others' tacit knowledge so it can be reflected upon and potentially revised. Faculty are most likely to change their beliefs and practices when "change is centered in their own disciplinary epistemologies, connects faculty to a community of practice, is data-driven, and becomes part of a faculty member's ongoing reflective teaching practice" (Condon et al., 2016, p. 6; Henderson, Beach, & Finkelstein, 2011). I have shown how communicative moves rooted in a view of change as transformative learning might operationalize these insights discursively and pedagogically in CCL conversations. The following section explores the nature of learners' transitions beyond liminal spaces.

Understanding the Postliminal State: Pursuing Multidirectional Transformation
According to Land, Meyer, and Baillie (2010), "as a consequence of [the] new understanding" earned in the liminal state, "the learner crosses a conceptual boundary into a new conceptual space and enters a postliminal state in which both learning and the learner are transformed" (p. xi). Postliminality may seem like an endpoint, a conclusion, the culmination of a journey; indeed Land, Meyer, and Baillie (2010) emphasize that "this is an irreversible transforma-

tion" (p. xi), for once learners fully grasp a threshold concept (following the oscillation that characterizes the liminal state) they will never see the subject matter, or in some cases the world, the way they did precomprehension. At the same time, Land and Meyer (2010) observe "considerable *post-liminal variation* in [learners'] level of new conceptual understanding and often much residual difficulty, misconception or partial understanding" (pp. 63–64). In CCL contexts, this observation has implications for how writing specialists understand and support content experts' extended learning trajectories. As Walvoord et al. (1997) and Condon et al. (2016) remind us, faculty do not learn from CCL experiences in isolation, and they do not stop learning when direct CCL interventions (such as workshops or consultations) are over. The concept of postliminality offers a lens for identifying and analyzing extended traces of transformative learning. Further, investigating the postliminal state illuminates ways writing specialists can ensure the goal of "irreversible transformation" does not perpetuate problematic views of change such as those inherent in missionary or critical approaches to CCL work.

According to Aidan Ricketts (2010) the promise of understanding "threshold experiences" as deep or transformative learning brings with it a "corresponding need to be cautious" (p. 47). He urges teachers not to take lightly "the potential ethical dilemmas" that emerge when accompanying learners on journeys of transformation (p. 47). Ricketts argues that reaching transformed understandings does not necessarily involve critical awareness, though it should; in fact, the process can actually close down "the capacity to critique those perspectives" (p. 45). Meyer and Land (2003) also admit threshold experiences can have a "colonizing" effect on learners (p. 10). To mitigate that possibility, Ricketts (2010) urges teachers to acknowledge and contend with another form of troublesome knowledge he calls "loaded knowledge." According to Ricketts, loaded knowledge refers to instances in which "the discipline itself attempts to mandate the acceptance of ideological or philosophical assumptions which privilege certain world views over plausible alternatives" (p. 47). Loaded knowledge does not refer to embedded worldviews, Ricketts clarifies, for all disciplines inherently have those, but it points to "particular situations in which the discipline appears to be demanding unquestioned acceptance of a contingent perspective as a precondition to success in the discipline" (Ricketts, 2010, p. 48). Often these incidents are invisible to core members of the discipline because they have so thoroughly internalized the worldviews inherent in disciplinary assumptions.

An example of loaded knowledge in WAC/WID might be the idea that writing should be the heart of undergraduate education because it is vital for student success in college, in the workplace, and in the communities to which students belong. Some scholars who study L2 (second-language) learners have begun to question this fundamental assumption undergirding the WAC/WID movement (Cox, 2011; Leki, 2003). Following intense case studies of L2 learners' experiences with writing in the disciplines and across the curriculum, Ilona Leki (2003) points out the often-dire consequences for L2 students of "placing such a high value on writing" (qtd. in Cox, 2011). Likewise, Cox asks if WAC/WID administrators "place the same overemphasis on writing" by paying "more attention to the potential benefits of integrating writing into curricula than the possible costs to some students?" By reflecting critically on the WAC/WID enterprise from the perspective of L2 student writers, Cox and Leki reveal an example of "loaded knowledge" and its implications. Another example of loaded knowledge might be the worldviews underlying writing studies TCs. For example, the expectation undergirding Bill's faculty seminar for teaching writing—that all student writers can improve, rooted in the writing studies TC "all writers have more to learn" (Rose, 2015)—might have constituted loaded knowledge for the psychology professor who used a bell curve to determine which students were (un)able to succeed.

According to Ricketts (2010) "there may be good reasons why a particular discipline chooses to adopt the world view that it has, (biology and evolution for instance)," and the idea of loaded knowledge "does not suggest that they should be jettisoned, but rather that every effort should be made to identify such assumptions, and make it explicit that the discipline proceeds from such an assumption" (p. 48). New learners should not "feel compelled to internalize the discipline's world view in place of their own prior equally plausible perspectives" but feel welcome to critically consider and critique it (Ricketts, 2010, p. 48) in relation to their own truths. Acknowledging the possibility of loaded knowledge in CCL contexts means resisting the treatment of TCs as static objects defined once and for all, and framing them instead as "final-for-now definitions of *some* of what our field knows" (Adler-Kassner & Wardle, 2015a, p. 4). Failing to allow that even knowledge for which there is "sufficient consensus" within a community of practice (Adler-Kassner & Wardle, 2015a, p. 4) can continue to evolve and change increases the chance of uncritically forwarding loaded knowledge, constrains the growth of the field, and limits CCL interactions. Alternatively, identifying and critically reflecting on loaded knowledge promotes the evolution of writing studies and keeps transformative learning in CCL contexts from becoming oppressive or unethical. Findings from my study suggest that while writing specialists used discursive strategies to create open learning environments, their efforts did not result in critical work with loaded knowledge as often as we might think.

Alicia, like many writing specialists in my study, demonstrated a commitment to self-reflection and a desire to be open to change. Referencing Nancie Atwell, she explained: "I'm always beginning, there's always new things to learn, there's new ways to consider. . . ." Alicia saw her role as a writing specialist as an opportunity to embrace a learner's stance. "I don't see my teaching as static in any way," she told me, "I like to approach things with new perspectives and try different things." When meeting with faculty from different disciplines, Alicia tried to learn from them in terms of "content," how they "are using writing to learn content," and "unique ways that they're writing in that discipline." Similarly, James described how much he enjoyed being surprised by what his disciplinary colleagues had to say about teaching and writing. "Because they're so self-reflexive," he explained "they have . . . these insights that really help me see things in some newer ways." Like Alicia, James strove to embrace a learner's stance by entering conversations with content experts expecting to learn from their insights rather than assuming he would only share his own.

Not only did writing specialists profess their openness to change, they worked to create atmospheres of change by modeling openness in conversations with disciplinary faculty. For example, James told Kim a story about giving his sister feedback on her writing because it was the first time he realized "why this relationship between the tutor and tutee can be so difficult." By sharing the story, he surfaced the challenge of building productive relationships with writers. As a discursive strategy, the story positioned James as a learner who once wrestled with the same complex writing-related concepts disciplinary faculty did. Modeling openness has the potential to unearth loaded knowledge—to make visible the contingent, constructed nature of writing studies threshold concepts and the underlying worldviews they imply—by acknowledging that writing specialists haven't always understood or embraced certain core disciplinary ideas. Ricketts (2010) suggests acknowledgment is a promising strategy for enacting and encouraging reflective thinking that can mitigate loaded knowledge: "The educator's own critical reflexivity . . . produces an atmosphere that invites [learners] to encounter new and potentially confronting critiques as a means of stimulating the [learners'] own processes of questioning" (p. 50). Likewise, Qualley (1997) submits, "if as teachers, we also share how we came to formulate our positions or how we came to hold the beliefs we do, we can model a way of approaching and thinking about ideas for [learners] to emulate" (p. 142). In other words, by referencing their own learning, and their evolving relationships with key concepts in the field, writing specialists can create atmospheres ripe for critical reflection and deep learning.

My research suggests that modeling openness can impact how faculty view their own learning and perceive writing specialists. For example, Bill presented himself as a teacher open to change by explaining how he used to promote the use of rubrics for writing assessment, but had recently moved away from rubrics in his own teaching. The move was salient for Lena. She explained:

The fact that [Bill] has gone from being a rubric man to not, shows me . . . I think that's one of the connections I have. I feel that, though he has this expertise, in terms of how we teach, we're similar. There's no one right way and what works one time may not work another time. Things change and you may have to just be adaptable. I see him as someone who is very flexible and adaptable, which has strengths and is problematic, too, I find for myself.

Lena saw Bill as "someone who is . . . open to trying different things if he thinks something is not working," which led her to reflect on the use of rubrics as well as on the benefits and drawbacks of her own tendency to constantly make changes in her teaching.

In addition to surfacing past learning experiences, writing specialists had opportunities to make real-time learning visible for disciplinary faculty. For example, Alicia told me about an "aha" moment she experienced in a conversation with Ann. Alicia had heard many faculty voice concerns similar to Ann's about how to make feedback and grading fair in large sections where students receive comments from several TAs in addition to the instructor. Alicia had been pondering the question for some time, but while talking with Ann, she grasped the value of multiple forms of feedback for students in a new way. She experienced a "lightbulb moment" when she thought about how faculty writers also get feedback from multiple reviewers when submitting their work for publication and how it can often be a benefit. Alicia's "discovery" could be indicative of liminal learning, of perceiving a threshold concept (perhaps "writing is a social and rhetorical activity" [Roozen, 2015] or "writing expresses and shares meaning to be reconstructed by the reader" [Bazerman, 2015]) in a new way. However, Alicia did not make the change in her thinking visible to Ann during the conversation. Thus while the exchange helped Ann brainstorm new ways to show students the value of multiple reviews, it did not engage loaded knowledge because it did not draw attention to the complex, constructed nature of key concepts in the field.

Bill went a bit further in highlighting subtle shifts in his thinking during conversation. When talking with Lena about techniques for grading and responding to student writing, Bill drew attention to a new way of understanding his approach to commenting that was emerging for him through their discussion.

> You know what, really, isn't this [teacher comments] also just a justification for this [grade]? This [grade] could have come first. Maybe that's an interesting thing, right? Maybe this is revealing something about me I never thought about before? That the grade always comes down at the bottom. What would it mean if the grade came here and then it was one, two, three? It would mean, "Here is your grade and here's why you got that grade." Instead it's, "Here's what my experience of your paper was like and that leads me [to] this." I don't know why I work that way but that's the way I work. Is that what you do too?

Statements such as "maybe that's an interesting thing, right?" and "maybe this is revealing something about me I never thought about before" suggest that Bill discovered a connection between form and philosophy of responding to student writing that he'd never consciously considered. Perhaps he was coming to understand the threshold concept, "assessing writing shapes contexts and instruction" (Scott & Inoue, 2015) in a more tangible way. Although Bill made his learning-in-process visible to Lena, he stopped short of interrogating loaded knowledge by unpacking the worldviews embedded in those disciplinary ideas.

These examples suggest the pedagogical potential of making learning visible. Modeling change in the moment can create a more flexible, collaborative environment where both writing specialist and content expert are open to changes in their thinking as a result of their interactions. Such an environment is necessary if loaded knowledge is to be revealed and investigated. An ethical approach to loaded knowledge is tricky, however, because it involves identifying principles "that are dearest to the discipline," and holding them up for challenge, critique, or even revision (Ricketts, 2010, p. 50). Bill and Alicia could have done more to show not only how their personal understandings of key concepts in the field were evolving as a result of CCL conversations, but how the concepts were rooted in particular worldviews that might be put productively in conversation with other "equally plausible perspectives" (Ricketts, 2010, p. 48).

The tendency not to be critical of disciplinary assumptions may be due, in part, to writing specialists' sense of their roles as change agents. For example, Bill explained his view that faculty should be the ones changing because "they're the ones who signed up for the seminar. If they signed up for the seminar then, in theory, they want something. They want to learn something." Presumably, writing expertise is *constitutive* for writing specialists—they are doing their work with the "content" of their disciplinary knowledge in the moment, demonstrating "knowing in action" (Schön, 1987, pp. 29–31). On the contrary, writing expertise is *prospective* for content experts—they have a chance to learn new insights and apply them in future contexts. This perspective doesn't necessarily prime writing specialists to look for opportunities to unearth loaded knowledge, to revisit what they thought they knew about (teaching) writing.

The tendency to avoid "critiquing . . . foundational assumptions" (Ricketts, 2010, p. 50) may also be rooted in writing specialists' commitment to validating writing expertise that has historically been devalued. Moreover, the challenge is intensified by the very nature of loaded knowledge. According to Ricketts (2010): "If we accept that as expert practitioners in [a] discipline we may have already been indoctrinated by loaded knowledge, then it requires an especially open mind to seriously engage in the process of locating, exposing, and critiquing the assumptions of our chosen discipline" (p. 50). Such difficulties can prevent writing specialists from interrogating loaded knowledge and embracing opportunities for personal and disciplinary transformation. Nevertheless, writing specialists have a stake in learning how to better engage loaded knowledge, for the continual evolution of "what we see as most important" is "inevitable and desirable if we are to continue to grow as a field" (Adler-Kassner & Wardle, 2015a, p. 5).

Cross-curricular literacy interactions provide ideal conditions for engaging loaded knowledge. Since "one is only likely to perceive [loaded knowledge] when it contradicts a strongly held personal perspective" (Ricketts, 2010, p. 48), interacting with disciplinary faculty can provide an exigency for writing specialists to make loaded knowledge visible for ourselves and others, thus opening it to reflection, critique, and even revision. A pedagogical view of faculty conversations in CCL contexts illuminates that exigency. It suggests that putting our disciplinary knowledge in conversation with others might keep writing specialists "from complacency with established learning in composition studies and from falling back into reiterating what we have learned rather than experiencing anew the often painful process of learning" (Bergmann, 2008, p. 530). A pedagogical view foregrounds the epistemological potential of CCL interactions by allowing for the possibility that "knowledge can be created on the spot, not merely transmitted" (p. 529). From this perspective, taking time to share and explore "light bulb moments" in conversation and consider how those moments might contribute to the evolution of writing expertise is one way writing specialists might enact openness, address the troublesomeness of loaded knowledge in postliminal states, and embrace mutually transformative learning by making new meaning with disciplinary faculty.

CONCLUSION

The pedagogical potential of discursive strategies writing specialists used to address troublesome knowledge suggests additional elements of a guiding ethic for CCL work. For example, writing specialists' attention to timing and circumstance when deciding when to encourage and when to challenge ritual knowledge suggests the need for tenets that scaffold pedagogical tact (Van Manen, 1991, 2015). Strategies for addressing conceptually difficult knowledge, such as planting seeds, indicate the need for habits of mind that promote relationality, such as patience, trust, and space-making. Writing specialists in my study illustrated the potential value of reflexive practice for embracing the epistemic dimension of CCL conversations when they employed strategies such as active listening, making cross-disciplinary connections, and emphasizing contextual application in response to inert knowledge. Reflexivity also emerged in strategies that responded to troublesomeness due to "foreign" and tacit knowledge, including offering compelling evidence and surfacing and animating. Finally, analyzing how and why writing specialists struggled to engage loaded knowledge suggests the need for guiding principles that promote a learner-centered approach to CCL work.

Examples in this chapter reveal how a guiding ethic that includes habits of mind and discursive strategies for supporting change as transformative learning could help writing specialists (1) usefully accompany content experts on their transformational journeys, (2) embark on transformational journeys ourselves, and (3) create opportunities for the transformation of knowledge about (teaching) writing. Relational attunement is central to these efforts, for as Perkins (2006) confirms, where transformational learning is sought, troublesome knowledge is involved, and when faced with the discomfort of liminality, learners need to be inspired and enticed to remain dedicated to the effort (p. 45). Walvoord et al.'s (1997) conclusions and findings from my research reinforce the sentiment: Learning must come from within, and learners in community are more likely to find the inner motivation to pursue transformative learning and lasting, meaningful change. A pedagogical view of relationality adds a useful dimension to the common trope of community building because it goes beyond cooperation to include the construction of a "collaborative self" that reinforces and supports individuals, yet is more than the sum of its parts (Gilly, 2004, p. 236). In that spirit, the following chapter further examines the challenge of sustaining collaborative investment in learning by examining playfulness as a relational sensibility with pedagogical potential.

4

Possibility of Play: Teaching and Learning in Liminal Spaces

TO INVESTIGATE THE THIRD SITE OF COMMUNICATIVE challenge and opportunity—embracing play—I focus on play in relation to the state of "liminality," the intense state of transformational learning that requires attunement to both cognitive and affective dimensions. Land, Meyer, and Baillie (2010) explain liminal space as "a suspended state of partial understanding, or 'stuck place'," which "can be exhilarating but might also be unsettling, requiring an uncomfortable shift in identity, or paradoxically, a sense of loss" (p. x). In what follows, I explore playfulness as an attitude and phenomenon that might offer unique benefits (and challenges) for faculty "stuck" in liminal learning spaces. First, I show how a pedagogical framework for interpreting CCL interactions draws attention to play by highlighting connections between play/playfulness, psychological development, and learning. Referencing writing center scholarship, I show how play can serve pedagogical purposes in the context of literacy learning in particular and speculate about why play has not been a focus of research on CCL interactions among faculty despite its potential. To fill this gap, I draw on my own research findings to identify three discursive forms of play that emerged in conversation between writing specialists and disciplinary content experts—metaphor, storytelling, and silliness. I then analyze possible cognitive and relational functions of these forms of play and suggest implications for learning transfer. Ultimately, I suggest that play—a source of motivation, creativity, imagination, and social interaction—can be a promising activity for writing specialists and disciplinary content experts floundering (or reveling) in the chaos of liminal learning spaces because it invigorates the epistemic, reflexive, and relational dimensions of pedagogical activity.

THE PHENOMENON OF PLAY: CONNECTIONS TO DEEP LEARNING

According to cultural anthropologist Johan Huizinga (1955), play is fundamental to human beings and exists across time and cultures. Essayist and poet Diane Ackerman (1999) explains:

> Every element of the human saga requires play. We evolved through play. Our culture thrives on play. [. . .] Ideas are playful reverberations of the mind. Language is playing with words until they can impersonate physical objects and abstract ideas. [. . .] [Play is] organic to who and what we are, a process as instinctive as breathing. Much of human life unfolds as play. (p. 4, 11)

In other words, play is vital to human existence; with cognitive, cultural, social, and emotional dimensions, play infuses our lives and relationships. Play has been studied from a range of disciplinary perspectives—biology, anthropology, psychology, sociology, education, etc. Psychiatrist and play researcher Stuart Brown outlines properties of play that capture generally accepted characteristics of the phenomenon: Play is "purposeless" or embraced for its own sake; play is considered "voluntary" as well as inherently fun or enjoyable; individuals immersed in play experience time differently, as somehow stopped or removed from reality; playful activities are unselfconscious, have "improvisational potential," and elicit the desire to continue playing (Brown & Vaughan, 2009, pp. 17–18). Psychologists associate play with cognitive, social, and emotional evolution and development in animals and children (see, for example, Bruner, Jolly, & Sylva, 1976); play is believed to stretch zones of proximal development (Vygotsky, 1978) and allow children to assimilate newly acquired schema (Piaget, 1962).

While play is often associated with the young, many researchers recognize it as an adult phenomenon as well. For example, Csikszentmihalyi (1979, 1990, 1996) offers the notion of flow to understand adult play as related to and distinguishable from children's play. Flow involves engrossment and lack of self-consciousness; adults in a state of flow are "living at [their] ultimate capacity" (Csikszentmihalyi, 1979, p. 268). For Csikszentmihalyi, play is a "culturally structured form, or an individually structured form, for experiencing flow" (p. 268). As with children, play can have pedagogical affordances for adults. David Tanis (2012) examines how forms of adult play, like flow, can be purposely structured in an institutional learning context, by studying manifestations of play in adult and higher education classrooms. He emphasizes the role of play in social interaction and meaning-making, associating "fun, spontaneity, relationship and connection, silliness or goofiness, creativity and imagination" with playfulness (p. iii). Adult play has also been tied to knowledge construction, framed as a state of mind, a means of understanding, and a way of coming to know (Kerr & Apter, 1991; Melamed, 1985).

Play can foster deep learning in adults because it includes elements such as "challenge, discovery, exploration, novelty, pushing one's limits, losing one's self in the activity" (Ackerman, 1999, p. 26). According to Margaret Macintyre Latta (2013), play brings out "the underlying possibilities of players and the underlying meanings of the world" (p. 5). Play is generative and revelatory because it invites embodied understanding and new ways of seeing. In adults as much as children, play can sponsor imagination, creativity, experimentation, and invention (Brown & Vaughan, 2009; Csikszentmihalyi, 1996; Duckworth, 1987; Lieberman, 1977). Importantly, adult play, insofar as it constitutes a state of flow, is not relegated to leisure activities or designated occasions (Csikszentmihalyi, 1979). In workplace settings, in educational contexts, and in life play can sponsor resilience, self-motivation, engagement, and solidarity (Bowman, 1987; Kane, 2004; Tanis, 2012).

Theoretical frameworks and practical approaches to CCL work expose the possible value of play in this context by highlighting the need for cognitive flexibility and collaborative meaning-making. Paretti et al.'s (2009) concept of integration, for example, "involves mutual learning across disciplinary boundaries and the willingness to engage not only with new knowledge, but with new ways of constructing and valuing knowledge" (p. 77). Because integration involves "knowledge synthesis and intellectual transformation" (p. 77), it calls for the conceptual pliancy, resilience, self-motivation, spirit of exploration, and trust that characterize playfulness. Yet play is not systematically explored as a strategy for developing and sustaining cross-disciplinary coalitions like the ones Paretti et al. (2009) describe. Similarly, while the creativity, connection, and engagement associated with play would certainly support the transdisciplinary collectives and collaborative partnerships among writing specialists and disciplinary instructors Jacobs (2007) studies, she does not explicitly examine playfulness as a factor. Likewise, though play is not a featured goal or articulated philosophy of Minnesota's Writing Enriched Curriculum, it could certainly invigorate the process of scaffolding knowledge synthesis and (cross) disciplinary collaboration as writing specialists consult with disciplinary liaisons and whole departments to create, implement, and assess comprehensive plans for "curricular integration of writing instruction" ("University of Minnesota WEC Home Page," n.d.). Although play is not typically emphasized in WAC/WID research studies and initiatives, it is clearly relevant and perhaps taking place in ways we would do well to understand.

One site of cross-disciplinary literacy work has embraced play as a means of teaching, learning, and community building: writing center scholarship and practice, a context that shares with CCL efforts a focus on teaching/learning/talking about writing as well as the challenge of communicating across disciplinary and institutional lines (see, for example, Boquet, 2002; Dvorak & Bruce, 2008; Geller, Eodice, Condon, Carroll, & Boquet, 2007). Dvorak and Bruce's collection (2008) *Creative Approaches to Writing Center Work* explores the role of play in the writing center, examining the relationship between work and play, how to mitigate potential dangers of play, and strategies for cultivating play. For example, Verbais (2008) explores play as a way to "energize the atmosphere" with a spirit of "whimsy and chance" that can be a "precursor for creativity and understanding" (pp. 136–38). He sees play as a way to relax frazzled, frustrated writers, to distance them from immediate, high stakes challenges so they may experience the space/process of learning as enjoyable and fun (p. 140). Disciplinary faculty can share many characteristics with the student writers Verbais (2008) describes: Often they are wrestling with new concepts and processes; they can be discouraged, pressed for time, insecure, and reluctant. It follows that play could be a useful strategy for supporting liminal learning experiences among faculty in CCL contexts as well.

Nevertheless, WAC/WID researchers have yet to fully attend to the possibilities of play in faculty interactions. I suspect this is the case for several reasons. First, traditional roles for writing specialists don't inherently suggest playful pursuits. Metaphors for writing specialists and our work, such as conqueror, diplomat, Peace Corps volunteer, change agent, missionary, anthropologist, cultural critic, and rhetorician (Jablonski, 2006; McLeod, 1995) don't necessarily value, emphasize, or in some cases even make room for play. Just as missionary, critical, or rhetorical models of CCL work can disrupt possibilities for negotiating expertise (see Chapter 2), or prompting transformative change (Chapter 3), they can thwart conditions for play. Second, there is a dark side of play that creates "an illusory fine line" between too far and just far enough (Melamed, 1985, p. 110). "Indeed, it is one of the vexing questions about playfulness to know how and when it is appropriate and productive" (Lieberman, 1977, p. 4). If actions are not channeled constructively (p. 4), are misinterpreted, or incite divergent reactions, "feelings of isolation, confusion, and shame" can result (Melamed, 1985, p. 110). Because adult learners especially need to see clearly how individual activities contribute to their learning, playful gestures in CCL contexts run the risk of seeming frivolous, unconnected, or distracting.

Worries about being playful—"fear of rejection, not wanting to appear incompetent, or of being viewed as childish or foolish" (Melamed, 1985, p. 113)—can be particularly poignant for writing specialists in WAC/WID contexts given the complicated ways our disciplinary expertise has been interpreted by our colleagues and institutions. In addition, play among faculty in WAC/WID contexts might not be a focus of research in the field because (1) we tend to associate play with children while faculty involved in WAC/WID initiatives are adults and (2) we tend to perceive play as the opposite of work while faculty involvement in WAC/WID initiatives is considered professional development, a specific type of work. However, by employing pedagogy as an interpretive framework, I treat CCL interactions as sites of teaching and learning that call for attention to play, revealing strategies for addressing the challenges that come with transformational learning by exploring how play works in liminal spaces as writing specialists and content experts grapple with one another's disciplinary worldviews and begin to collaboratively construct meaning through pedagogical engagement. Attending to play as an important dimension of teaching and learning in CCL contexts illuminates otherwise imperceptible elements of a guiding ethic for this work.

FORMS OF PLAY

Three forms of play emerged discursively in conversations among writing specialists and content experts in my study: metaphor, storytelling, and silliness. When interpreting my data, I put in the metaphor category moments when a speaker suggested "understanding and [/or] experiencing one kind of thing in terms of another" (Lakoff & Johnson, 1980, p. 5). The second form of play, storytelling, I defined as the construction of a narrative with a beginning, middle, and end. Storytelling episodes were often signaled by conversational cues such as "So, when my son was four," or "By the way, when we drove to Kansas" or "Did I ever tell you how I. . . ." Storytellers tended to accomplish many of the discourse tasks Schiffrin (1987) identifies, including: "initiating the story, reporting events within the story, conveying the point of the story, accomplishing an action through the story" (p. 15). The third form of play I call silliness. Silly episodes were ones in which speakers seemed to "get off topic" in a frivolous or improvisational way. Silliness was marked by smiling, laughter, and expressions of enjoyment about a topic that did not directly bear on the topic at hand (writing/teaching writing). In what follows, I examine how writing specialists and content experts used metaphors, told stories, and engaged in silliness during conversations, and investigate how certain discursive strategies invite play and scaffold learning in liminal spaces.

Metaphor

More than an extraordinary "device of the poetic imagination and rhetorical flourish," metaphor is fundamental to "our ordinary conceptual system," and thus a powerful heuristic for organizing and constructing meanings and perceptions (Lakoff & Johnson, 1980, p. 3). Metaphor constitutes a discursive moment in which conversation partners might co-create meaning as they work to make sense of objects or ideas that are both similar and disparate. In this way, metaphor is more than a linguistic maneuver; "pervasive in everyday life," it is a powerful driver and framework for language, thought, and action (p. 3). Given these links, researchers study metaphor because it offers insight into speakers' conceptual systems, cognitive processes, and social relations (Cameron et al., 2009; Low, Todd, Deignan, & Cameron, 2010; MacArthur, Oncins-Martinez, Sanchez-Garcia, & Piquer-Piriz, 2012). For example, metaphor can be part of a critical approach to language study that seeks to unmask racist and other oppressive ideologies in discourse (Hart, 2008; Musolff, 2012). Taking a different tack, educational researchers examine how metaphor serves teaching and learning as a way of framing the pedagogical enterprise (Marshall, 1990a; Shuell, 1990) and pedagogical relationships (Berliner, 1990; Cohen & Lotan, 1990), and as an instructional tool for reflection and professional development (K. Carter, 1990; Mahilos & Maxson, 1998; Marshall, 1990b; Munby & Russell, 1990; Tobin, 1990). In the spirit of these approaches, I examine metaphor as a discursive move that offers insight into conceptual and relational processes involved with teaching and learning. Before moving to analyze specific instances of metaphor use, I situate metaphor as a dynamic form of play.

Metaphor as play can be associated with Sutton-Smith's (1997) rhetoric of the imaginary. This type of play is linked to learning that draws on right-brain thinking and intuition and involves creativity and improvisation (Melamed, 1985; Tanis, 2012). In her exploration of play through art in the form of film, installation, quilts, multimodal/media exhibits, and performance art, Latta's (2013) observations about the nature of inquiry as aesthetic play capture the playful qualities of metaphor. For example, metaphor is generative by nature; it "assumes participatory engagement through making and relating, perceiving and responding, and connecting and understanding" (Latta, 2013, p. 15). In conversation, metaphor can allow speakers to participate in collaborative inquiry and meaning-making by wrestling with how ideas are both alike and different. Like art, metaphor entails an "act of recreation" that is participatory and playful (p. 16). Both metaphor and art "deman[d] the work of imagination" conjuring "opportunities afforded by wandering, interacting, deliberating, and re-imagining" (p. 17). Imagination, in turn, necessitates cognitive flexibility, spontaneity, "mindful trust in process, [and] embracing the contingencies and the significances as the meanings to be found and made are more apt to be unknown" (p. 20). In other words, metaphor can create a playful spirit of spontaneity that leads to collaborative, creative meaning-making. Melamed (1985) found metaphor to be a common cognitive and communicative strategy among playful participants in her study of adult learners. In fact, metaphoric thought and language have been explicitly used as (playful) means to encourage teacher learning through reflection and creative problem solving (Marshall, 1990b) and "offe[r] great potential for understanding play/playfulness in adult learning" (Tanis, 2012, p. 66). Findings from my study build on these observations by elaborating on how metaphor constitutes a form of play that can sponsor pedagogical relationships in the context of CCL work.

For example, Bill used metaphor in response to Lena's limited sense of why she should develop detailed writing assignments for students in her political science courses. Early in their second recorded conversation, Lena explained how she had tried to be more explicit about her expectations on assignment sheets as a result of participating in Bill's summer seminar on teaching writing. "Especially when they are first-year students," she professed, "they don't have the experience. They do need a lot more guidance, a lot more hand-holding." While Lena acted on a specific takeaway from the workshop (write detailed assignments), her reason for doing so (first-year students need hand-holding) glossed over the underlying message about how students, how all writers, learn to write. She separated a central aspect of sound writing pedagogy from the principle informing it, a principle grounded in disciplinary concepts from the field of writing studies including genre, activity theory, and an understanding of how writers learn to write. However, Bill did not challenge Lena's reasons for developing detailed writing assignments by sharing theories in strictly disciplinary terms that Lena might well have found complicated or "foreign"; instead, Bill used metaphor to invite Lena to play with the ideas.

Bill slowly worked his way up to the metaphor: "assignment sheet is like an instruction manual" by starting with the idea of "genre" and then using the tenure binder as an example to prompt Lena to recall her own firsthand experience learning a new genre.

> BILL: But there's another reason why [students] need more [guidance] too. So, if you think about writing for a second from the perspective of the word *genre* . . . if you think of the different types of writing that we have to do here at [Public College], my promotion and tenure binder, our annual personnel report, the report that the chairs have to write on each of us, a syllabus. Right? These are all our workplace genres. Whenever we want to or need to produce those, a new one for example, there's a process of learning that genre.

Bill pointed out that when faced with a new genre even he, an experienced writer, looked to instructions and models—in fact he had dossiers from senior colleagues in his office to help him compile his tenure portfolio. "So you're making up a genre," Bill told Lena, "that's what we give students. We make up genres. Outside of here, institutions make up genres, and then we acquire them." Finally, he presented the metaphor: "*so the assignment sheet is really like an instruction manual* [emphasis added]. That's really what it is. It's just amazing to think of it in those terms."

I see metaphor as a form of play in this instance because it invited personal association, cognitive flexibility, and interpersonal connection. Since Lena had recently earned tenure, the tenure binder example likely resonated with her. While Lena's memories may have been about a high-stakes writing moment (much as students often perceive college writing assignments), because she'd successfully earned tenure the stakes were low for her in the conversational moment, making it more likely she could draw unselfconscious connections between her experience and students' experiences. Finally, the metaphor drew personal connections. Since Bill was creating his own tenure binder at the time, he could joke about the process, adding that "for institutional reasons" few instructions existed for this type of workplace genre, an observation that made Lena laugh in commiseration. The metaphor appeared to be a more lighthearted and playful way to engage Lena's perspective than a lecture about the value of detailed writing assignments.

Later in the conversation, Bill extended the initial instance of play by using another metaphor about fixing a faucet. He explained that assignment sheets can guide students to complete writing tasks the same way he relied on an instruction manual to install his kitchen faucet. He acknowledged that the process of completing a writing assignment was "enormously complicated" for both Lena and students: for Lena "because it requires this level of explicitness and clarity about things for which you may not have figured out yet" and for students because "everything hinges on what you say here, because this is what they're holding onto when they're sitting there writing." Associating the connection between assignment sheets and student writing with his reliance on a manual to complete a plumbing project highlighted the complexity of the relationship and invited engagement through conceptual play. Bill's extended metaphor was playful in a different way than the original because it located Bill in a nonprofessional context. We can almost picture Bill, wet and filthy, head under the sink as he consults a soggy instruction booklet to install his new faucet. By referencing the world outside academia in an amusing way, the metaphor had the potential to forge a more human, as opposed to purely professional, connection.

By revisiting and extending his initial metaphor, Bill urged Lena to play with her original assumptions about why students might need detailed assignment sheets and to draw imaginative connections between students' struggle to complete her assignments and her own struggle to write the assignment sheets. Lena's response indicated her willingness to play along. "It's funny," she told him:

> When I was doing that [creating the assignment], I can't tell you how much time I spent Googling, searching for something that I could use as a model. . . . So I'm looking at lesson plans and I'm searching for . . . I could find nobody doing the kind of project that I wanted to do. So, yeah, once I gave up on that, then I had to create it . . . from scratch.

While it's difficult to say whether the metaphor prompted Lena to reconsider her initial frustration with assignment sheets as a form of "hand-holding" only novice writers required, at the very least she began to consider her struggle to create an assignment from scratch in relation to students' struggle to respond to her assignment prompt. Thus, the exchange incited new connections through conceptual play. Although the metaphor seemed to emerge spontaneously in this case, spontaneity isn't necessary for metaphors to be a form of play. Writing specialists might well have several "go to" metaphors they use to illustrate certain concepts in conversations with disciplinary experts. Metaphors, even routinely used ones, can have playful potential if they invite conceptual play and foster a sense of enjoyment and/or connection.

Whereas Bill used metaphor as a playful teaching tool, Chuck, the computer science professor, used metaphor as a heuristic to explore how students' relationship with the undergraduate writing fellow in his first-year seminar differed from the traditional teacher-student dynamic. Prompted by his struggle to articulate "the difference between authority and respect," Chuck offered the following:

I would make the analogy where, if you're a musician, and you're opening for another band that's bigger than you, you can go and feel, like, "I'm opening for them, so I can go chat with them." If you were a member of the audience, and then you got to meet that big band, you would be more of like a fanboy, and you'd feel different about that.

Encouraged by Frank, Chuck continued:

> You'd try to present yourself in a different way. You wouldn't speak freely, when you're the other opening band, you're like, well, they asked me to open, and so, whatever, you know. It's kind of being equals, but yet, understanding the other person might have more knowledge.

I interpret Chuck's metaphor as a form of play because he offered it voluntarily as an imaginative way to explore concepts of interest. In this case, the metaphor also referenced a playful event, attending a concert, that resonated loosely with Chuck's course on '80s music and culture.

While Chuck clearly associated students with the audience in the analogy, it was less clear how he saw the teacher and writing associate in relation to the headliner and opening act. Accepting the metaphor as an invitation to play, Frank responded by putting gentle pressure on the connections Chuck was making.

> FRANK: But would it also be the case that the people in the audience would feel more relaxed talking to the band that's opening?
> CHUCK: Yeah, that too. I think so.
> FRANK: So are the consult—
> CHUCK: Maybe not. Maybe not. I think that depends.
> FRANK: OK, I'm just trying to figure out the writing fellows, are they the opening band?
> CHUCK: Oh, I don't know what they are. That's why I said I don't think the analogy fits with the terms I was using as far as respect and . . .
> FRANK: Authority.

CHUCK: Authority, yeah. So, I think when they interact with J or K [writing associates], they're peers, but they respect that the other person is in charge. Whereas, when I'm in the classroom, they may be hesitant to ask questions because they think I'm passing this judgment on them or
. . .
FRANK: Yes. After all, you are the grade giver.
CHUCK: Yeah, yeah.

With his pointed questions, Frank played alongside Chuck to imagine different associations and the implications each would suggest for the relationships among the concepts Chuck wanted to unpack. As in Latta's (2013) analysis of art as aesthetic play, Chuck's band metaphor was potentially playful in that it raised new conceptual possibilities in an effort to uncover meaning in the world—in this case the meaning of the relationships unfolding in his classroom. By playing along, Frank engaged Chuck's questions in a generous, exploratory way. As Chuck and Bill's examples illustrate, the playful potential of metaphor emerges through interaction, when speakers engage them as invitations for conceptual play and interpersonal connection.

Storytelling
Storytelling is a second form of play that emerged during conversations among participants in my study. Karen Tracy (2002) characterizes everyday stories by three features: talk about a time when someone experienced an event; talk about an event that is "newsworthy" or worth telling/hearing; and evaluation of the event (p. 152). These characteristics accurately describe stories told in my study as well. Storytelling often arose spontaneously in loose connection with something mentioned in conversation. As Tracy suggests, episodes of storytelling tended to feature the speaker's interesting or unusual experience and the teller either implied or explicitly shared an evaluation of the story's message. According to Stuart Brown "storytelling has the capacity to produce a sense of timelessness, pleasure, and an altered state of vicarious involve-

ment that identifies narrative and storytelling with states of play" (Brown & Vaughan, 2009, p. 92). What makes stories playful, says Tanis (2012), is a focus on elements such as "fun, spontaneity (or the unexpected), goofiness, and the importance of relationship" (p. 150). Tanis found storytelling to be one of the most frequent ways play and playfulness were manifested in the adult and higher education classroom he studied (p. iii). Like the teachers Tanis observed, writing specialists in my study (especially Frank) told stories that featured playful elements such as humor, suspense, and embellishment.

For example, in conversations with both Thomas and Chuck, Frank told a story about taking dictation from his five-year-old son as the child revised the tale of "Little Red Riding Hood." In one conversation, Chuck prompted the story by admitting he hoped he could be "the worst writer and a great writing teacher." Frank explained to Chuck that what we think of as writing "actually combines two quite different skills"—writing and scribal skills—and then proceeded to share this story by way of illustration:

> So, when my son was four or five years old, he decided that he wanted to rewrite the story of "Little Red Riding Hood." He wasn't pleased with the version he had been reading or had been read to him. And so he came down to my office one night at home, and he dictated [a] new version of "Little Red Riding Hood." Which I thought was kind of interesting because it sort of combined "Little Red Riding Hood" with "Goldilocks and The Three Bears." Became one story. And, so, I mean, pretty long dictation. Probably took us a half hour. This was precomputers. So I was doing all this on [a] typewriter. And when we got finished, he was very proud of what he had written. You know, but in one sense he wasn't old enough to write, I mean he couldn't type, he couldn't [gesture like writing with a pen]. And it was one of those moments "Oh my gosh" it really kind of sank in for the first time. Of this, how much difference there is between being the writer—my son was clearly the writer, he wrote the story his new version, and I was a scribe. It was my job to [gestures

like writing with pen] and what we want students to do is to combine those two skills into one. And a lot of the times our criticisms of students are not for the writing side, are for the scribal errors. Failure to have an apostrophe in the right place, comma missing, whatever. My son when he was writing, he didn't have to worry about periods, commas, and spelling. He was free of all that, he could just concentrate on writing, just composing this text.

Frank's narrative meets the discursive criteria for storytelling. He opens with a linguistic cue signaling the forthcoming recollection of an event he'd experienced: "So, when my son was. . . ." The event was interesting because Frank's son behaved in an unusual way and worth telling because it clearly impacted Frank's understanding of writing and teaching writing. Indeed, Frank told the story because it captured a significant moment in his own learning:

> It's a story certainly I've told a number of times. [. . .] It was that experience with my son, that moment of discovery when I realized, "Oh my gosh! Here I've been teaching composition for all these years, and I've really confused one dimension of writing with another dimension of writing. This could be important in my own teaching, but also important in now trying to help the faculty think about the writing."

Frank recounted the story for Chuck, for Thomas, and for me during an interview, demonstrating just how important it is to his own thinking and how much he trusted it to communicate a disciplinary value to others. As with most stories, Frank explicitly identified the message or moral of the story in relation to the conversation he was having with Chuck, specifying how the event he recalled—transcribing his son's retelling of "Little Red Riding Hood"—illustrated how composing and scribal skills constitute different aspects of writing.

Further, Frank's story exhibited many characteristics of play. The story was fun; it recounted an event that happened outside of a professional context and described a child's imaginative behavior. Frank also embellished the story—gently poking fun at his age by noting his use of the typewriter in a precomputer age. Frank's decision to tell the story and Chuck's involvement in the telling were voluntary; each engaged willingly. Frank could have chosen to make his point about composing/scribal skills in any number of ways but told the story presumably for its playful qualities. The story seemed to create a comfortable atmosphere within a larger context in which both Frank and Chuck might have felt self-conscious about communicating (Frank) and understanding (Chuck) ideas about teaching writing. Finally, the story seemed to support relationship building, as playful moments often do. Because it dealt with Frank's home life and recounted the moment when an idea crystalized for him, the story humanized Frank and invited a more intimate interaction with Chuck than would have a strictly professional focus on disciplinary concepts.

Some stories, like Frank's story about his son, were closely related to issues of writing and teaching writing. Other times, stories seemed mainly intended for relationship building and playful interaction. For example, in their first recorded conversation, as Thomas and Frank discussed readings for the first-year seminar on water and place, Thomas explained how water issues are current and topical as evidenced by numerous newspaper articles on water-related topics like fracking, and listed readings he planned to assign—a book about a recent flood, a popular work on America's water crisis, several selections accessible online. Frank interrupted Thomas with a story about his experience with fracking. Again, Frank discursively initiated the story with a linguistic cue ("by the way, when we drove to Kansas . . ."), personalized and embellished the story with details, and evaluated the story by emphasizing that it highlighted how expensive and wasteful fracking can be. The fracking story is striking in how far afield it moved from teaching writing. Frank sprinkled the story with particulars that weren't immediately relevant—his wife boarded in town during high school, they were attending a ninetieth birthday party, direct quotes from a truck driver, etc. The story was rather long, and the message seemed to be simply that Frank realized how expensive fracking must be.

At first glance, an off-topic story may seem unnecessary and unimportant given the larger goals of the conversation. However, the story is interesting *because* it was not explicitly about (teaching) writing. Frank told me he shared the story because it was fresh in his memory, he thought it would appeal to Thomas's disciplinary interest in water, and he was curious how Thomas would respond. Frank's expressed desire to connect with Thomas's disciplinary interests illuminates the story's playful potential—it was spontaneous, improvised, voluntary, and relatively purposeless (at least in terms of teaching writing). The story allowed Frank and Thomas to connect over a shared stance on an issue that was not writing related by sparking lighthearted interaction. Thomas contributed to the narrative momentum with enthusiastic exclamations ("Oh my God, yes!" and "Just huge!"), attesting to the interactive and immersive features of storytelling as a form of conversational play. Interestingly, Thomas brought the conversation back around to his teaching, emphasizing his goal to make students aware of water issues such as fracking. As Frank's two stories show, storytelling, even (especially) when it seems disconnected from writing and teaching, can be a flexible discursive strategy for cultivating comfortable relationships and (in)directly sponsoring thinking and learning about teaching writing through meaningful play.

Silliness

A third type of play I identified in my data, silliness, epitomizes Sutton-Smith's (1997) rhetoric of frivolity—play associated with "activities of the idle or the foolish" (p. 11). Many play scholars distinguish serious theories of play from common lay perceptions of play as childish and inconsequential. Play is *not* frivolous, trivial, or silly this body of work argues; it is serious, vital, with implications for learning and development. Frivolity, or silliness, might easily become the "bad" type of play that makes articulation of "good" types of play possible (Sutton-Smith, 1997, p. 204). However, educators in Tanis's (2012) study identified "silliness or goofiness" as central elements of playfulness and play (p. iii). As demonstrated through classroom observation and interviews, these educators embraced silliness, lightheartedness, and foolishness through stories, songs, dance, impersonations, physical gestures, acts, humor, etc. What made these behaviors silly was their spontaneity, their divergence from participants' expectations for the context, the joy they cultivated for participants. Likewise, moments of silly play emerged among participants in my study, particularly between Frank and Chuck.

One example of silliness occurred near the end of Frank and Chuck's second recorded conversation in which Chuck tried to explain a particular assignment in his course on '80s music and culture. Students were to choose a song from the Bruce Springsteen album *Born in the USA* and tell a personal story related to the song. Chuck mentioned the song "Dancing in the Dark" as an example and Frank asked if it was similar to Ray Conniff's song by the same name. When Chuck admitted he didn't know the Conniff song, Frank began to sing it aloud. Laughing good-naturedly, Chuck felt compelled to sing the Springsteen version, which he described as "'80s dancey." Doing his best to imitate the gravelly rocker, Chuck tried his hand at other songs, referencing the crazy music videos they inspired. "You've got a good singing voice," he told Frank, "you need to break that out." The singing was boisterous and both men clearly enjoyed themselves, as evidenced by their laughter and the sustained participation in the exchange. Their conversation ended shortly after this episode, never returning to a discussion of Chuck's assignment, though revising the assignment didn't seem to be the point of the exchange.

During an interview, Chuck described how strange it was for him as a young faculty member to sing with a senior colleague. "It's odd for me to sing in front of [Frank], that's for sure." He went on to explain: "I think at the time I was kind of a little embarrassed, but I was like what the hell what are we doing here. . . ." While the disconnect between what Chuck expected to happen in conversations with Frank and the singing episode that actually took place felt risky and embarrassing, because it occurred in a silly, rather low stakes environment, Chuck found it invigorating; he was willing to play (sing) along. Although unfulfilled expectations might seem pedagogically unproductive, research suggests that embracing activities that seem out of place or even rebellious can stimulate psychological arousal associated with learning through play. Michael Apter (1991) explains the transgressive nature of certain devices used "to obtain the pleasures of play, and especially to achieve high arousal" (p. 18). His structural phenomenology of play outlines several "psychological strategies," including negativism, or "deliberate and provocative rule-breaking" (p. 19). A wide range of transgressions can inspire playful pleasure, he points out, and rule-breaking need not be extreme—examples might include "taking a perverse line at a committee meeting, making a risqué joke at a formal party, being catty, or parking where you are not supposed to" (p. 20). Indeed, Frank and Chuck's spontaneous choice to sing during a professional conversation in Frank's university office likely felt playful because it defied expectations for professional behavior, demonstrating how even a moderate transgression can inspire play.

While Frank and Chuck unabashedly embraced a boisterous form of silly play, other instances of silliness were subtler. One brief silly encounter among James, Liliana, and Kim occurred when Kim asked if she and other instructors of the writing course she taught could have WAs in future semesters. Liliana and James teased Kim about accepting bribes to place WAs with certain instructors. Kim laughed and played along, implying she was open to bribery. Less jubilantly silly than Frank and Chuck's gleeful vocalizing, the exchange similarly demonstrates Apter's (1991) notion of negativism as a playful device. James jokingly identified bribery as a "gray line" they didn't want to cross. Happily embracing the transgression of imaginary rule-breaking, Kim followed James's comment with a promise to outdo her fellow instructor's offer to provide cupcakes. She reiterated the deliciously transgressive nature of the bribe by admonishing the others not to tell anyone. Noting they were not being recorded, Liliana strengthened their bond as partners in crime who might get away with their dealings. Laughingly, James reminded the group that they were in fact being recorded and moved to turn off the recording device. The recorder strengthened the jubilant deviousness of the groups' shared transgression, solidifying their witty exchange as an instance of silliness as play.

Perhaps more understated than Frank and Chuck's musical example, the silly playfulness among Kim, James, and Liliana was still obvious. The group's banter about culinary bribery was "pointless" in that it did not have a purpose related to Kim's teaching of the course or ideas about (teaching) writing. It was also spontaneous. The conversation could have ended with James's explanation about how the program was limited in its ability to expand due to lack of funding. However, Liliana interjected with a silly comment about accepting bribes. The laughter from all three participants suggests the playful potential of the interaction. The fact that the instance came at the end of their conversation and the group was quick to end the recording suggests that these slices of silliness may have happened more often than my data indicates. It might also suggest that writing specialists don't necessarily recognize the importance of silly, playful interactions to the work they do and might benefit from closer examination of the value of play.

FUNCTIONS OF PLAY: SUPPORTING EXPERIENCES OF LIMINALITY

By examining instances of play in the context of participants' larger conversations and analyzing what they had to say about these moments, I identify cognitive and relational functions of playful moves in CCL exchanges and explore their potential for supporting faculty experiences of liminality in the process of transformative learning (see Figure 4.1). More specifically, I examine implications of playful strategies for learning transfer in CCL contexts. I conclude by extrapolating additional principles to inform a guiding ethic for CCL work.

Cognitive Functions

If CCL work is about embracing interdisciplinarity (Jacobs, 2007; Paretti et al., 2009), and if (as I have argued here) it's about pedagogy as an epistemic, reflexive, and relational activity, then cognitive flexibility, intellectual pliancy, creativity, and imagination are necessary components. In my study, I defined cognitive functions of play as those that helped faculty explore a complex concept, ex-

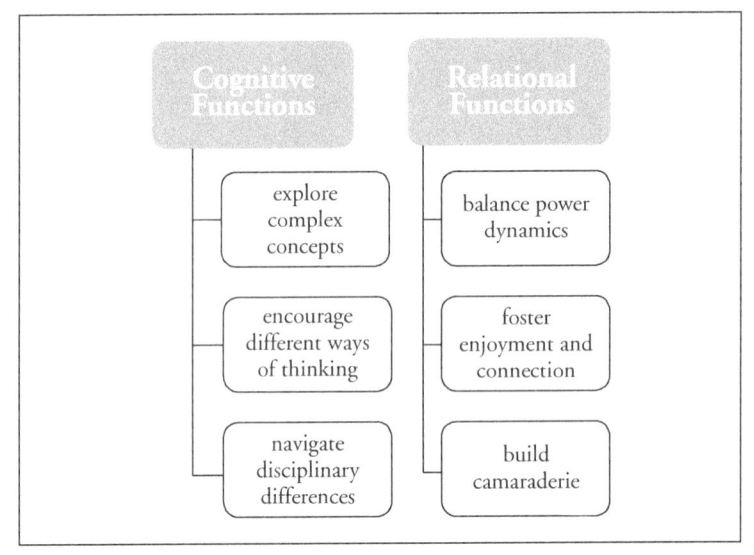

```
                Cognitive              Relational
                Functions              Functions

                  explore              balance power
                  complex                dynamics
                  concepts

                 encourage               foster
               different ways        enjoyment and
                 of thinking            connection

                  navigate                build
                 disciplinary          camaraderie
                 differences
```

Figure 4.1. Functions of play.

periment with different ways of thinking about an idea or practice, and navigate disciplinary differences in thinking or perception. Bill's extended metaphor about the assignment sheet as instruction manual provides one example of how play might serve a cognitive function in CCL contexts. Lena's initial sense that she should create detailed assignment sheets because novice writers needed "hand-holding" suggested that she hadn't fully internalized the writing studies TC "all writers have more to learn," or accepted that all "writers [not just novices] must struggle to write in new contexts and genres" (Rose, 2015, p. 60; see also: Anson & Moore, 2016a, p. 338; Anson, 2016). From a pedagogical perspective, Lena was in a state of liminality, which the metaphor addressed by urging her to explore a "troublesome" concept from different angles and make connections between how experienced writers, including herself, wrestle with new genres and her students' struggle with her writing assignments. Bill could have responded by using the immediate schema of students in Lena's disciplinary writing course to make a point about why detailed assignment sheets are important, a move that may or may not have addressed characteristics of liminality such as the feeling of "stuckness" that precedes a perspective shift or the inability to recognize tacit assumptions that restricts integration of new knowledge into existing worldviews. Instead, Bill's playful metaphor referenced a writing situation Lena had successfully traversed (learning new workplace genres, particularly the tenure binder) giving her a different, experiential angle for considering the change in perspective he proposed. The metaphor encouraged a deeper understanding of (teaching) writing by prompting Lena to reflect on connections between a new idea and familiar experiences and by exposing the logic underlying her initial assumption. This example suggests the pedagogical potential of playful metaphor as a valuable tool for supporting the (meta)cognitive work of connecting complex new concepts to existing knowledge/experiences.

Metaphors can lead to cognitive shifts that foster changes in behavior as well as perspective. As Lakoff and Johnson (1980) point out in *Metaphors We Live By*: "we act according to the way we conceive things" (p. 5). Consequently, metaphors are not just concepts that govern and shape thought; they also "govern our everyday functioning . . . what we perceive, how we get around in the world, . . . how we relate to other people . . . what we experience, and what we *do* [emphasis added]" (p. 3). Because we both think with and "live by" metaphors, altering how we perceive and conceive metaphors can also change individual actions and long-term behaviors. Contributors to a special edition of *Theory into Practice* explain how metaphor can be used explicitly with teachers as a reflexive heuristic for identifying problematic patterns in teaching and learning processes and as a means of "creat[ing] possibilities for new modes of interacting" by shifting perspective on the problem (Marshall, 1990b, p. 129; Munby & Russell, 1990; Tobin, 1990). Marshall (1990b) demonstrated how "cued metaphor" can be used to help teachers identify their underlying assumptions about teaching and learning, reflect on those assumptions, and explore alternative frameworks (p. 129). Although Bill did not use metaphor in quite the same way, his comparisons did prompt Lena to explore complex concepts from different angles and draw connections between her teaching and writing practices. Such careful reflection can be a precursor to meaningful transformation. Tobin (1990) goes so far as to deem metaphors "master switches" that have the potential to "help teachers reconceptualize teaching roles and change instructional practices" (p. 123). In a similar vein, my research suggests that metaphor as a form of play has the potential to shift faculty learners' ways of thinking and acting, making it a promising mechanism for supporting (meta)cognitive work in liminal states of transformation.

The cross-disciplinary nature of CCL contexts means transformative shifts in thought involve the navigation of disciplinary differences, and the cognitive functions of play have the potential to ease the troublesomeness of that process. When Bill's faucet metaphor, for example, enacted a playful spirit by tapping into the everyday realm, it likely facilitated disciplinary boundary crossing. Nancy Welch (1999) extols the value of bringing perceptions "into play" by considering relationships between situations (i.e., fixing a faucet and completing a writing assignment) and between "spheres of living" (i.e., academic and home) (pp. 62–63). These are "crucial relationships," she argues, because people "more often experience gaps between, not possible connections among, the different spheres, activities, and values that make up their lives" (pp. 62–63). In Welch's terms, metaphors can foster cognitive flexibility by crossing work/home spheres of living. Thus, Bill's metaphor may have bridged disciplinary gaps by framing writing studies concepts in ways that connected with activities from daily life outside the academy. According to Melamed (1985), the grounded abstraction of metaphor allows learners to "mediate diverse experiences enabling us to explore connections which were otherwise unsuspected" (p. 177). The bridging ability of cognitive functions of metaphors may seem surprising, for according to MacArthur and Oncins-Martinez (2012), metaphor can be a source of difficulty when it comes to navigating the disciplinary divide because "different academic discourse communities use metaphor in different ways" and the metaphors or models used to frame disciplinary theories and problems vary vastly from field to field (p. 2). In Bill's case, however, carefully chosen metaphors seemed to span rather than sharpen disciplinary differences, suggesting that playful metaphor may be a valuable communicative strategy for supporting liminal learning *because* it can straddle disciplinary cultures. The creative, playful aspect of juxtaposing concepts or spheres can conjure profound insights and lead to deeper, more intuitive cultural (or in this case disciplinary) understandings (Sapir, 1977, p. 32). As Chuck put it, metaphor is a way to "talk in someone else's language."

Frank's story about recording his son's composition illustrates how storytelling as play might serve similar (meta)cognitive functions by scaffolding complex concepts and encouraging reflection as a means of bridging disciplinary divides. In sharing the narrative, Frank created an opportunity for Chuck to explore the difference between composing and scribal skills by removing it from the immediate context of Chuck's classroom and teaching, while also grounding the concept in the reality of Frank's lived experience. Frank and Chuck were wrangling with (perhaps several) writing studies TCs—"writing is a social and rhetorical activity" (Roozen, 2015), "writing is a technology" (Brooke & Grabill, 2015), "writing is (also always) a cognitive activity" (Dryer, 2015b), "writing is an expression of embodied cognition" (Bazerman & Tinberg, 2015)—that did not seem to be intuitive for Chuck, who worried about his ability to be a good writing teacher when he wasn't confident in his own writing. Addressing these concepts in the context of Chuck's own courses and teaching might have led to defensiveness or resistance. At the same time, dealing with the concept in the abstract might have been disorienting or unconvincing. Alternatively, Frank's story seemed to address sources of troublesomeness by couching the message in an enjoyable, playful narrative.

That stories can function to playfully cultivate cognitive flexibility and deeper understanding in liminal learning spaces is likely no surprise for seasoned teachers. After all, "storytelling has been identified as *the* unit of human understanding" beginning in childhood and extending well beyond (Brown & Vaughan, 2009, p. 91). Like teachers in Tanis's (2012) study who attested to the value of storytelling, Thomas reported using stories in his classroom to help students develop rich, flexible understanding of complex chemistry concepts. For him, storytelling is a way to make abstract concepts concrete by grounding them in reality. Likewise, because Frank's story about his son did not involve the exact situation Chuck was facing, Chuck was free to extrapolate a range of understandings from the narrative and apply them multitudinously to his own current and future circumstances. When I asked Chuck about his experience of Frank's story he explained:

> When [Frank] was telling the story about his son writing that paper by telling him, I would say my brain was churning in that, I had this moment where I was like, I could have the students do this in pairs. I really hadn't formalized it in my head, or what that would look like, or was it feasible. Then this goes back to the expertise where he was able to say, "Yeah, you could do that." It's more one of those moments where somebody is saying something and you find this other idea, or something you want to apply, while they're talking.

Chuck's comments suggest that playful storytelling might address potential sources of troublesomeness before they become issues. Chuck's evolving understanding of the difference between composing and scribal skills was not likely to become inert, for example, because Frank's story made the concept relevant to Chuck's teaching, invited Chuck to make his own connections by sponsoring reflection, and tethered the abstract idea to a memorable real-world example. As I have shown, in a (meta)cognitive sense play has the potential to encourage exploration of complex concepts, experimentation with different ways of thinking, and creative navigation of disciplinary differences. In this way, play can be a particularly effective way to scaffold liminal learning by mitigating the uncomfortable experience of troublesomeness that characterizes transformation.

Relational Functions

Findings from my study suggest that play can also function on a relational level to address conditions of liminal learning by balancing power dynamics, fostering enjoyment and connection, and building camaraderie. For example, Bill's instruction manual metaphor seemed to serve a relational function by balancing a power dynamic that otherwise skewed toward him as the writing expert. First, Bill's move to compare the construction of his tenure binder with students' efforts to compose writing assignments simultaneously worked against the infantilizing of first-year writers and humanized Bill as a writer who, like all writers, struggled to learn a new genre. Further, by choosing his tenure case as an example, Bill subtly, and perhaps unconsciously, shifted authority away from himself, a pretenure faculty member, toward Lena, who had successfully earned tenure. He did this despite his feeling that their "relationship was somewhat asymmetrical" based on Lena's senior ranking and time at Public College. "While it may not have come up or shown," Bill told me, "I always did feel that asymmetricality on some level." In this instance, leveraging that "asymmetricality" likely mitigated Bill's power as "expert" and framed his offer to think differently about assignment sheets as an invitation, rather than an authoritative move to persuade. In this way, metaphor as a form of play suggests a relational function that tempers power dynamics and promotes collaborative inquiry as opposed to one-directional instruction.

Like metaphor, silliness as a form of play can also cultivate pedagogical relationships by mitigating unequal power dynamics. Frank's desire to be playful and have a good time, for instance, allowed him to break down potential barriers separating him as an administrator with writing expertise from faculty in other disciplines. While many of Frank's colleagues invested him with authority due to his writing-related expertise and institutional position, Frank often wanted disciplinary faculty to see him as a fellow learner committed to intellectual exploration, out to have a good time. Frank's willingness to be silly and playful, manifested in his decision to sing with Chuck, seemed to communicate that he was "just another faculty member" rather than an authority figure with an agenda. By agreeing to sing along, Chuck responded to Frank's playful persona, reciprocating his openness and spontaneous spirit.

"It's because both of us are crazy," Chuck laughingly told me, "That's why no one else would do it [sing together]." He explained:

[T]o sing in front of somebody else is kind of an exposing moment. It's kind of an opening moment where you have to feel relaxed or trusting in the other person . . . it's tough because being a new faculty member I do feel judged. I feel like there is some evaluation going on and there is some assessment of how well I do things. [. . .] I guess with Frank I don't. . . . He has the same goals and he is very serious about the outcome in the work he does. I think he puts a lot of effort into it and all that. At the same time, understanding that you can be serious and still feel comfortable. You have to kind of trust in the person that's evaluating you, in a sense. You have to trust that they're a human being and that they're very relaxed.

As Chuck suggests, silliness bonded him and Frank on a human level. That connection is vital for pedagogical activity, for Chuck couldn't be open to the uncertainty of inquiry and experimentation, markers of the generative potential of liminality, if he felt evaluated and judged. Instead, the relational function of silliness as a means of fostering joy and connection seemed to allow Frank to be "good company" for Chuck as Chuck lingered at the "edge of [his] knowing" about teaching writing (Berger, 2004, p. 346, 347).

Along with equalizing power dynamics and encouraging joyful connection, forms of play can serve a relational function by fostering camaraderie. J. David Sapir's (1977) discussion of the element of the commonplace in "The Anatomy of Metaphor" reiterates how metaphors, at their core, are designed to tap into shared understandings. Although "commonplaces can vary" widely (Sapir, 1977, p. 10), their connection-forging potential demonstrates how play can foster camaraderie by making ideas accessible and reiterating experiences or ways of thinking that individuals have in common. For example, Bill's metaphor seemed to build camaraderie with Lena by referring to their shared plight as faculty members required to internalize unfamiliar, high stakes workplace genres such as the tenure binder. Similarly, Frank's story about fracking used a shared interest to reinforce his relationship with Thomas and remind him of the joy he experienced when talking with Frank. When I asked Thomas about his experience of the fracking story, his response indicated the relational value of storytelling:

> I enjoy talking with [Frank] a lot and that's part of it, is that shared interests, shared experiences. You know, I think. . . . When he asked me about doing this, that was clearly part of the attraction for me because, frankly, anytime I have the opportunity to sit down and have a conversation with him, it's generally both enjoyable and worthwhile in some way.

Likewise, the playful exchange among James, Liliana, and Kim constructed a commonplace around their immediate shared performance, which they all found entertaining and enjoyable. Subtle humor and gentle sarcasm—Liliana's request for bribery and Kim's tongue-in-cheek acquiescence—indicate a level of comfort and mutual participation as well as a sense of togetherness. These instances are perfect examples of how "play relationships [can] serve as a symbol of group membership and perform the integrative function of helping to create and maintain group solidarity" (Bowman, 1987, p. 69). Camaraderie, whether between individuals or within groups, can have a sustaining effect, bolstering determination and renewing the commitment needed to weather the uncertainty, frustration, and doubt that comes with liminality. As these examples show, all three forms of play—metaphor, storytelling, and silliness—have the potential to be useful strategies for attending to the relational dimension of pedagogical activity. They can address affective aspects of liminality by mitigating feelings of anxiety, defensiveness, insecurity, and doubt that characterize learning thresholds. The relational functions of play—equalizing power dynamics, cultivating connection, and building camaraderie—in particular throw into relief all that is enjoyable, invigorating, and fun about teaching and learning. They remind us that pedagogy is a *human* endeavor and elucidate the importance of frivolity and spontaneity for pedagogical activity.

Implications for Learning Transfer

So far, I have suggested how cognitive and relational functions of play might support transformational learning in liminal spaces. In this section, I explore implications of the forms and functions of play for learning transfer in CCL contexts. Debates about the nature of transfer, how/why/when it happens, how to study it, and how to sponsor it have intensified recently, including in the realm of writing studies (Anson & Moore, 2016b; Tuomi-Gröhn, Engeström, & Young, 2003; Wardle, 2012). Transfer has been described as "creative repurposing for expansive learning" (Wardle, 2012; drawing on Prior & Shipka, 2003; Roozen, 2010; and Engeström, 1987), generalization or "consequential transitions" (Beach, 1999, 2003), transformation (Wardle, 2007), boundary-crossing (Tuomi-Gröhn et al., 2003), and integration (Nowacek, 2011). The range of perspectives, rooted in different epistemologies and learning frameworks, represent "overlapping paths that lead through transfer's theoretical [and experiential] thickets" (Qualley, 2016, p. 102). Task-based conceptions take a cognitive perspective focused on reconceptualizing knowledge and skills across contexts; individual conceptions locate responsibility for transfer in individual learners and emphasize their dispositions; and context-based conceptions consider the learner in relation to sociocultural environments or activity systems (for detailed summaries of these perspectives see Tuomi-Gröhn et al., 2003; Wardle, 2007). Although various perspectives constitute distinct approaches to transfer, they are not mutually exclusive (Tuomi-Gröhn & Engeström, 2003, p. 35; Wardle, 2007, p. 66). Therefore, while cognitive and relational functions of play I have examined in this chapter resonate most deeply with individual conceptions of transfer and lead me to focus on dispositional aspects, I hope my brief discussion of transfer in CCL contexts prompts further research across frameworks.

Transfer researchers studying student writers and teachers of writing have identified dispositions as a vital component in individuals' "sensitivity toward and willingness to engage in transfer" (Driscoll & Wells, 2012; Jarratt, Mack, Sartor, & Watson, 2009; Qualley, 2016; Wardle, 2012). According to Perkins, Tishman,

Ritchhart, Donis, and Andrade (2000), dispositions are distinguishable from knowledge, skill, and intellectual ability in that they "concern not only what people can do, but how they tend to invest their capabilities—what they are disposed to do" (p. 270). In the context of complicated, real world circumstances, traits such as "curiosity, open-mindedness, and skepticism" don't just contribute to learning, but can actually "*allow* or *prevent* successful development from taking place" (Perkins et al., 2000, p. 269; Driscoll & Wells, 2012). Some research suggests that dispositions can be context specific (Driscoll & Wells, 2012; Hofer, 2000), which means that faculty who embrace transfer-supporting dispositions in their own disciplinary work may not bring those same dispositions to bear in the context of teaching writing. Therefore, exploring ways to foster transfer-focused dispositions in CCL contexts can enhance writing specialists' ability to facilitate meaningful learning and change. In what follows, I investigate how cognitive and relational functions of play might cultivate dispositions conducive to learning transfer (see Figure 4.2).

According to Driscoll and Wells (2012), "willingness to engage in transfer-focused thinking, [is] both crucial and precarious." This is particularly true for what Salomon and Perkins (1989) call high-road transfer, a transfer mechanism that "involves the explicit conscious formulation of abstraction in one situation that allows making a connection to another" as opposed to the low-road mechanism, which "involves the spontaneous, automatic transfer

Cognitive Functions
- Problem-exploring dispositions
- Bridging dispositions

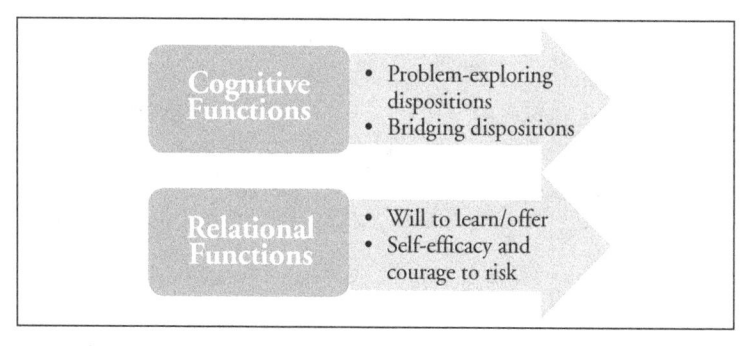

Relational Functions
- Will to learn/offer
- Self-efficacy and courage to risk

Figure 4.2. Implications of play for learning transfer in CCL contexts.

of highly practiced skills, with little need for reflective thinking" (p. 118). High-road transfer, and thus the need for transfer-focused thinking, is most crucial in the context of ill-structured situations like writing and teaching writing. Within the realm of high-road transfer, Salomon and Perkins (1989) further distinguish between backward-reaching and forward-reaching transfer. Cognitive functions of play seem to encourage dispositions that support transfer-focused thinking in both cases.

Bill's instruction manual metaphor, for example, seemed to encourage backward-reaching transfer, a form of high-road transfer that occurs when a learner "formulates an abstraction guiding his or her reaching back to past experience for relevant connections" (Salomon & Perkins, 1989, p. 119). In this case, Bill formulated the abstraction (writers composing in a new genre) and reached back to his own past experience finding guidelines for tenure portfolios and using a manual to fix his faucet to forge relevant connections. Doing so encouraged backward-reaching transfer by prompting Lena to consider her initial perception (that novice writers need "handholding" in the form of detailed assignment sheets) in terms of her own experience figuring out how to compose her tenure argument and craft writing assignments.

In a slightly different vein, Frank's story about his son seemed to prime Chuck for forward-reaching transfer, the process of generally forming a concept with the intent to find "new application spontaneously later" (Salomon & Perkins, 1989, p. 119). Frank's story abstracted the difference between scribal skills and composing by removing it from Chuck's local context and usefully (re)grounded the abstract idea by rooting it in a personal context. By setting up a general principle in a memorable, accessible way, Frank primed Chuck to find new, appropriate applications later on. Chuck's comment that his brain was "churning" in the moment suggests the stimulating effects of such priming. His interview comments about his experience talking with Frank reinforces the interpretation:

> [T]here's not gonna be one solution to [disciplinary faculty's] problem. So, in the case that they're walking away with a solution, that's great, that's a temporary fix. . . . Because what

are they gonna do the next time they have one of these problems? Have they talked about a general solution or a general mindset for attacking these situations that they're in? [. . .] [I]t reminds me of a student coming in with a paper and learning how to revise this paper but you're not asking them to think about why they're revising it and how this would apply, in a general sense, to every paper they're gonna do in the future. And so, I guess every time we've left the conversation, I've had a solution to two or three of the problems I've been dealing with in other classes. So it's like, even though we're not conversing about those problems, in my mind I'm applying them to all these problems.

Here, Chuck demonstrates a "problem-exploring disposition," one that inclines him "toward curiosity, reflection, consideration of multiple possibilities, a willingness to engage in a recursive process of trial and error, and toward a recognition that more than one solution can 'work'" (Wardle, 2012). Chuck made connections between teaching and writing as activities that require adaptable responses to changing circumstances, as well as ongoing growth and development through reflection. One cannot learn finally and exactly how to write or how to teach (writing), he suggests; instead, we need ideas to think and play with as we approach unknowable future situations. Frank facilitated Chuck's grappling with these ideas, fostering a problem-exploring disposition and the "reflective thought [involved] in abstracting from one context and seeking connections with others" (Perkins & Salomon, 1988, p. 26).

In addition to sponsoring backward-reaching and forward-reaching transfer, the cognitive function of playful strategies might sponsor transfer-focused thinking by forging mental bridges. Metaphors, in particular, seem to support transfer through bridging, which Perkins and Salomon (1988) describe as "'mediat[ing]' the needed processes of abstraction and connection making" (p. 28). Their detect-elect-connect model of transfer includes three particular "bridges": First the learner detects a "possible link" between a current problem or situation and past learning; then the learner must elect to further explore the link; finally, the learner must make the effort to connect past learning to the details of present circumstances (Perkins & Salomon, 2012, p. 250). Examples in the previous section suggest metaphor has the potential to strengthen mental bridges of each kind. For instance, Bill's faucet metaphor might have facilitated detection of possible links between current situations and past learning by revealing the assumptions hidden beneath personal or disciplinary values. It likely urged Lena to elect to pursue those links by using grounded abstraction to mediate experiences that might initially seem vastly unrelated—such as fixing a faucet and composing a tenure argument and/or writing a paper for class. Finally, by putting into play various perceptions across spheres of living, the metaphor likely sustained interest and motivation to pursue conceptual bridges.

Any of the bridges described in the transfer model above "can be a bridge too far" (Perkins & Salomon, 2012, p. 250). While researchers often turn to learners' lack of ability to explain failed bridging, Perkins and Salomon (2012) argue that "in the wild," in the context of ill-structured problems, motivations and dispositions play an important role (p. 253). Examples from my study suggest the relational functions of play might have the potential to act as motivational and dispositional drivers sustaining learners struggling to forge the long bridges involved in high-road transfer. Put differently, playful strategies might encourage transfer by inspiring and sustaining the will (Barnett, 2007) or desire to learn (McCune & Entwistle, 2011).

According to Barnett's theory (2007), a will to learn must be accompanied by a "will to offer" or "a readiness to put personal understanding into a public arena for critical consideration by others" (McCune & Entwistle, 2011, p. 305). The offering up is necessary, say McCune and Entwistle (2011), for "private will to learn leads nowhere" (p. 305). However, to forward understanding-in-process is to make oneself vulnerable to criticism, judgment, and rejection: Offering is "an act of courage" (Barnett, 2007, p. 83). Because "the world of play favors exuberance, license, abandon" (Ackerman, 1999, p. 6), it can lessen feelings of anxiety and self-consciousness that stifle the will to offer and learn. In a playful world, Ackerman

(1999) explains, "shenanigans are allowed, strategies can be tried, selves can be revised" (p. 6). Chuck suggested the relational value of play when he explained how silly play fostered "exposing" or "opening moment[s]" for him with the potential to temper anxiety and bolster the courage needed to be vulnerable.

In a similar vein, relational functions of play—including balancing power dynamics and building camaraderie—can promote transfer by encouraging a spirit of risk-taking needed to expand "prior knowledge and practice" (Qualley, 2016, p. 101). Donna Qualley's (2016) use of the concept of the "corridor of tolerance" helps clarify the connection between risk-taking, transfer, and play (p. 98). She explains that the construct was originally used to describe how teachers decided to make changes in their practice based on self-reflection. When teachers determined that a particular teaching practice lay outside their "corridor of tolerance," they made changes to that practice, while positive evaluations of practice rarely led to change. As Qualley (2016) puts it: "The smaller the corridor for acceptability, the more likely teachers will decide to revise and modify their practices" (p. 99). Thus, in order to notice and feel compelled to pursue opportunities for change, individuals "may need to 'shrink' the size of their corridors" (p. 99). Shrinking corridors is risky business because it means opening one's practice up to wider scrutiny. Nevertheless, as Barnett (2007) points out, risk is "inevitable" if intellectual, practical, and ontological growth is to take place (p. 145). According to Qualley (2016), dispositional and motivational drivers "seem to play a role in the size of . . . corridors and the speed at which they expand or contract" (p. 100); it follows that drivers can inhibit or bolster the courage to risk shrinking corridors of tolerance.

Playful strategies, such as equalizing power dynamics and building camaraderie, can encourage the shrinking of corridors despite the risk by cultivating trust among writing specialists and content experts. Literacy scholarship supports the notion that playfulness can sponsor risk-taking and encourage new possibilities for learning. Miller (2008), for example, suggests that creative play can be a means of "enhance[ing] individualized meaning-making" and cultivating learners' confidence so they are more willing to take risks in the future (pp. 88–89). In the context of CCL work, Chuck's experience crooning with Frank might have laid the groundwork for Chuck to narrow his corridor of tolerance and embrace the risk of scrutinizing and changing his teaching practice in future conversations with Frank. Cultivating camaraderie is key here, for as Geller (2008) points out, creative risk-taking takes practice and thus demands sustained support and endorsement (p. 172). Boquet and Eodice (2008) use the "double-entendre of 'hanging out'" to make sense of the interactive element in creativity and learning: "Engaging in risky behaviors, pursuing the unknown," they explain, "can certainly leave us feeling as though we are hanging out (on a limb) or worried that we will be hung out (to dry)" (p. 15). At the same time, "hanging out" with fellow learners (perhaps in playful ways) "is a start to building the support networks we all need to feel emboldened to take chances now and then" (p. 15). Relational dimensions of play can communicate camaraderie, a form of "hanging out," and sponsor the dispositions that make risk-taking, and high-road transfer, possible.

In particular, play can cultivate self-efficacy, a disposition Driscoll and Wells (2012) identify as key for learning transfer. As Tanis (2012) explains, "play/playfulness keeps [learners] off guard, engaged, motivated, and moves them to a place where they take ownership and responsibility for their own learning" (p. 154). Encouraging ownership is especially important in the context of adult learning; adults must take an active role in their learning; they need space and motivation to self-monitor through metacognitive practice and to participate in the negotiation of new understanding (Bransford et al., 2000; Cranton, 1996; Mezirow, 1991). By creating "occasion[s]" for learners to construct knowledge, to have "wonderful ideas" (Duckworth, 1987, p. 1), playfulness can prompt active learning, ownership, and self-efficacy. We see the potential for this in Lena's "aha" moment when she applied the concept of genre to her own struggle to compose an assignment sheet. We see it in Chuck's tendency to build on Frank's ideas in conversation, exploring them to flexibly and imaginatively apply them for his own purposes. According to Duckworth (1987) this is the very best teachers can do for learners, to make knowledge "seem interesting and accessible" so as "to let them raise and answer their own questions, to let them realize that their ideas are significant—so they have the interest, the ability, and the self-confidence to go on by themselves" (p. 8).

My initial speculation about how cognitive and relational functions of play might encourage transfer-focused dispositions reveals the pedagogical promise of playful discursive strategies that can be adapted in a range of CCL contexts. Workshop leaders, for instance, might incorporate metaphor or storytelling more purposefully into traditional activities such as case studies, scenarios, and role play to cultivate transfer-focused dispositions, or be more attuned to moments that invite humor, spontaneity, or improvisation as opportunities to embrace silliness as a form of play. Doing so would not only more fully embrace the pedagogical potential of CCL work, but might also model playful strategies for faculty participants, encouraging them to be more playful in their own classroom pedagogies. Moreover, revealing the promise of play for learning transfer suggests a need for more comprehensive investigations of transfer in CCL contexts. Driscoll and Wells (2012) identify areas for "future inquiry into the nature of dispositions" that apply to faculty in CCL contexts as well. Inspired by the areas of inquiry identified by Driscoll and Wells (2012), I propose future research that more systematically explores which faculty dispositions facilitate and inhibit transfer; determines if, how, and when faculty dispositions change; and examines the role of pedagogical interaction in encouraging transfer-oriented dispositions.

CONCLUSION

Throughout this chapter, I have explored play as a communicative challenge and opportunity in the context of CCL consultations. Seasoned (and perhaps even not-so-seasoned) writing specialists might recognize the discursive strategies—metaphor, storytelling, and silliness—as moves they make intuitively in conversation with faculty to establish rapport. By foregrounding the pedagogical potential of these discursive practices, however, I hope to prime writing specialists to employ them more deliberately for pedagogical purposes. Moreover, I imagine that not all writing specialists automatically bring these rather amorphous interpersonal communication strategies to their work. Delineating the moves and their functions makes them available and accessible as pedagogical practices for those of us who might not be inherently playful. While a fine line (or in some cases no line at all) may exist between the accounts of play I have examined here and common interactional practices such as exchanging pleasantries, sharing food, or asking about family, examples in this chapter suggest that the same moves can function more or less playfully and pedagogically; play and pedagogy are achieved through interaction. By highlighting the pedagogical potential of play, I urge writing specialists to attend more intentionally to playful possibilities in CCL contexts and begin to embrace them as part of the work of teaching and learning rather than as unrelated activities.

My investigation of play, as a valuable if not yet fully intentional aspect of CCL work, contributes to a guiding ethic for writing specialists working with faculty in other disciplines. Findings indicate that cognitive functions of metaphor and storytelling have the potential to prompt reflection, reveal assumptions and underlying logics, and forge connections with prior knowledge and experience. These strategies suggest the value of shared openness and collaborative meaning-making. Along with silliness, metaphor and storytelling can also have relational functions such as fostering an atmosphere of enjoyment and cultivating the courage and persistence to pursue transformational learning. To capitalize on these pedagogical possibilities of play, a guiding ethic for CCL work might support reflexive habits of mind and encourage a willingness to accompany fellow learners in their experiences of liminality. The ethic might also respect and scaffold relational attunement to inform decisions about how, when, and why to embrace playfulness with particular learners. In the final chapter I flesh out principles of a guiding ethic for CCL work and examine implications of the ethic for this unique professional practice.

5

A Guiding Ethic for Cross-Curricular Literacy Work

IN THIS BOOK, I HAVE TREATED CCL WORK AS A pedagogical activity—one that is epistemic, reflexive, and relational. Through that lens, I have investigated sites of communication challenge and opportunity in conversations among writing specialists and faculty in other disciplines—places where the possibility of embracing pedagogical potential can be thwarted or strengthened. By analyzing discursive strategies used to address these challenges/opportunities from the perspective of teaching and learning, I have begun to suggest ways to capitalize on pedagogical possibilities in CCL contexts. In this chapter, I synthesize my observations into a guiding ethic for CCL work, elaborating key principles I have only gestured toward in previous chapters and reiterating particular techniques for enacting each principle during faculty conversations about (teaching) writing. In detailing a guiding ethic for CCL work, this chapter transitions from analyzing professional practice as it *is* to proposing and enabling how it *ought to be*,[1] crystalizing research-based insights in order to make them implicative for action. Moving "back and forth between practical suggestions and moral principles, ideals for action and concrete communicative techniques," I describe both habits of mind and discursive strategies for enacting an ethic for CCL work as pedagogical activity (Tracy, 1997, p. 133). I propose three guiding principles: (1) commit to reflexive practice; (2) maintain a learner's stance; and (3) approach CCL conversations as pedagogical performance. I will briefly describe each principle before examining implications and applications of a pedagogical ethic for responding to the challenges of negotiating expertise, pursuing transformational change, and enacting pedagogical play in a range of CCL contexts.

PRINCIPLE 1: COMMIT TO REFLEXIVE PRACTICE. Reflexivity is widely acknowledged by writing teacher-scholars as a cornerstone of teaching and learning (Gallagher, 2002; Qualley, 1997; Stenberg, 2005); it resonates with arguments about the value of reflection and metacognition for composing and learning to write (Yancey, 1998), for sponsoring transfer of writing knowledge across contexts (Nowacek, 2011; Yancey, Robertson, & Taczak, 2014), for deliberative processes of expert practitioners faced with unfamiliar situations (Schön, 1987), and for making new knowledge meaningful and personally relevant for adult learners (Mezirow & Associates, 1990). Based on my research, reflexive practice—reflecting systemically on one's own values and assumptions in relation to new, sometimes counterintuitive ideas—seems potentially useful for negotiating expertise, pursuing change and transformative learning, and embracing play in pedagogical ways. In terms of expertise, Frank demonstrated reflexive practice when he drew on his knowledge of institutional context to acknowledge and respect Thomas's complicated feelings about changes to the first-year seminar program. Writing specialists also had to be reflexive to make the methodology and epistemology of teaching writing accessible for disciplinary faculty, a crucial condition for establishing an expert techne. They had to negotiate their own values and understandings with their colleagues' to recognize faculty members' existing expertise and productively shift or expand it. These examples illustrate how particular discursive strategies can employ reflexive practice to negotiate expertise in CCL contexts. The first row in Appendix A lists specific discursive moves for negotiating expertise along with purposes for each move.

Reflexive habits of mind could also support change as transformational learning. Writing specialists in my study created opportunities for active learning, reflection, and cross-disciplinary connection-making by temporarily withholding advice. Alicia's use of active listening strategies such as minimal response and say backs, her decision not to advise Ann to "flip" her classroom, and her choice to mention KWL only after Ann had developed a reasoned response to her own problem, are good examples. Reflexive practice can also be invaluable for addressing troublesome knowledge that can inhibit transformational learning. Bill tempered the foreignness of the worldview expressed in his faculty workshop by supporting teaching advice with evidence the psychology professor found compelling; Frank used "surfacing and animating" to unearth Thomas's tacit knowledge about writing and make it available for reflexive reconsideration; and Alicia urged Ann to imagine hypothetical outcomes that might result from changes in her teaching to animate insights and resist inert knowledge. These examples suggest how demonstrating and/or encouraging reflexive practice can support transformational learning by putting individuals' knowledge and experience in conversation (see Appendix A, Row 2).

Finally, reflexive practice can be a mechanism for embracing pedagogical play just as play can sponsor reflexivity. Bill both enacted and prompted reflexivity when he employed interlocking metaphors as a teaching tool in his conversation with Lena. To create the metaphors, he had to think reflexively about the relationship between his understanding of how writers develop and Lena's perception of detailed assignment sheets as handholding. At the same time, his metaphors guided Lena's reflexive engagement with the concepts, potentially fostering backward-reaching transfer by creating an opportunity for her to forge mental bridges between her own experience as a writer and her current challenge to support students in successfully completing her writing assignments. In a slightly different vein, Frank and Chuck engaged the concert metaphor as a heuristic for shared inquiry. By engaging the comparison between student-teacher-peer relationships and the relationship between audience, opening act, and main performer at a concert, they reflexively put their tentative understandings in conversation. The reflexive process encouraged "problem-exploring" dispositions that acknowledge multiple alternative possibilities (Wardle, 2012). The cognitive function of storytelling also suggests the value of reflexive practice. By both grounding and abstracting complex concepts, Frank's story about composing "Little Red Riding Hood" primed Chuck for forward-reaching transfer, as evidenced by Chuck's comment that his "brain was churning" after hearing the story. See Appendix A, Row 3 for discursive practices that enact the principle of reflexive practice for the purpose of pedagogical play. Based on my analysis of faculty conversations and interviews, reflexivity is a promising habit of mind for achieving the epistemic, reflexive, and relational dimensions of CCL work. Communicative strategies that enact and/or encourage reflexive practice enable faculty to "ear[n] [their] insights" through a process of critical questioning, exploration, and connection making (Qualley, 1997, p. 35). At the same time, reflexive practice can be difficult to encourage and perform. Highlighting a commitment to reflexive practice as a guiding principle for CCL work and identifying practical strategies for achieving it make visible and achievable the dialogue at the heart of the pedagogical process. Reflexivity becomes more than a value we tout as educators, but part of an ethic writing specialists can animate through daily professional practice.

PRINCIPLE 2: MAINTAIN A LEARNER'S STANCE.

The notion that writing specialists should strive to maintain a learner's stance during conversations with disciplinary faculty is the second principle of a guiding ethic for CCL work. A learner's stance is one that articulates itself and can account for its evolution, while simultaneously remaining open to reconsideration and revision (Qualley, 1997). A version of the learner's stance appears in scholarship across educational contexts. Donna Qualley (1997) advocates a learner's stance as integral to the process of reflexive inquiry at the heart of teaching writing. Toohey and Waterstone (2004) promote a version of the learner's stance when they acknowledge multiple sites of (shifting) expertise in collaborative teacher research, and Barbara Rogoff (1994) describes a "community of learners" in which expert old-timers learn from and with novices, enhancing community-based knowledge and opportunities for new understanding (p. 213). Alicia invoked the learner's stance when she described Nancie Atwell's (1998) notion of "always beginning" as a mantra driving her work with teachers. As these examples suggest, maintaining a learner's stance is a vital part of engaging in pedagogical activity because it promotes knowledge production and transformation within individual and collaborative meaning-making frameworks.

A learner's stance actualizes the epistemic dimension of CCL conversations as pedagogical activity by opposing traditional views of teaching and learning as one-directional transactions from expert to novice. Writing specialists can usefully trouble imbalanced perceptions of power and expertise through a learner's stance by discursively acknowledging the knowledge and experience others bring to CCL conversations and to teaching writing. Alicia's attention to language difference, for example, allowed that faculty practices might already include the activities she suggested, such as assigning learning letters, even if faculty understood or named those practices differently. Alicia didn't assume she was the only expert writing teacher or that her suggestions were always novel; taking a learner's stance, she was open to considering her practices in relation to others'. Similarly, writing specialists employed matchmaking and strategically used pronouns to shift the locus of expertise and discursively construct a wider community of writing teachers. Finally, by positioning themselves as fellow faculty or fellow human beings, writing specialists highlighted shared experiences, inviting collective inquiry and meaning-making. See Appendix B, Row 1 for a list of discursive strategies that enact a learner's stance to negotiate expertise.

Of course, a learner's stance is vital for supporting and embracing change as transformational learning. Actively engaging and mapping a range of alternative viewpoints can bridge disciplinary divides and promote deep learning for all involved. Bill illustrated the difficulty of engaging others' disciplinary perspectives, especially when the underlying assumptions vary greatly or conflict with our own. Nevertheless, juxtaposing alternatives can lead to new discoveries and insights, particularly in CCL contexts like faculty workshops where many different viewpoints are likely in play. Taking a learner's stance can mean modeling openness to change by sharing memories of learning or making visible experiences of learning in real time. That writing specialists rarely went beyond mentioning insights that emerged during conversation to investigate and interrogate loaded knowledge in their fields suggests that taking a learner's stance may be easier said than done. While writing specialists may espouse, and even model, openness as a central value, more concrete strategies and habits of mind are needed to enact the philosophy of a learner's stance. Several communicative techniques for supporting transformational learning with a learner's stance are outlined in Appendix B, Row 2.

Lastly, a learner's stance can enable and be enabled by pedagogical play. Playful strategies—metaphor and silliness in particular—can facilitate the articulation and reconsideration of ideas through conversation with others. As Chuck pointed out, silly, playful experiences foster openness and trust, which can mitigate the vulnerability that comes with learning. Frank and Chuck's singing episode, for instance, seemed to cultivate trust by equalizing power dynamics, humanizing each man in the eyes of the other. Silliness can also foster camaraderie, communicating a willingness to stand with or come along, to "be good company" (Berger, 2004, p. 346) for one another on recursive journeys of liminal learning, as illustrated by James, Liliana, and Kim's playful discussion of hypothetical culinary bribery. In a slightly different vein, playful strategies such as metaphor can encourage and enact a learner's stance by inviting collaborative sense-making. Frank and Chuck inhabited a learner's stance when they embraced the concert metaphor as a heuristic for shared inquiry, offering and revising tentative ideas about complex relationships. As these examples suggest, maintaining a learner's stance can be a valuable principle for enacting CCL work as pedagogical activity. Identifying specific discursive practices will ideally facilitate more purposeful engagement in day-to-day faculty interactions, slowly shifting assumptions about the nature of CCL work, and alleviating factors that might make a learner's stance in service of pedagogical activity so difficult to realize. Appendix B, Row 3 outlines ways to use a learner's stance to embrace pedagogical play.

PRINCIPLE 3: APPROACH CCL CONVERSATIONS
AS PEDAGOGICAL PERFORMANCE.

The third principle of my guiding ethic for CCL work urges writing specialists to approach CCL conversations as pedagogical performances. Inspired by writing teacher-scholars who have challenged the notion of static teaching roles, this principle advocates "a more rhetorical approach in which teachers *perform* varied, overlapping, difficult-to-pin-down roles for varied rhetorical situations, taking into account audience, context, and purpose" (Bartlett, 2015, p. 40).[2] In *Revisionary Rhetoric, Feminist Pedagogy, and Multigenre Texts*, Julie Jung (2005) understands teacher behaviors not as the natural consequence of identity, style, or institutional structure but as performance genres that can be strategically manipulated, juxtaposed, employed, etc., for particular pedagogical effects (2005, p. 147). A performance approach to teaching and learning foregrounds agency, shifts focus from who teachers are or should *be* to what they *do* and "invites teachers to attend to *what is possible* for themselves and [fellow learners]" (Bartlett, 2015, p. 40). In CCL contexts, the idea of pedagogical performance reinforces the reality that conversations about (teaching) writing are themselves sites of teaching and learning and empowers faculty to choose to communicate in ways that foreground pedagogical purpose.

The principle of pedagogical performance prompts writing specialists to tease out the teaching-learning subjectivities that unconsciously shape our interactions with disciplinary colleagues and illuminate the "pedagogical genres they inspire" so we can "rhetorically choose from among them rather than unconsciously summon them" (Jung, 2005, p. 147). For example, identifying subjectivities associated with stages of the WAC movement reveals their underlying goals and values as well as possible communicative techniques for enacting them. The "missionary" who values self-discovery, process pedagogy, and writing to learn might pose probing questions to spark reflection, while the "anthropologist" who is interested in social constructionism and enculturation into disciplinary discourse communities might employ ethnographic strategies of defamiliarization and open-ended "interview" questions that invite thick description of experience. We could go on mapping subjectivities, values, and communicative techniques for other traditional writing specialist roles as well as for personal subjectivities individual writing specialists might bring to CCL work. In this way, the lens of pedagogical performance links "performativity to enactment and reflection," associating identities and ideologies with communicative strategies and interactive behaviors (Bartlett, 2015, p. 41). Tracing this relationship exposes for critical consideration potential sources and consequences of our actions.

The principle of pedagogical performance might guide writing specialists to make more informed decisions about when, why, and how to enact particular communication strategies to negotiate expertise, pursue change as transformational learning, and embrace play. For instance, considering the pedagogical potential of urging acquiescence or inviting participation in a given moment might compel a writing specialist to contemplate circumstantial factors such as teaching load, timing, a faculty member's home life, as well as relational factors such as mutual honesty and trust. The notion of pedagogical performance can facilitate attunement to prior knowledge, prompting writing specialists to notice types of faculty writing expertise and decide whether to reframe or build on it. As an ethical principle, pedagogical performance acknowledges and respects locations of expertise and inspires communicative decisions based on how individuals are positioned in relation to one another. Appendix C, Row 1 outlines discursive practices for embracing pedagogical performance to negotiate expertise.

This principle can also help writing specialists respond flexibly to the nuances of troublesome knowledge in pursuit of transformative learning. For instance, when Thomas found troublesome the notion that (teaching) writing is like a conversation, Frank chose to take a long view of learning. He planted the seed of an idea without pushing for immediate changes in Thomas's teaching practice, demonstrating the patience needed to nurture change as slow, messy learning that evolves over time. Based on a holistic view of Thomas as a complex person with rich experiences, Frank's pedagogical performance paid off. While Thomas's assignments didn't immediately change, Frank's ideas impacted him on a "higher level" by provoking him to reflect on why he did what he did in his writing classes. Ann's experience also indicates how pedagogical performance might reinforce the long view of learning by enabling writing specialists to address the needs and circumstances of unique learners. As a new faculty member, Ann needed to ritualize basic knowledge and practices to teach writing in her new WI course. Later, Alicia recognized Ann's desire to de/ritualize knowledge and make changes to her teaching. These examples emphasize that faculty members come to CCL exchanges as complicated people and multifaceted learners. Embracing pedagogical performance enables writing specialists to respond to that complexity pedagogically, as teachers and learners. See Appendix C, Row 2 for ways to promote change as transformative learning through pedagogical performance.

Finally, pedagogical performance helps writing specialists decide when and how to seize opportunities for meaningful, generative play and recognize when playful elements (spontaneity, frivolity, transgression, etc.) might work against the goals of relationality and long-term teaching and learning. Frank's willingness to embrace humility, silliness, and frivolity by singing with Chuck, for instance, shows how purposeful performances of play can sponsor transfer-focused dispositions, such as the will to learn and offer, self-efficacy, and risk-taking. Frank's sense of Chuck's goals for their conversations, his attitude toward learning, and his anxieties as a new faculty member, likely informed his decision to incorporate silly play into their conversations. By the same token, Alicia's decision not to make play part of her time with Ann and Bill's move to use subtler forms of play, such as metaphor and storytelling, to establish personal connection in conversations with Lena, model pedagogical performances attuned to individual needs and learning styles.

The principle of pedagogical performance can provide a method for more deliberately actualizing pedagogical engagement. Such a mechanism is vital, for as I have shown, principles of a guiding ethic for CCL work—reflexivity and a learner's stance—can be difficult to realize in practice. Pedagogical performance gives writing specialists both the structure and the versatility to address real challenges and find creative ways to enact and reflect on the principles we hold most dear. Appendix C, Row 3 identifies discursive strategies that employ the principle of pedagogical performance to address the challenge and opportunity of play.

These three principles—(1) commit to reflexive practice; (2) maintain a learner's stance; and (3) approach CCL conversations as pedagogical performance constitute a *pedagogical ethic* for CCL work. Rather than providing a static model or method for professional practice, the ethic calls for attunement to the relational, "locat[ing] motive energy" within teacher-learners and their "interests and purposes" and encouraging varying approaches to teaching and learning rather than "accepting one best way" (Noddings, 2004, p. vii). The ethic is pedagogical because it supports activity that is epistemic—engenders collaborative meaning-making; reflexive—involves critical questioning, self-exploration, and connection; and relational—inspires interpersonal attunement and long-term engagement. Principles of the ethic and features of pedagogical activity enable one another. Rather than a set of linear relationships (principle informs action, action embodies a feature of pedagogy, features combine to constitute pedagogical activity), they are nodes and pathways in a complex rhizome that represents a constant striving toward pedagogical relationship building. Given this (inter)relationship, it is fitting that pedagogy informs both the analytical lens at the heart of this study and the principles for practice that have emerged from it. As a situational frame, a pedagogical lens provided a way to interpret what *is*; it allowed me to investigate the habits of mind and discursive strategies faculty use to achieve (or not) the pedagogical potential of CCL work. As a driving force behind principles of practice, pedagogy also crystalizes, and suggests a means for achieving, what *ought to be*. By distilling key principles and conceptualizing them as part of a cohesive, dynamic ethic, I aim to guide practitioners engaged in the rich range of activities constituting CCL work to more purposely and fully achieve pedagogical ends.

APPLICATIONS: WHO SHOULD TAKE UP A PEDAGOGICAL ETHIC?

A pedagogical ethic is not only valuable for writing specialists in CCL context; it also has applications for faculty and administrators (WPAs, writing center directors, and faculty developers) outside WAC/WID programs who facilitate cross-disciplinary conversations; postsecondary educators responding to an educational landscape that demands cross-disciplinary research, writing, teaching, and service work; and for education and training programs preparing the next generation of academic consultants.

Applications for Cross-Disciplinary Consultants

As a former writing program administrator (WPA) directing first-year composition (FYC), I'm struck by the relevance of the ethic to my daily work facilitating conversations about (teaching) writing with instructors, graduate TAs, undergraduate students, advisors, administrators, and other faculty and staff across the university. For example, in response to an administrative mandate to redesign the first-year writing program to align with large-scale general education reform at my institution, I spent two years working with a team of faculty, GTAs, instructors, and administrators to overhaul FYC curriculum, labor structures, teacher support, and public relations strategies. The project presented countless opportunities to negotiate expertise (with central administrators, senior colleagues, instructors, and students), navigate myriad possibilities for pursuing meaningful change, and contemplate possibilities for play within a process that was consuming, maddening, and risky as well as invigorating and generative. As a young, untenured, female assistant professor who simultaneously and unexpectedly inherited both the program directorship and the remodeling project, I would have appreciated a guiding ethic in my first meeting with the dean and provost. Treating our interactions and the differences shaping them (including discipline, professional rank, gender, and age) as opportunities for pedagogical engagement might have revealed more possibilities and pathways for collaboration. Moreover, had I been armed with communicative strategies for traversing the unfamiliar rhetorical landscape, I might have felt less intimidated and more empowered to inhabit and encourage an environment for teaching and learning. My experience suggests a pedagogical ethic can provide WPAs informed approaches to uniquely challenging conversations, particularly when it comes to negotiating expertise (Tarabochia, 2013).

Likewise, Jackie Grutsch McKinney's (2013) robust representation of the theoretically and pedagogically complex reality of writing center work attests to the promise of a pedagogical ethic for writing center tutors and administrators facing the challenges and opportunities of cross-disciplinary conversations about (teaching) writing in that institutional context. Collaboration with various departments and units is a central aspect of writing center work. Directors are often considered "the" writing person on campus, as was the case with Frank, and deal regularly with faculty across the curriculum in various capacities. In their study of the working lives of writing center directors, Caswell, Grutsch McKinney, and Jackson (2016) note the "emotional labor" of directors who regularly engage in tasks that "involv[e] nurturing, encouraging, and building relationships or resolving conflict" (p. 55) Habits of mind and communicative strategies that resonate with writing center philosophies could support tutors, directors, and staff in navigating these rich and varied interactions.

In a slightly different vein, a pedagogical ethic may be useful in the field of faculty development, "a profession dedicated to helping colleges and universities function effectively as teaching and learning communities," (Felten et al. qtd in Artze-Vega et al., 2013, p. 164). Based on a survey of five hundred faculty developers from across institution types, Sorcinelli and her colleagues identified several unique challenges and opportunities for faculty developers that highlight the potential benefit of a pedagogical ethic for this professional practice, including expanding faculty roles, the shifting needs of a "changing professoriate," and the changing nature of teaching, learning, and scholarship (Sorcinelli, 2007). The shifts mean faculty developers must negotiate expertise across institutional positions and ranks, determine kairotic approaches for sponsoring transformative learning, and find creative ways to encourage long-term investment in professional growth and development. Additionally, to "guide colleagues along a *developmental continuum* of scholarly teaching," developers must address troublesome threshold concepts in scholarly teaching by negotiating expertise, modeling and inviting critical self-reflection, and scaffolding interdisciplinary conversations around teaching inquiry (Bunnell & Bernstein, 2012, p. 17). Moreover, continued diversification of higher education in terms of student and faculty body mean developers must be cognizant of how the unique experiences of underrepresented faculty along axes such as campus climate, teaching, access to appropriate mentoring and support, demands and pressures for service, and (de)valuing of scholarly credentials (Tuitt, 2010) call for attuned communicative and pedagogical strategies.

Given the complex nature of this work, communicative capacities are vital for developers who regularly interact with individual faculty; facilitate interdisciplinary groups in committees, workshops, and learning communities; and counsel administrators responsible for areas, systems, and budgets across the institution (Zakrajsek, 2010, pp. 90–93). In her study of directors and supervisors of teaching and learning centers, Connie M. Schroeder found that faculty developers are enabled in their role as "change agents" by (among other factors) pedagogical knowledge, collaborative style, established credibility and trust, and building close contacts with faculty, departments, and institutional leadership (Schroeder, 2011a, pp. 33–39; Schroeder, 2011b, p. 116). The relational, interactional nature of these factors suggests faculty development work would benefit from careful negotiation of expertise, nuanced approaches to change, and a felt sense for if, when, and how play might inform development efforts. Embracing the principles (reflexivity, learner's stance, pedagogical performance) and communication practices (e.g., metaphor, storytelling, withholding advice, attending to language difference) associated with a pedagogical ethic would allow faculty developers to facilitate pedagogical conversations and foster the pedagogical habits of mind all faculty need to meet the demands of a changing educational landscape.

Applications for All Faculty

Although a pedagogical ethic is designed for consultants, forces of change identified by Sorcinelli, Austin, Eddy, and Beach (2006) suggest that all faculty will be called upon to "engage in more interdisciplinary work" (Sorcinelli, 2007) and could thus benefit from a pedagogical ethic as well. In the realm of research, academic institutions are beginning to incentivize the development of skills and sensibilities to confront the world's most unresolvable problems. Colleen Flaherty (2015) points out a growing trend among research universities to fund "grand challenge" research programs focused on big ideas. Addressing problems on local, national, and global levels, grand challenge programs "involve collaborative, interdisciplinary research and partnerships with community organizations, industry and government." In addition to expertise in their fields, faculty researchers need pedagogical sensibilities to contribute productively to interdisciplinary grand challenge teams. When faculty are able to collaborate across disciplines and sectors they mitigate many difficulties inherent in grand challenge projects—including poor communication, lack of organization, and inefficient use of resources (Flaherty, 2015).

A pedagogical ethic could support faculty in this crucial work. For example, through reflexive practice, faculty could learn to "surface and animate," often tacit, disciplinary logics and deliberately reveal counterproductive disciplinary assumptions. By learning to maintain a learner's stance, faculty could employ strategies (such as metaphor and storytelling) to bridge disciplinary divides and seek opportunities to identify and celebrate perspective transformations. Deliberately utilizing interactional techniques toward pedagogical ends could cultivate environments ripe for serious play—a generative condition for creativity and innovation, as well as long-term relationship building and the persistence to sustain work on "lifeworld challenges . . . that arise from an age of supercomplexity" (Barnett, 2004, p. 250). In short, faculty who are able to be reflexive, take a learner's stance, and make communicative decisions with teaching and learning in mind are better prepared to flourish on interdisciplinary research teams by negotiating expertise, defining and pursuing meaningful change, and engaging in innovative play to positive effect.

A pedagogical ethic would also benefit classroom teaching across the curriculum by reinforcing habits of mind and relational strategies faculty need to teach students to work and collaborate meaningfully across disciplinary lines. In *The Meaningful Writing Project*, Eodice, Geller, and Lerner (2016) argue that agency, engagement, and learning for transfer should be key terms in ongoing discussions of student writing and learning (p. 22). Indeed, as the student body at postsecondary institutions becomes larger and more diverse each year in terms of "educational background, gender, race and ethnicity, class, age, and preparation," faculty must learn how to support students with various learning styles in developing "capacities for problem-solving, teamwork, and collaboration—skills required in a rapidly changing and increasingly global world" (Sorcinelli, 2007). Toward those ends, principles of a pedagogical ethic can help "cultivate teachers and students who value diverse ideas, beliefs, and worldviews, and promote more inclusive [teaching and] learning" (Sorcinelli, 2007). Applying reflexive practice in the classroom through minimal response and say backs, for example, can prompt students to draw on prior knowledge, avoid ritualizing new knowledge, and draw connections across disciplines. By approaching classroom teaching as pedagogical performance, faculty could purposefully juxtapose pedagogical genres, making deliberate decisions about when and how to employ particular communicative practices. Teaching based on these principles would support students' learning transfer and perspective transformation as well as model the ethic by example. In terms of both research and teaching, then, a pedagogical ethic can help prepare faculty to utilize, model, and teach habits of mind needed to "think beyond the assumptions and practices of our disciplinary or departmental contexts to consider what other disciplines and settings may have to offer as a source of reflection on our own practices" (McCune, 2009, pp. 231–32).

The ethic can be useful for faculty in the context of service commitments as well, for the call to participate in cross-disciplinary, interdisciplinary, or transdisciplinary work extends beyond teaching and research. Assessment initiatives, for example, demand cross-disciplinary collaboration as faculty work across subdisciplines within departments, or in the case of general education assessment across disciplines and departments within an institution. John Bean and his colleagues describe the discourse-based approach to university outcomes assessment at Seattle University as a process that "focuses primarily on rich faculty talk about ways to improve curriculum and instruction in light of strengths and weaknesses in student performance" (Bean, Carrithers, & Earenfight, 2005, p. 7). Because processes like these involve faculty in multiple "kinds of inquiry: 1) learning themselves what learning is taking place; 2) considering how to stage increased learning opportunities" for students (Kistler, Yancey, Taczak, & Szysmanski, 2009); and (I would add) (3) identifying learning opportunities for themselves, assessment initiatives are particularly relevant sites for engaging a pedagogical ethic. Approaching assessment conversations as pedagogical performance would position faculty to share and appreciate many types of expertise, cultivate the patience to nurture seeds of change, and take the long view of assessment. Faculty could attend to language differences in order to build bridges across (sub)disciplines and use surfacing and animating to unearth tacit knowledge for examination and reconsideration. In short, pedagogical habits of mind and communication strategies are valuable for assessment projects because they enrich and enable conversations across disciplines or subdisciplines about how to observe and document student learning and how to design rich opportunities for (student and faculty) learning.

Despite the fact that faculty are called upon with increasing frequency to engage in cross-disciplinary endeavors, research suggests we still tend to struggle to communicate productively across disciplinary lines. In her study of interdisciplinary faculty seminars, Myra H. Strober (2011) found that faculty "had developed disciplinary habits of mind that severely hampered interdisciplinary conversation. They were blind to the rules they used to engage in scholarly dialogue and blindsided by the fact that others' rules were so different from theirs" (p. 31). Given these tendencies, faculty must develop "new ways of being" (McCune, 2009, p. 232) to engage productively in cross-disciplinary projects. We must learn to contend with unconscious fears and negative disciplinary stereotypes; fundamental differences in disciplinary discourse and culture; power dynamics created by institutional positioning, gender, race, and culture; and institutional structures that work against the conditions for meaningful boundary-crossing (Strober, 2011, pp. 154–58). A pedagogical ethic could help faculty meet the demands of cross-disciplinary interactions and collaboration.

While nonconsultants may be less likely to encounter the pedagogical ethic in formal training contexts or seek it out on their own, writing specialist and faculty developers can foster the principles implicitly and explicitly during consultations and development events. As teacher educators know, modeling can be an extremely effective way to expose teachers to practices we hope they'll incorporate in their classrooms, especially when accompanied by metacognitive elements. In the spirit of the "show, don't tell" philosophy (Fulwiler, 1981) that has long informed approaches to WAC/WID faculty development, consultants might draw attention to principles of the ethic as they are enacted in faculty development contexts, guiding reflection on the value and potential uses of particular strategies. Depending on campus culture and faculty interest, instructional developers might also consider incorporating the ethic into faculty learning communities or workshops.

IMPLICATIONS: EDUCATING FUTURE CROSS-DISCIPLINARY CONSULTANTS

A pedagogical ethic has implications beyond the direct applications I have outlined above. The ethic is accessible in that it extends and animates many terms, concepts, and theories of teaching and learning that writing specialists and faculty developers will likely find familiar; yet it isn't necessarily intuitive. For individuals to enact it in local contexts it must be taught, practiced, and consistently revisited and revised, especially given the range of "pathways and motives" that lead to cross-disciplinary consultancy work (Artze-Vega et al., 2013, p. 163). As a result, we must look for opportunities to prepare future academic consultants. Toward that end, I suggest writing center tutor training and graduate education in composition and rhetoric as sites for teaching a pedagogical ethic for CCL work.

Implications for Writing Center Consultant Training
Like faculty consultants, writing center tutors regularly face the complicated task of communicating about (teaching) writing across disciplinary lines with complications related to "the incredible variety" of talk, activities, and contexts they engage, and the power dynamics they experience as a result of institutional positioning, among other factors (Nowacek & Hughes, 2015, p. 172). In addition to consulting with student writers, writing center staff also engage in many "non-tutoring activities" that demand communication or collaboration across disciplines and other axes of difference, including: conducting class, faculty, staff, and community workshops; running programs for basic and ESL writers; facilitating faculty and student writing groups; collaborating with departments, writing programs, WAC, WID, or CAC programs, and/or National Writing Project sites; and supporting TA and teacher education (McKinney, 2013, pp. 77–79). These activities call for negotiating expertise, embracing and sponsoring change as transformative learning, and making decisions about the role of play.

Writing center consultants must learn to inhabit the role of "expert outsider," to share their expertise in writing even as they "capitalize on lack of content knowledge" and do so in spaces "where negotiation of academic, social, cultural, and political identities are ubiquitous" (Nowacek & Hughes, 2015, p. 181; Denny, 2010, p. 96). Moreover, because the individual/social processes of writing and identity development inevitably intersect in the spaces of writing center work, consultants must attend to the politics of identity production, learning to navigate "structuring binaries" including directive/nondirective, expert/novice, teacher/student, professional/peer, as well as woman/man, white/people of color, and straight/gay (Denny, 2010, p. 97). They must learn to develop a nuanced expertise that is "simultaneously confident enough to work with writers from a wide range of disciplines and levels of experience and humble enough to remain open to constantly learning" (Nowacek & Hughes, 2015, p. 71).

Writing center consultants also face the challenge of supporting transformative change as writers and teachers of writing experience liminal learning spaces. Like the disciplinary faculty in my study, students and faculty come to the writing center immersed in various stages of learning about/in/with their disciplinary subject matter as well as learning about writing. Like the writing specialists in my study, writing center tutors are also always in states of transformational learning in terms of the disciplines they encounter and in terms of their (shifting) orientations to (teaching) writing. Nowacek explains that tutors must learn to "understand and contextualize their own views of writing" as well as "their interactions with writers" (Nowacek & Hughes, 2015, p. 177). They need to be "flexible and patient," and "able to see the potential value of incremental progress or planting the seed" of learning (p. 178). They must be able to "create a welcoming space for writers," to reconsider "the nature of resistance" and to reflect on sources of writers' frustrations (p. 178). Because tutors not only work with student writers but also with disciplinary faculty teaching writing, they also must "develop schema for listening analytically for faculty beliefs about writing" and learn to "accept and expect realistic progress [from faculty] on perhaps only a single concept at a time" (p. 180). These are sophisticated capacities, to be sure, especially given that writing center consultants can range from first-year undergraduates to postdocs and faculty.

Given these challenges, writing center consultants are also in a unique position to embrace the possibilities of pedagogical play in and through CCL interactions. As I mentioned in Chapter 4, writing center praxis leads the way when it comes to embracing play in support of meaningful CCL interactions (Boquet, 2002; Dvorak & Bruce, 2008; Geller et al., 2007), tutor education (Geller, 2008) and writing center work more broadly (Boquet & Eodice, 2008). Just like faculty writing consultants in my study, tutors can learn when, why, and how to use playfulness to promote learning as they respond to the range of assumptions, goals, and expectations in situations that often blur the lines between work and play. Learning to embrace a pedagogical ethic would position writing center consultants to respond to the challenges of cross-disciplinary communication and relationship building by more deliberately approaching interactions with faculty and peers as opportunities for pedagogical engagement.

A pedagogical ethic would bolster contemporary approaches to consultant education by foregrounding the interactional, relational dimensions of CCL work and by offering communicative strategies for enacting particular habits of mind both in tutor development contexts and during writing center consultations of all kinds. For instance, R. Mark Hall (2011) advocates "an inquiry stance toward writing center practice" and tutor training that "involves relentless questioning, asking *why*, wondering, researching, generating alternatives, testing, reviewing, and revising options" the purpose of which is to "examine both what [consultants] do and the rules and reasoning—the habits of mind—that determine what [they] do" (pp. 84–85). Principles and practices of a pedagogical ethic, in particular committing to reflexive practice, clearly resonate with the sustained inquiry Hall describes and provide directors and tutors with interactional strategies (such as juxtaposition, hypothesizing outcomes, and storytelling) for engaging in the process. Likewise, teaching a learner's stance would supplement threshold-based approaches to tutor education (Nowacek & Hughes, 2015) by giving consultants tools (such as metaphor, emphasizing other's expertise, and interrogating light bulb moments) for engaging "foreign" knowledge, unearthing loaded knowledge, and collaboratively constructing new knowledge as they use threshold concepts in writing studies to (re)consider their own views on writing.

Furthermore, a pedagogical ethic, particularly the third principle—approaching CCL work as pedagogical performance—speaks to the move in writing center and WAC scholarship to develop and engage critical praxis for equity and racial justice (Godbee, Ozias, & Tang, 2015; Poe, 2013; Young & Condon, 2013; Zhang et al.,

2013). Extending "calls to pedagogical action" from writing center scholars Nancy Grimm (1999, 2009); Anne Ellen Geller, Michele Eodice, Frankie Condon, Meg Carroll, and Elizabeth Boquet (2007); Harry Denny (2010); and Tiffany Rousculp (2014) among others, Godbee, Ozias, and Tang (2015) argue that in writing centers committed to "more equitable relations and practices," "tutor education [must] engage with issues of identity and power, as well as the material conditions of language, learning, and writing" (p. 63, 61, 62). Toward that end they advocate for "'critical tutor education,'" that "acknowledges the importance of bodies as spaces and sites for knowledge-making in order to more fully understand the intersecting and systemic nature of people's lived experiences with literacies and learning" (pp. 62–63). They propose movement-based workshops rooted in "feminist self-reflexivity," a "simultaneity" of "intentional and open" and a commitment to "creative movement" as "a productive mode of analysis for critiquing and intervening into race, racism, and racial formation" (p. 86, 99). The alignment between such workshops (and social justice commitments more broadly) and principles of a pedagogical ethic is clear. Specifically, discursive moves for engaging in pedagogical performance—including attunement to timing, trusting fellow learners, taking a holistic view, and embracing frivolity—have the potential to reinforce workshop elements and foundational habits of mind for critical tutor education. In sum, a pedagogical ethic both resonates with and builds on contemporary approaches to tutor development by associating broad principles with concrete communicative goals and practices and synthesizing them under the principles of reflexivity, learner's stance, and pedagogical performance. It provides a coherent, flexible structure for learning the habits of mind, rhetorical dexterity, and relational attunement tutors need to capitalize on the pedagogical potential of writing center work.

Implications for Graduate Student Education

A pedagogical ethic should be incorporated into graduate education in composition and rhetoric because comp/rhet graduate students are the writing specialists—the WAC/WID consultants, WPAs, and/or faculty developers—of tomorrow. Artze-Vega et al. (2013) point out that faculty members with comp/rhet backgrounds are increasingly called upon to fill "interdisciplinary faculty development leadership positions at their institutions" (p. 162). They do this work "wittingly and willingly or not, through their leadership in WAC and WID initiatives, general education curriculum development and assessment efforts, and common writing program administration (WPA) tasks" (Artze-Vega et al., 2013, p. 164; Rutz & Wilhoit, 2013; Willard-Traub, 2008). Yet comp/rhet graduate programs don't always prepare students for this work, particularly in terms of the communicative, relational dimensions so vital to cross-disciplinary interactions. Bill's comment during an interview that he was "shooting from the hip" during his interactions with faculty captures the experience of many WAC/WID leaders; likewise faculty developers (Zakrajsek, 2010, p. 83) and writing center administrators (McKinney, 2013, pp. 52–53) are not always formally trained to take on the cross-disciplinary collaborations those positions entail. Thus, comp/rhet students, in particular, would benefit from graduate pedagogy and curriculum designed to foster the habits of mind they need to do cross-curricular faculty development work.

The writing pedagogy course, mandatory in many comp/rhet programs, is an ideal site for teaching future writing specialists to embrace a pedagogical ethic because it often already promotes the belief that "teaching matters," develops "insights into teaching that are relevant across disciplines," promotes rhetorical dexterity for communicating across difference, inspires understanding of learning and passion for supporting learners (Artze-Vega et al., 2013, pp. 166–69), emphasizes reflective problem solving, and invests in an "uncoverage" model that values the experience of deep learning (Reid, 2013, p. 202). At the same time, the course can fall short of preparing future writing specialists for CCL work in three ways. First, it might not necessarily urge students to perceive the pedagogical potential in contexts beyond the writing classroom. Because graduate students enrolled in pedagogy courses are often simultaneously teaching writing for the first time, the need to prepare them for the immediate teaching context is urgent. Most research focuses on if/how pedagogy education accomplishes that purpose (Estrem & Reid, 2012a; E. Reid et al., 2012). However, given the changing nature of faculty work, especially for comp/rhet graduates, I propose that efforts to reconsider what pedagogy education "is" (Estrem & Reid, 2012b) should include applications beyond FYC. Graduate students should learn to consider the work they do (or will/might do) outside the composition classroom, including cross-disciplinary conversations with faculty, as pedagogical endeavors.

The second way writing pedagogy courses could better prepare graduate students for CCL work is by more directly emphasizing the relational in teaching and learning. Admittedly these courses, whether seminars or workshops at the graduate or undergraduate level, can be "impossible to teach" because they are expected to accomplish myriad objectives from orienting new students to graduate school to introducing writing theory, practice, and research, to transmitting standardized writing curriculum (Reid, 2013, p. 198; Trubek, 2005, p. 160). However, as Bingham and Sidorkin (2004) argue, there is "no education without relation," no pedagogy without pedagogical relationships. Thus comp/rhet graduate students would benefit from exposure to "a philosophy of relational pedagogy" (Noddings, 2004, p. vii) and practice enacting it in the context of teaching and learning across multiple sites.

Last, many writing pedagogy seminars don't make it a point to grapple with the challenges of cross-disciplinary communication and their relevance for future comp/rhet faculty. Given the likelihood that they will be called to CCL work (formally or informally), comp/rhet graduate students not only need to cultivate pedagogical habits of mind, but also learn to employ, adapt, and create discursive practices that enact them in cross-disciplinary contexts. That is, they must develop the rhetorical and pedagogical versatility to negotiate long- and short-term goals for conversations about (teaching) writing and pursue those goals with disciplinary colleagues through face-to-face interactions.

In addition to better preparing comp/rhet graduate students for the range of potential pedagogical relationships they will undoubtedly find as faculty, incorporating a pedagogical ethic into graduate pedagogy courses can impact the nature and practice of our discipline (Dobrin, 2005, p. 4). In that vein, I conclude the book by exploring how a pedagogical ethic might usefully shift how we understand and study CCL work and suggest directions for future research.

DIRECTIONS FOR FUTURE RESEARCH

A pedagogical ethic for CCL work has implications for WAC/WID as a movement and field of study. Rooted in practitioner experience, the ethic can deepen our understanding of the "ontology" (Paretti, 2011) of cross-disciplinary exchanges and urge a focus on the value of teaching and learning among colleagues across disciplinary lines. The ethic foregrounds the knowledge that faculty are complex, dynamic teacher-learners—a belief that has always been at the heart of WAC/WID as a faculty-centered movement, even if/when it was not embraced in practice. As I have suggested, that perspective troubles rigid interpretations of roles, relationships, and purposes undergirding many traditional approaches to CCL work and usefully complicates the linear progression of "stages" in the historical evolution of the WAC movement. It changes how we perceive, pursue, and measure the success of faculty exchanges in WAC/WID contexts, favoring evidence of slow transformation of writing specialists, disciplinary faculty, and the "subject matter" at the center of the work through deep learning and persistent efforts to nurture long-term pedagogical relationships. Through these shifts, a pedagogical ethic opens up new pathways for research in the field, two of which I will imagine here.

Additional Discourse-Based Studies of Cross-Disciplinary Conversations

Jablonski's (2006) observation that little WAC/WID scholarship addresses day-to-day interactions among faculty still rings true (p. 4). Recent publications focusing on important but broad institutional and programmatic approaches to improving writing instruction across disciplines continue the trend (see, for example, Melzer,

2014; Soliday, 2011). Rebecca Nowacek's (2011) discourse-based approach to understanding the challenges faculty face when teaching for transfer in an interdisciplinary seminar reinforces the need for a closer look at the discursive strategies faculty use (with colleagues and with students) when teaching and learning across disciplinary lines. My study responds to this need by examining cross-disciplinary interactions at the level of faculty conversation to identify and link habits of mind (reflexivity, learner's stance, relational pedagogy) and broad discursive moves (storytelling, metaphor, planting seeds, minimal response, etc.) into a guiding ethic for approaching face-to-face conversations in CCL contexts.

However, a more robust understanding of the nature of CCL work as a professional practice calls for micro-level analysis of interpersonal cross-disciplinary communication among faculty. For example, my research suggests that issues of power, privilege, and difference are implicated in cross-disciplinary conversations in ways that call for critical micro-level discourse analysis. How does gender shape cross-disciplinary conversations about teaching writing? How do the micro-level linguistic choices of Bill and Lena (man and woman) compare with those of Alicia and Ann (two women) or those of Frank and Thomas (two men)? How might differences in age and rank feature in Frank and Chuck's conversations? Liliana identified as Latina and bisexual, raising questions about how difference based on race, ethnicity, and sexual orientation might come to bear on cross-disciplinary conversations about (teaching) writing. What are the communicative implications of differences such as native language, nationality, and sexuality? Does the globalization and internationalization of higher education have implications for communicating across difference in CCL contexts? How might studying multilingual faculty in face-to-face conversations about teaching writing make visible the complexity of their rich language lives and extend arguments like Geller's (2011) against language standardization? Broadly speaking, my research surfaces issues of difference and inclusivity in the field of WAC/WID, issues foregrounded recently at the 2016 IWAC conference. While it is beyond the scope of this book to interrogate these forces in depth, micro-level linguistic analyses, driven by critical methodologies, have the potential to "facilitate studies of inequality, ethics, higher education . . . and institutional practices" in CCL contexts (Huckin, Andrus, & Clary-Lemon, 2012, p. 112; Godbee, 2012; Tarabochia, 2016a).

Studies of Transformative Learning Experiences of Faculty

My research also suggests the need for studies that further investigate faculty learning in and through CCL initiatives as a unique professional context. In Chapter 3, I use transformative learning theory to shed light on the dynamics of writing specialist and disciplinary faculty learning during CCL conversations. In particular, I map stages of liminality onto the learning experiences of faculty in my study and tease out discursive moves that (1) indicate faculty are wrestling with certain types of troublesome knowledge associated with each liminal stage and (2) support transformational learning by responding to unique experiences of troublesomeness. Rooted in these findings, a pedagogical ethic is designed to scaffold attunement and response to the "stuckness" of troublesome learning. This preliminary examination of liminal learning experiences, however, raises questions about what faculty involved in CCL initiatives should be learning, and what common patterns, if any, characterize their experiences of transformative learning. At least two research trajectories emerge from such questions.

First, we need studies that investigate meaningful content or curriculum for CCL work and identify strategies for teaching and learning for transfer in this context. This line of inquiry asks: What theories, ideas, practices, etc. prompt transformational learning for faculty involved in WAC/WID efforts and can we identify an ideal curriculum for CCL work? My focus on face-to-face interactions among faculty did not allow me to study how and why faculty transfer learning about (teaching) writing across contexts. Longitudinal research designed to track faculty transfer over time could build on my pedagogical focus and update/extend seminal WAC studies such as Walvoord et al.'s (1997) *In the Long Run*. Future research inspired by questions about curriculum and transfer in CCL contexts might look to recent transfer-related scholarship in writing studies for inspiration. For example, in the spirit of Yancey, Robertson, and Taczak's (2014) comparative study of first-year composition curricula, future research might test transfer-focused curriculum for faculty in CCL contexts. We might explore the potential for the WAC/WID specific threshold concepts Chris Anson (2015) outlines for faculty development, determine what "content" the concepts suggest, and experiment with the order and means by which they are introduced.

Second, we need studies that investigate how faculty experience change as transformational learning, the edge of their understanding. To make decisions about the curricular content and pedagogy most likely to sponsor learning transfer for faculty in CCL contexts, we must continue to deepen our understanding of faculty as teacher-learners. While a pedagogical ethic is designed to attune writing specialists to liminal learning experiences and equip them to respond to learners' needs, the nature of transformation means experiences of liminality will always vary widely. Therefore, the more we can learn about the nature of transformative learning in CCL contexts, the better writing specialists will be able to engage the ethic to pedagogical effect. Future studies might look to research in adult education and teacher preparation for ways to investigate transformational learning among faculty in CCL contexts. For example, researchers could adapt Berger's (2004) theoretical and methodological lenses for analyzing learners' experiences on the edge of understanding—Robert Kegan's (1982) constructive-developmental theory of adult learning and the Subject-Object Interview (SOI) method (Lahey, Souvaine, Kegan, Goodman, & Felix, 2011) growing out of that theory—to examine how and why some faculty in CCL contexts "appreciate the opportunity to dance on the edge" while others "seem reluctantly dragged there and scramble to get back to familiar ground" (Berger, 2004, p. 343). Findings could help WAC leaders map "our own orientation toward transformation" as well as develop additional communicative and pedagogical strategies for supporting and including a range of individual differences in "patience for and excitement about transformation" (Berger, 2004, p. 344).

The principles and practices of a pedagogical ethic forwarded in this book are grounded in systematic analysis of how several practitioners respond to the challenges and opportunities presented by CCL work in WAC/WID contexts. As I have shown, the necessary limitations of my study open the door for future research that continues to investigate the pedagogical promise of cross-disciplinary interactions among faculty.

CONCLUSION

During our final interview, James perfectly portrayed the dynamism of cross-disciplinary collaboration:

> [E]very discipline has a particular set of values about how knowledge should be produced. . . . A certain set of institutional norms for good or for bad that defines how they teach and how they think about the processes of inquiry [or] the habits of thought that they have. [. . .] We should try to reach across these boundaries but we should recognize that there are boundaries and explore them, that there are always connections that can be made that you don't think can be made, and that the people in different disciplines will make those connections in ways that you don't expect.

The research reported in this book further testifies to the challenges and opportunities that emerge when faculty attempt to "reach across boundaries" and illuminates the pedagogical potential of cross-boundary interactions. I have focused on CCL work as a professional practice and my findings certainly have implications for writing specialists (WPAs, writing center directors, WAC/WID consultants) who must often learn on the job how to navigate complicated conversations about (teaching) writing. At the same time, as I have demonstrated in this final chapter, findings have applications and implications beyond WAC/WID consultations. Indeed, the principles and communicative strategies associated with a pedagogical ethic have the potential to cultivate "habits of thought" all faculty and students need to function in shifting educational, workplace, and global environments (Strober, 2011).

The pedagogical ethic is implicative for action; it offers a promising focal point from which to navigate unpredictable challenges involved in cross-disciplinary interactions. It encourages writing specialists "to be more attentive to how conversations take place and to consider the array of options available to [us] at a given moment rather than constructing [our] choices as oppositional and mutually exclusive" (Lee, 2000, p. 265). It scaffolds what Paul Lynch (2013) calls "inspired adhockery" (pp. xx, 22–25) or "pedagogical imagination" (p. 25)—the ability to respond in the moment to situations that "present incommensurable choices" (p. 23). It animates the mysterious capacity long ascribed to inspired teacher-learners— professional artistry (Schön, 1987), phronesis or casuistry (Lynch, 2013, pp. 104–5, 111), and pedagogical tact[3] (Van Manen, 1991, 2015). Recent trends reinforce the urgency of this guiding ethic. The 2016 IWAC Conference saw a flurry of energy and excitement from graduate students focusing their academic careers on CCL work. At the same time, as more and more institutions build assessment, Quality Enhancement Plans (QEPs), and accreditation efforts around writing, early career comp/rhet faculty are called upon to initiate and sustain CCL collaborations on their campuses. As a field, we have an opportunity and a responsibility to embrace this work deliberately and ethically. Theorizing and enacting reflexive practice, learner's stance, and pedagogical performance as part of a cohesive ethic for cross-disciplinary work empowers practitioners to attend pedagogically to the complexities of cross-disciplinary work, to put the principles and practices described here in conversation with individual goals and experiences to apply, adapt, repurpose, and/or develop new communicative strategies that foster pedagogical relationships across disciplines.

APPENDIXES: DISCURSIVE MOVES FOR ENACTING PRINCIPLES OF A PEDAGOGICAL ETHIC FOR CCL WORK

APPENDIX A

Principle 1: Commit to reflexive practice.

Communicative Challenge/ Opportunity	Discursive Moves	Purposes
(1) Negotiate Expertise	Reference local knowledge and past work with faculty	Put knowledge/experience in context
	Counter assumptions	Shift false assumptions from popular understanding or primary source knowledge
	Share examples from teaching	Make methodology accessible
	Put writing principles in faculty member's terms	Make epistemology accessible
(2) Pursue Change as Transformational Learning	Imagine hypothetical outcomes in context	Actualize insights and resist inert knowledge
	Listen actively: minimal response and say backs	Create space for reflecting on past experience
	Wait to make cross-disciplinary connections	Establish value and relevance of connection; resist ritualized knowledge
	Withhold advice	Create opportunity for active learning
	"Surface and animate"	Unearth tacit knowledge for reconsideration
	Provide appropriate evidence	Make foreign worldview accessible

continued on next page

(3) Embrace Pedagogical Play	Use metaphor as teaching tool	Present connections
		Guide reflection on related concepts
		Forge mental bridges
		Foster backward-reaching transfer
	Use metaphor as heuristic for inquiry	Explore connections
		Encourage problem-exploring dispositions
	Incorporate storytelling	Ground and abstract complex concepts
		Prime forward-reaching transfer

Appendix B

Principle 2: Maintain a learner's stance.

Communicative Challenge/ Opportunity	Discursive Moves	Purposes
(1) Negotiate Expertise	Use pronouns strategically	Construct a community of teacher-learners
	Practice matchmaking	Shift locus of expertise
	Position self as fellow faculty/human being	Emphasize shared experience and humanity
	Allow for language differences	Acknowledge others' expertise
(2) Pursue Change as Transformational Learning	Actively engage alternative worldview	Bridge disciplinary divides
	Share stories about your learning	Model openness to change
	Acknowledge "light bulb" moments in conversation	Make real-time learning visible
	Take time to explore "light bulb" moments	Interrogate loaded knowledge
(3) Embrace Pedagogical Play	Be silly	Humanize yourself
		Equalize power dynamics
		Foster camaraderie
		Be good company on the edge of understanding
	Use metaphor as a heuristic for inquiry	Prompt collaborative exploration of complex concepts

Appendixes / 177

APPENDIX C

Principle 3: Approach CCL conversations as pedagogical performance.

Communicative Challenge/ Opportunity	Discursive Moves	Purposes
(1) Negotiate Expertise	Present guidelines and/or forward personal values	Teach product
		Build relationship based on honesty and trust
		Validate writing expertise
	Address prior knowledge	Reframe or build on what is known
	Acknowledge different types of expertise	Invite participation
		Create community of differently positioned experts
(2) Pursue Change as Transformational Learning	Plant seeds	Nurture slow, messy learning
		Respect learner's process
	Reinforce or complicate ritual knowledge	Address the needs and circumstances of unique learners
(3) Embrace Pedagogical Play	Be silly (defy situational expectations)	Encourage risk-taking and the will to learn/offer
	Tell stories or craft metaphors	Establish personal connection
		Highlight shared interests/experiences

NOTES

1. Cross-Curricular Literacy Work as Pedagogical Activity

1. Taking my cue from Jeffrey Jablonski, who draws on David Russell, I use *cross-curricular literacy* to mean writing that happens in academic contexts outside of English departments or composition classrooms. I use the term to encompass a range of writing initiatives including WAC, WID, and WEC (Writing Enriched Curriculum).

2. Exploding the Dilemma of Expertise

1. I use [. . .] to indicate one or more sentences of omitted material and . . . to signify material omitted within a sentence, a break in speaking, or speech trailing off.

5. A Guiding Ethic for Cross-Curricular Literacy Work

1. In my use of this term, I want to acknowledge Kirk Branch (2007) who borrows the term from Myles Horton, leader of the Highlander Folk School, whose mission was to "focus on the world as it ought to be, rather than on the world as it is" (p. 8). Branch argues that "because teaching [and I'd add learning] has in mind a future world" all educational endeavors project a vision of ought to be. I hope my project engages the hopefulness of this sentiment and likewise inspires ongoing discussion about "what that 'ought to be' should be" (p. 8).
2. Writing scholars often examine performance in relation to difference—class (LeCourt & Napoleone, 2011) and gender (Waite, 2009). Although it is beyond the scope of this study, embodied performance in the context of CCL conversations is a rich area for future research. See Tarabochia (2016b) for a discussion of the role of gender identity in pedagogical relationship building in CCL contexts.

3. Van Manen (2015) writes about pedagogy in a more traditional sense in terms of an adult (parent, teacher, therapist) caring for a young person. However, his notion of "pedagogical tact"—as instant, intuitive, and sensitive to the uniqueness of child, adult, and context—is relevant for the pedagogical interactions I explore here between teacher-learners of all kinds.

REFERENCES

Ackerman, D. (1999). *Deep play*. New York: Random House.
Addison, J., & McGee, S. J. (2010). Writing in high school/writing in college: Research trends and future directions. *College Composition and Communication, 62*(1), 147–79.
Adler-Kassner, L., & Estrem, H. (2015). Threshold concepts of writing, of writing in learning, and of teaching: "Negotiating the trifecta" and "Graduate student learning and conceptual stasis." Presented at the Conference on College Composition and Communication, Tampa, FL.
Adler-Kassner, L., Estrem, H., & Brennan, S. (2016, June). Disciplinarity and its discontents. Presentation at the International Writing Across the Curriculum Conference, Ann Arbor, MI.
Adler-Kassner, L., Majewski, J., & Koshnick, D. (2012). The value of troublesome knowledge: transfer and threshold concepts in writing and history. *Composition Forum, 26.*
Adler-Kassner, L., & Wardle, E. (2015a). Naming what we know: The project of this book. In L. Adler-Kassner & E. Wardle (Eds.), *Naming what we know: Threshold concepts of writing studies* (pp. 1–11). Logan: Utah State University Press.
Adler-Kassner, L., & Wardle, E. (Eds.). (2015b). *Naming what we know: Threshold concepts of writing studies*. Logan: Utah State University Press.
Anson, C. M. (2015). Crossing thresholds: What's to know about writing across the curriculum. In L. Adler-Kassner & E. Wardle (Eds.), *Naming what we know: Threshold concepts of writing studies* (pp. 203–19). Logan: Utah State University Press.
Anson, C. M. (2016). The Pop Warner chronicles: A case study in contextual adaptation and the transfer of writing ability. *College Composition and Communication, 67*(4), 518–49.
Anson, C. M., & Dannels, D. (2009). Profiling programs: Formative uses of departmental consultations in the assessment of communication

across the curriculum [Special issue on Writing Across the Curriculum and Assessment]. *Across the Disciplines, 6*. Retrieved from http://wac.colostate.edu/atd/assessment/anson_dannels.cfm

Anson, C. M., & Moore, J. L. (2016a). Afterword. In C. M. Anson & J. L. Moore (Eds.), *Critical transitions: Writing and the question of transfer* (pp. 331–39). Fort Collins, CO: The WAC Clearinghouse and University Press of Colorado. Retrieved from http://wac.colostate.edu/books/ansonmoore/

Anson, C. M., & Moore, J. L. (Eds.). (2016b). *Critical transitions: Writing and the question of transfer*. Fort Collins, CO: The WAC Clearinghouse and University Press of Colorado. Retrieved from http://wac.colostate.edu/books/ansonmoore/

Apter, M. J. (1991). A structural-phenomenology of play. In J. H. Kerr & M. J. Apter (Eds.), *Adult play: A reversal theory approach* (pp. 13–29). Amsterdam: Swets & Zeitlinger.

Artze-Vega, I., Bowdon, M., Emmons, K., Eodice, M., Hess, S. K., Lamonica, C. C., & Nelms, G. (2013). Privileging pedagogy: Composition, rhetoric, and faculty development. *College Composition and Communication, 65*(1), 162–84.

Atwell, N. (1998). *In the middle: New understandings about writing, reading, and learning*. Portsmouth, NH: Boynton/Cook.

Barnett, R. (2004). Learning for an unknown future. *Higher Education Research & Development, 23*(3), 247–60.

Barnett, R. (2007). *A will to learn: Being a student in an age of uncertainty*. Maidenhead: Society for Research into Higher Education and Open University Press.

Bartlett, L. E. (2015). Performing pedagogy: Negotiating the "appropriate" and the possible in the writing classroom. *Teaching/Writing: The Journal of Writing Teacher Education, 4*(2), 38–56. Retrieved from http://scholarworks.wmich.edu/wte/vol4/iss2/3

Bazerman, C. (1991). The second stage in writing across the curriculum. *College English, 53*(2), 209–12. https://doi.org/10.2307/378203

Bazerman, C. (2015). Writing expresses and shares meaning to be reconstructed by the reader. In L. Adler-Kassner & E. Wardle (Eds.), *Naming what we know: Threshold concepts of writing studies* (pp. 21–23). Logan: Utah State University Press.

Bazerman, C., Little, J., Bethel, L., Chavkin, T., Fouquette, D., & Garufis, J. (2005). *Reference guide to writing across the curriculum*. West Lafayette, IN: Parlor Press and the WAC Clearinghouse.

Bazerman, C., & Tinberg, H. (2015). Writing is an expression of embodied cognition. In L. Adler-Kassner & E. Wardle (Eds.), *Naming what*

we know: Threshold concepts of writing studies (pp. 74–75). Logan: Utah State University Press.
Beach, K. (1999). Consequential transitions: A sociocultural expedition beyond transfer in education. *Review of Research in Education, 24*(1), 101–39. https://doi.org/10.3102/0091732X024001101
Beach, K. (2003). Consequential transitions: A developmental view of knowledge propagation through social organizations. In T. Tuomi-Gröhn & Y. Engeström (Eds.), *Between school and work: New perspectives on transfer and boundary-crossing* (pp. 39–61). Boston: Pergamon.
Bean, J. C., Carrithers, D., & Earenfight, T. (2005). Transforming WAC through a discourse-based approach to university outcomes assessment. *The WAC Journal, 16,* 5–21.
Belenky, M. F., & Stanton, A. V. (2000). Inequality, development, and connected knowing. In J. Mezirow (Ed.), *Learning as transformation: Critical perspectives on a theory in progress* (pp. 71–102). San Francisco: Jossey-Bass.
Berger, J. G. (2004). Dancing on the threshold of meaning: Recognizing and understanding the growing edge. *Journal of Transformative Education, 2*(4), 336–51. https://doi.org/10.1177/1541344604267697
Bergmann, L. S. (1998). Missionary projects and anthropological accounts: Ethics and conflict in writing across the curriculum. In S. I. Fontaine & S. Hunter (Eds.), *Foregrounding ethical awareness in composition and English studies* (pp. 144–59). Portsmouth, NH: Boynton/Cook Publishers.
Bergmann, L. S. (2008). Writing centers and cross-curricular literacy programs as models for faculty development. *Pedagogy, 8*(3), 523–36.
Berlin, J. A. (1987). *Rhetoric and reality: Writing instruction in American colleges, 1900–1985.* Carbondale: Southern Illinois University Press.
Berliner, D. C. (1990). If the metaphor fits, why not wear it? The teacher as executive. *Theory Into Practice, 29*(2), 85–93.
Billig, M., Condor, S., Edwards, D., Gane, M., Middleton, D., & Radley, A. (1988). *Ideological dilemmas: A social psychology of everyday thinking.* London: SAGE Publications.
Bingham, C., & Sidorkin, A. M. (Eds.). (2004). *No education without relation.* New York: Peter Lang.
Black, L. J. (1998). *Between talk and teaching: Reconsidering the writing conference.* Logan: Utah State University Press.
Boquet, E. H. (2002). *Noise from the writing center.* Logan: Utah State University Press.
Boquet, E. H., & Eodice, M. (2008). Creativity in the writing center: A terrifying conundrum. In K. Dvorak & S. Bruce (Eds.), *Creative*

approaches to writing center work (pp. 3–20). Cresskill, NJ: Hampton Press.

Bowman, J. R. (1987). Making work play. In G. A. Fine (Ed.), *Meaningful play, playful meaning* (Vol. 11, pp. 61–71). Champaign, IL: Human Kinetics Publishers.

Boyd, R. D., & Myers, J. G. (1988). Transformative education. *International Journal of Lifelong Education*, *7*(4), 261–84.

Branch, K. (2007). *"Eyes on the ought to be": What we teach about when we teach about literacy*. Cresskill, NJ: Hampton Press.

Bransford, J. D., Brown, A. L., & Cocking, R. R. (Eds.). (2000). *How people learn: Brain, mind, experience, and school*. Washington, DC: National Academy Press.

Brooke, C., & Carr, A. (2015). Failure can be an important part of writing development. In L. Adler-Kassner & E. Wardle (Eds.), *Naming what we know: Threshold concepts of writing studies* (pp. 62–64). Logan: Utah State University Press.

Brooke, C., & Grabill, J. T. (2015). Writing is a technology through which writers create and recreate meaning. In L. Adler-Kassner & E. Wardle (Eds.), *Naming what we know: Threshold concepts of writing studies* (pp. 32–34). Logan: Utah State University Press.

Brown, S., & Vaughan, C. (2009). *Play: How it shapes the brain, opens the imagination, and invigorates the soul*. New York: Avery.

Bruner, J. S., Jolly, A., & Sylva, K. (Eds.). (1976). *Play: Its role in development and evolution*. New York: Basic Books.

Bunnell, S. L., & Bernstein, D. J. (2012). Overcoming some threshold concepts in scholarly teaching. *Journal of Faculty Development*, *26*(3), 14–18.

Cameron, L., Maslen, R., Todd, Z., Maule, J., Stratton, P., & Stanley, N. (2009). The discourse dynamics approach to metaphor and metaphor-led discourse analysis. *Metaphor & Symbol*, *24*(2), 63–89. https://doi.org/10.1080/10926480902830821

Carter, K. (1990). Meaning and metaphor: Case knowledge in teaching. *Theory Into Practice*, *29*(2), 109–15.

Carter, M. (1990). The idea of expertise: An exploration of cognitive and social dimensions of writing. *College Composition and Communication*, *41*(3), 265–86. https://doi.org/10.2307/357655

Carter, M. (2003). A process for establishing outcomes-based assessment plans for writing and speaking in the disciplines. *Language and Learning Across the Disciplines*, *6*(1), 4–29.

Caswell, N. I., Grutsch McKinney, J., & Jackson, R. (2016). *The working lives of new writing center directors*. Logan: Utah State University Press.

Clark, I. L., & Hernandez, A. (2011). Genre awareness, academic argument, and transferability. *WAC Journal, 22*, 65–78.
Cohen, E. G., & Lotan, R. A. (1990). Teacher as supervisor of complex technology. *Theory Into Practice, 29*(2), 78–84.
Collins, H., & Evans, R. (2007). *Rethinking expertise*. Chicago: University of Chicago Press.
Condon, W., Iverson, E. R., Manduca, C. A., Rutz, C., & Willett, G. (2016). *Faculty development and student learning: Assessing the connections*. Bloomington, IN: Indiana University Press.
Condon, W., & Rutz, C. (2012). A taxonomy of writing across the curriculum programs: Evolving to serve broader agendas. *College Composition and Communication, 64*(2), 357–82.
Cox, M. (2011). WAC: Closing doors or opening doors for second language writers? *Across the Disciplines, 8*(4). Retrieved from http://wac.colostate.edu/atd/ell/cox.cfm
Craig, R. T., & Tracy, K. (1995). Grounded practical theory: The case of intellectual discussion. *Communication Theory, 5*(3), 248–72. https://doi.org/10.1111/j.1468-2885.1995.tb00108.x
Cranton, P. (1996). *Professional development as transformative learning: New perspectives for teachers of adults*. San Francisco: Jossey-Bass.
Cranton, P. (2000). Individual differences and transformative learning. In J. Mezirow (Ed.), *Learning as transformation: Critical perspectives on a theory in progress* (pp. 181–204). San Francisco: Jossey-Bass.
Cranton, P. (2006). *Understanding and promoting transformative learning: A guide for educators of adults* (2nd ed.). San Francisco: Jossey-Bass.
Csikszentmihalyi, M. (1979). The concept of flow. In B. Sutton-Smith (Ed.), *Play and learning* (pp. 257–74). New York: Gardner Press.
Csikszentmihalyi, M. (1990). *Flow: The psychology of optimal experience*. New York: HarperCollins.
Csikszentmihalyi, M. (1996). *Creativity: Flow and the psychology of discovery and invention*. New York: HarperCollins.
Denny, H. (2010). Queering the writing center. *The Writing Center Journal, 30*(1), 95–124.
Dobrin, S. I. (Ed.). (2005). *Don't call it that: The composition practicum*. Urbana, IL: National Council of Teachers of English.
Downs, D. (2015). Revision is central to developing writing. In L. Adler-Kassner & E. Wardle (Eds.), *Naming what we know: Threshold concepts of writing studies* (pp. 66–67). Logan: Utah State University Press.
Driscoll, D. L., & Wells, J. (2012). Beyond knowledge and skills: Writing transfer and the role of student dispositions. *Composition Forum*,

26. Retrieved from http://compositionforum.com/issue/26/beyond-knowledge-skills.php

Dryer, D. B. (2015a). Writing is not natural. In L. Adler-Kassner & E. Wardle (Eds.), *Naming what we know: Threshold concepts of writing studies* (pp. 27–29). Logan: Utah State University Press.

Dryer, D. B. (2015b). Writing is (also always) a cognitive activity. In L. Adler-Kassner & E. Wardle (Eds.), *Naming what we know: Threshold concepts of writing studies* (pp. 71–74). Logan: Utah State University Press.

Duckworth, E. R. (1987). *"The having of wonderful ideas" and other essays on teaching and learning*. New York: Teachers College Press.

Dvorak, K., & Bruce, S. (Eds.). (2008). *Creative approaches to writing center work*. Cresskill, NJ: Hampton Press.

Engeström, Y. (1987). *Learning by expanding: An activity-theoretical approach to developmental research*. Helsinki: Orienta-Konsultit OY.

Eodice, M., Geller, A. E., & Lerner, N. (2016). *The meaningful writing project: Learning, teaching, and writing in higher education*. Logan: Utah State University Press.

Estrem, H., & Reid, E. S. (2012a). What new writing teachers talk about when they talk about teaching. *Pedagogy*, *12*(3), 449–80.

Estrem, H., & Reid, E. S. (2012b). Writing pedagogy education: Instructor development in composition studies. In *Exploring composition studies: Sites, issues, and perspectives* (pp. 223–40). Logan: Utah State University Press. Retrieved from http://www.jstor.org/stable/j.ctt4cgjsj.17

Farris, C. (1992). Giving religion, taking gold: Disciplinary cultures and the claims of writing across the curriculum. In J. A. Berlin & M. J. Vivion (Eds.), *Cultural studies in the English classroom* (pp. 112–22). Portsmouth, NH: Boynton/Cook Heinemann.

Flaherty, C. (2015, October 7). Grand challenges all around. *Inside Higher Ed*. Retrieved from https://www.insidehighered.com/news/2015/10/07/big-ideas-oriented-science-exciting-will-recent-initiatives-live-hype?

Fulwiler, T. (1981). Showing, not telling, at a writing workshop. *College English*, *43*(1), 55–63. https://doi.org/10.2307/377317

Gallagher, C. W. (2002). *Radical departures: Composition and progressive pedagogy*. Urbana, IL: National Council of Teachers of English.

Gallagher, C. W., Gray, P. M., & Stenberg, S. (2002). Teacher narratives as interruptive: Toward critical colleagueship. *symploke*, *10*(1), 32–51. https://doi.org/10.1353/sym.2002.0011

Gayle, B. M., Randall, N., Langley, L., & Preiss, R. (2013). Faculty learning processes: A model for moving from scholarly teaching to the scholarship of teaching and learning. *Teaching and Learning Inquiry*, *1*(1), 81–93.

Geller, A. E. (2008). Drawing the (play)spaces of conferences. In K. Dvorak & S. Bruce (Eds.), *Creative approaches to writing center work* (pp. 159–76). Cresskill, NJ: Hampton Press.

Geller, A. E. (2009). The difficulty of believing in writing across the curriculum. *The Journal of the Assembly for Expanded Perspectives on Learning*, *15*(1), 27–36. Retrieved from http://trace.tennessee.edu/jaepl/vol15/iss1/6

Geller, A. E. (2011). Teaching and learning with multilingual faculty. *Across the Disciplines*, *8*(4). Retrieved from http://wac.colostate.edu/atd/ell/geller.cfm

Geller, A. E., & Eodice, M. (Eds.). (2013). *Working with faculty writers*. Logan: Utah State University Press.

Geller, A. E., Eodice, M., Condon, F., Carroll, M., & Boquet, E. H. (2007). *The everyday writing center: A community of practice*. Logan: Utah State University Press.

Gere, A. R., Swofford, S. C., Silver, N., & Pugh, M. (2015). Interrogating disciplines/disciplinarity in WAC/WID: An institutional study. *College Composition and Communication*, *67*(2), 243–66.

Gilly, M. S. (2004). Experiencing transformative education in the "corridors" of a nontraditional doctoral program. *Journal of Transformative Education*, *2*(3), 231–41. https://doi.org/10.1177/1541344604265273

Godbee, B. (2011). *Small talk, big change: Identifying potentials for social change in one-with-one talk about writing* (Unpublished doctoral dissertation). The University of Wisconsin, Madison.

Godbee, B. (2012). Toward explaining the transformative power of talk about, around, and for writing. *Research in the Teaching of English*, *47*(2), 171–97.

Godbee, B., Ozias, M., & Tang, J. K. (2015). Body + power + justice: Movement-based workshops for critical tutor education. *The Writing Center Journal*, *34*(2), 61–112.

Grimm, N. M. (1999). *Good intentions: Writing center work for postmodern times*. Portsmouth, NH: Boynton/Cook-Heinemann.

Grimm, N. M. (2009). New conceptual frameworks for writing center work. *The Writing Center Journal*, *29*(2), 11–27.

Gustafsson, M., Eriksson, A., Räisänen, C., Stenberg, A.-C., Jacobs, C., Wright, J., Wyrley-Birch, B., & Winberg, C. (2011). Collaborating for content and language integrated learning: The situated character of faculty collaboration and student learning. *Across the Disciplines*,

8(3). Retrieved from http://wac.colostate.edu/atd/clil/gustafsson etal.cfm

Hall, R. M. (2011). Theory in/to practice: Using dialogic reflection to develop a writing center community of practice. *The Writing Center Journal*, *31*(1), 82–105.

Haring-Smith, T. (1992). Changing students' attitudes: Writing fellows programs. In S. H. McLeod & M. Soven (Eds.), *Writing across the curriculum: A guide to developing programs* (pp. 123–31). Newbury Park, CA: SAGE Publications. Retrieved from http://wac.colostate.edu/books/mcleod_soven/chapter11.pdf

Harrington, S., MacKenzie, I., & DeSanto, D. (2016). Traversing uncommon ground: Cases in WID consulting at Dawson College and UVM. Presented at the International Writing Across the Curriculum Conference, Ann Arbor, MI. Retrieved from https://iwac2016.org/session-h/

Hart, C. (2008). Critical discourse analysis and metaphor: Toward a theoretical framework. *Critical Discourse Studies*, *5*(2), 91–106. https://doi.org/10.1080/17405900801990058

Hartelius, E. J. (2011). *The rhetoric of expertise*. Lanham, MD: Lexington Books.

Henderson, C., Beach, A., & Finkelstein, N. (2011). Facilitating change in undergraduate STEM instructional practices: An analytic review of the literature. *Journal of Research in Science Teaching*, *48*(8), 952–84. https://doi.org/10.1002/tea.20439

Hillocks, G., Jr. (1984). What works in teaching composition: A meta-analysis of experimental treatment studies. *American Journal of Education*, *93*(1), 133–70.

Hofer, B. K. (2000). Dimensionality and disciplinary differences in personal epistemology. *Contemporary Educational Psychology*, *25*(4), 378–405. https://doi.org/10.1006/ceps.1999.1026

Huber, M. T. (2016). Foreword: Pathways from faculty learning to student learning and beyond. In W. Condon, E. R. Iverson, C. A. Manduca, C. Rutz, & G. Willett, *Faculty development and student learning: Assessing the connections* (pp. vii–xi). Bloomington, IN: Indiana University Press.

Huckin, T., Andrus, J., & Clary-Lemon, J. (2012). Critical discourse analysis and rhetoric and composition. *College Composition and Communication*, *64*(1), 107–29.

Hughes, B., & Hall, E. B. (2008). Guest editors' introduction [Special issue on Writing Fellows]. *Across the Disciplines*, *5*. Retrieved from http://wac.colostate.edu/atd/fellows/intro.cfm

Huizinga, J. (1955). *Homo ludens: A study of the play-element in culture*. Boston: Beacon Press.

References / 189

Jablonski, J. (2006). *Academic writing consulting and WAC: Methods and models for guiding cross-curricular literacy work*. Cresskill, NJ: Hampton Press.

Jacobs, C. (2007). Towards a critical understanding of the teaching of discipline-specific academic literacies: Making the tacit explicit. *Journal of Education*, *41*(1), 59–81.

Jacoby, S., & Gonzales, P. (1991). The constitution of expert-novice in scientific discourse. *Issues in Applied Linguistics*, *2*(2), 149–81.

Jarratt, S. C., Mack, K., Sartor, A., & Watson, S. E. (2009). Pedagogical memory: Writing, mapping, translating. *WPA: Writing Program Administration*, *33*(1–2), 46–73.

Jones, R., & Comprone, J. J. (1993). Where do we go next in writing across the curriculum? *College Composition and Communication*, *44*(1), 59–68. https://doi.org/10.2307/358895

Jung, J. (2005). *Revisionary rhetoric, feminist pedagogy, and multigenre texts*. Carbondale: Southern Illinois University Press.

Kameen, P. (2000). *Writing/teaching: Essays toward a rhetoric of pedagogy*. Pittsburgh: University of Pittsburgh Press.

Kane, P. (2004). *The play ethic: A manifesto for a different way of living*. London: Macmillan.

Kaufer, D., & Young, R. (1993). Writing in the content areas: Some theoretical complexities. In L. Odell (Ed.), *Theory and practice in the teaching of writing: Rethinking the discipline* (pp. 71–104). Carbondale: Southern Illinois University Press.

Kegan, R. (1982). *The evolving self: Problem and process in human development*. Cambridge, MA: Harvard University Press.

Kerr, J. H., & Apter, M. J. (Eds.). (1991). *Adult play: A reversal theory approach*. Amsterdam: Swets & Zeitlinger.

Kinchin, I. M. (2010). Solving Cordelia's Dilemma: Threshold concepts within a punctuated model of learning. *Journal of Biological Education*, *44*(2), 53–57.

Kistler, R., Yancey, K. B., Taczak, K., & Szysmanski, N. (2009). Introduction: Writing across the Curriculum and assessment. *Across the Disciplines*, *6*. Retrieved from http://wac.colostate.edu/atd/assessment/kistleretal.cfm

Kolb, A. Y., & Kolb, D. A. (2010). Learning to play, playing to learn: A case study of a *ludic* learning space. *Journal of Organizational Change Management*, *23*(1), 26–50. https://doi.org/10.1108/09534811011017199

Kolb, D. A. (2015). *Experiential learning: Experience as the source of learning and development* (2nd ed.). Upper Saddle River, NJ: Pearson Education.

Kuriloff, P. C. (1992). The writing consultant: Collaboration and team teaching. In S. H. McLeod & M. Soven (Eds.), *Writing across the curriculum: A guide to developing programs* (pp. 94–108). Newbury Park, CA: SAGE Publications. Retrieved from http://wac.colostate.edu/books/mcleod_soven/chapter9.pdf

Lahey, L., Souvaine, E., Kegan, R., Goodman, R., & Felix, S. (2011). *A guide to the subject-object interview: Its administration and interpretation.* Cambridge, MA: Minds at Work.

Lakoff, G., & Johnson, M. (1980). *Metaphors we live by.* Chicago: University of Chicago Press.

Land, R. (2015). Preface. In L. Adler-Kassner & E. Wardle (Eds.), *Naming what we know: Threshold concepts of writing studies* (pp. xi–xiv). Logan: Utah State University Press.

Land, R., Meyer, J. H. F., & Smith, J. (Eds.). (2008). *Threshold concepts within the disciplines.* Rotterdam: Sense Publishers.

Land, R., & Meyer, J. H. F. (2010). Threshold concepts and troublesome knowledge (5): Dynamics of assessment. In J. H. F. Meyer, R. Land, & C. Baillie (Eds.), *Threshold concepts and transformational learning* (pp. 61–80). Rotterdam: Sense Publishers.

Land, R., Meyer, J. H. F., & Baillie, C. (2010). Editor's preface: Threshold concepts and transformational learning. In J. H. F. Meyer, R. Land, & C. Baillie (Eds.), *Threshold concepts and transformational learning* (pp. ix–xlii). Rotterdam: Sense Publishers.

Latta, M. M. (2013). *Curricular conversations: Play is the (missing) thing.* New York: Routledge.

LeCourt, D. (1996). WAC as critical pedagogy: The third stage? *JAC, 16*(3), 389–405.

LeCourt, D., & Napoleone, A. R. (2011). Teachers with(out) class. *Pedagogy, 11*(1), 81–108. https://doi.org/10.1215/15314200-2010-018

Lee, A. (2000). *Composing critical pedagogies: Teaching writing as revision.* Urbana, IL: National Council of Teachers of English.

Leki, I. (2003). A challenge to second language writing professionals: Is writing overrated? In B. Kroll (Ed.), *Exploring the dynamics of second language writing* (pp. 315–32). Cambridge, UK: Cambridge University Press.

Lerner, N. (2015). Writing is a way of enacting disciplinarity. In L. Adler-Kassner & E. Wardle (Eds.), *Naming what we know: Threshold concepts of writing studies* (pp. 40–41). Logan: Utah State University Press.

Lieberman, J. N. (1977). *Playfulness: Its relationship to imagination and creativity.* New York: Academic Press.

Lillis, T., & Rai, L. (2011). A case study of a research-based collaboration around writing in social work. *Across the Disciplines, 8*(3). Retrieved from http://wac.colostate.edu/atd/clil/lillis-rai.cfm

Lord, B. (1994). Teachers' professional development: Critical colleagueship and the role of professional communities. In N. Cobb (Ed.), *The future of education: Perspectives on national standards in America* (pp. 175–204). New York: College Entrance Examination Board.

Low, G., Todd, Z., Deignan, A., & Cameron, L. (Eds.). (2010). *Researching and applying metaphor in the real world*. Amsterdam: John Benjamins.

Lynch, P. (2013). *After pedagogy: The experience of teaching*. Urbana, IL: National Council of Teachers of English.

MacArthur, F., & Oncins-Martinez, J. L. (2012). Introduction: Metaphor in use. In F. MacArthur, J. L. Oncins-Martinez, M. Sanchez-Garcia, & A. M. Piquer-Piriz (Eds.), *Metaphor in use: Context, culture, and communication* (pp. 1–18). Amsterdam: John Benjamins.

MacArthur, F., Oncins-Martinez, J. L., Sanchez-Garcia, M., & Piquer-Piriz, A. M. (Eds.). (2012). *Metaphor in use: Context, culture, and communication*. Amsterdam: John Benjamins.

Magnotto, J. N., & Stout, B. R. (1992). Faculty workshops. In S. H. McLeod & M. Soven (Eds.), *Writing across the curriculum: A guide to developing programs* (pp. 23–34). Newbury Park, CA: SAGE Publications. Retrieved from http://wac.colostate.edu/books/mcleod_soven/chapter3.pdf

Mahala, D., & Swilky, J. (1994). Resistance and reform: The functions of expertise in writing across the curriculum. *Language and Learning Across the Disciplines, 1*(2), 35–62.

Mahilos, M., & Maxson, M. (1998). Metaphors as structures for elementary and secondary preservice teachers' thinking. *International Journal of Educational Research, 29*(3), 227–40.

Malinowitz, H. (1998). A feminist critique of writing in the disciplines. In S. C. F. Jarratt & L. Worsham (Eds.), *Feminism and composition studies: In other words* (pp. 291–312). New York: Modern Language Association of America.

Marshall, H. H. (1990a). Beyond the workplace metaphor: The classroom as a learning setting. *Theory Into Practice, 29*(2), 94–101.

Marshall, H. H. (1990b). Metaphor as an instructional tool in encouraging student teacher reflection. *Theory Into Practice, 29*(2), 128–32.

McCarthy, L. P., & Fishman, S. M. (1991). Boundary conversations: Conflicting ways of knowing in philosophy and interdisciplinary research. *Research in the Teaching of English, 25*(4), 419–68.

McCarthy, L. P., & Walvoord, B. E. (1988). Models for collaborative research in writing across the curriculum. In S. H. McLeod (Ed.), *Strengthening programs for writing across the curriculum* (pp. 77–89). San Francisco: Jossey-Bass.

McConlogue, T., Mitchell, S., & Peake, K. (2012). Thinking writing at Queen Mary, University of London. In C. Thaiss, G. Bräuer, P. Carlino, L. Ganobcsik-Williams, & A. Sinha (Eds.), *Writing programs worldwide: Profiles of academic writing in many places* (pp. 203–11). Fort Collins, CO: The WAC Clearinghouse and Parlor Press. Retrieved from https://wac.colostate.edu/books/wpww/chapter18.pdf

McCune, V. (2009). Teaching within and beyond the disciplines: The challenge for faculty. In C. Kreber (Ed.), *The university and its disciplines: Teaching and learning within and beyond disciplinary boundaries* (pp. 231–37). New York: Routledge.

McCune, V., & Entwistle, N. (2011). Cultivating the disposition to understand in 21st century university education. *Learning and Individual Differences*, *21*(3), 303–10. https://doi.org/10.1016/j.lindif.2010.11.017

McKinney, J. G. (2013). *Peripheral visions for writing centers*. Logan: Utah State University Press.

McLeod, S. H. (1989). Writing across the curriculum: The second stage, and beyond. *College Composition and Communication*, *40*(3), 337–43. https://doi.org/10.2307/357778

McLeod, S. H. (1995). The foreigner: WAC directors as agents of change. In J. Janangelo & K. Hanssen (Eds.), *Resituating writing: Constructing and administering writing programs* (pp. 108–16). Portsmouth, NH: Boynton/Cook.

Melamed, E. (1985). *Play and playfulness in women's learning and development* (Unpublished doctoral dissertation). The University of Toronto, Toronto, Canada.

Melzer, D. (2014). *Assignments across the curriculum: A national study of college writing*. Logan: Utah State University Press.

Meyer, J., & Land, R. (2003). Threshold concepts and troublesome knowledge: Linkages to ways of thinking and practising within the disciplines. *Enhancing teaching-learning environments in undergraduate courses*. Edinburgh: University of Edinburgh. Retrieved from http://www.etl.tla.ed.ac.uk/docs/ETLreport4.pdf

Meyer, J. H. F., & Land, R. (Eds.). (2006). *Overcoming barriers to student learning: Threshold concepts and troublesome knowledge*. New York: Routledge.

Meyer, J. H. F., Land, R., & Baillie, C. (Eds.). (2010). *Threshold concepts and transformational learning*. Rotterdam: Sense Publishers.

Mezirow, J. (1978). *Education for perspective transformation: Women's reentry programs in community colleges*. New York: Center for Adult Education, Teachers College, Columbia University.

Mezirow, J. (1991). *Transformative dimensions of adult learning*. San Francisco: Jossey-Bass.

Mezirow, J., & Associates. (1990). *Fostering critical reflection in adulthood: A guide to transformative and emancipatory learning*. San Francisco: Jossey-Bass.

Miller, sj. (2008). "Literativity": Reconceptualizing creative literacy learning. In K. Dvorak & S. Bruce (Eds.), *Creative approaches to writing center work* (pp. 85–96). Cresskill, NJ: Hampton Press.

Moore, J. (2012). Mapping the questions: The state of writing-related transfer research. *Composition Forum, 26*.

Mortensen, P. (1992). Analyzing talk about writing. In G. Kirsch & P. A. Sullivan (Eds.), *Methods and methodology in composition research* (pp. 105–29). Carbondale: Southern Illinois University Press.

Mullin, J. A. (2001). Writing centers and WAC. In S. H. McLeod, E. Miraglia, M. Soven, & C. Thaiss (Eds.), *WAC for the new millennium: Strategies for continuing writing-across-the-curriculum-programs* (pp. 179–99). Urbana, IL: National Council of Teachers of English.

Munby, H., & Russell, T. (1990). Metaphor in the study of teachers' professional knowledge. *Theory Into Practice, 29*(2), 116–21.

Musolff, A. (2012). The study of metaphor as part of critical discourse analysis. *Critical Discourse Studies, 9*(3), 301–10. https://doi.org/10.10 80/17405904.2012.688300

Noddings, N. (2004). Foreword. In C. W. Bingham & A. M. Sidorkin (Eds.), *No education without relation* (pp. vii–viii). New York: Peter Lang.

Norgaard, R. (1999). Negotiating expertise in disciplinary "contact zones." *Language and Learning Across the Disciplines, 3*(2), 44–63.

Nowacek, R. S. (2005). A discourse-based theory of interdisciplinary connections. *JGE: The Journal of General Education, 54*(3), 171–95.

Nowacek, R. S. (2007). Toward a theory of interdisciplinary connections: A classroom study of talk and text. *Research in the Teaching of English, 41*(4), 368–401.

Nowacek, R. S. (2011). *Agents of integration: Understanding transfer as a rhetorical act*. Carbondale: Southern Illinois University Press.

Nowacek, R. S., & Hughes, B. (2015). Threshold concepts in the writing center: Scaffolding the development of tutor expertise. In L. Adler-Kassner & E. Wardle (Eds.), *Naming what we know: Threshold concepts of writing studies* (pp. 171–85). Logan: Utah State University Press.

Paretti, M. C. (2011). Interdisciplinarity as a lens for theorizing language/content partnerships. *Across the Disciplines*, *8*(3). Retrieved from http://wac.colostate.edu/atd/clil/paretti.cfm

Paretti, M., McNair, L., Belanger, K., & George, D. (2009). Reformist possibilities? Exploring writing program cross-campus partnerships. *WPA: Writing Program Administration*, *33*(1–2), 74–113.

Paretti, M. C., & Powell, K. M. (2009). Bringing voices together: Partnerships for assessing writing across contexts. In M. C. Paretti & K. M. Powell (Eds.), *Assessment of writing* (Vol. 4, pp. 1–9). Tallahassee, FL: Association for Institutional Research.

Perkins, D. (2006). Constructivism and troublesome knowledge. In J. H. F. Meyer & R. Land (Eds.), *Overcoming barriers to student learning: Threshold concepts and troublesome knowledge* (pp. 33–47). New York: Routledge.

Perkins, D. (2010). Foreword. In J. H. F. Meyer, R. Land, & C. Baillie (Eds.), *Threshold concepts and transformational learning* (pp. xliii–xlv). Rotterdam: Sense Publishers.

Perkins, D. N., & Salomon, G. (1988). Teaching for transfer. *Educational Leadership*, *46*(1), 22–32.

Perkins, D. N., & Salomon, G. (2012). Knowledge to go: A motivational and dispositional view of transfer. *Educational Psychologist*, *47*(3), 248–58. https://doi.org/10.1080/00461520.2012.693354

Perkins, D., Tishman, S., Ritchhart, R., Donis, K., & Andrade, A. (2000). Intelligence in the wild: A dispositional view of intellectual traits. *Educational Psychology Review*, *12*(3), 269–93.

Piaget, J. (1962). *Play, dreams and imitation in childhood*. New York: Norton.

Poe, M. (2013). Re-framing race in teaching writing across the curriculum. *Across the Disciplines*, *10*(3). Retrieved from http://wac.colostate.edu/atd/race/poe.cfm

Polanyi, M. (1966). *The tacit dimension*. Garden City, NY: Doubleday.

Prior, P., & Shipka, J. (2003). Chronotopic lamination: Tracing the contours of literate activity. In C. Bazerman & D. R. Russell (Eds.), *Writing selves/Writing societies* (pp. 180–238). Fort Collins, CO: WAC Clearinghouse. Retrieved from http://wac.colostate.edu/books/selves_societies/prior/prior.pdf

Qualley, D. J. (1997). *Turns of thought: Teaching composition as reflexive inquiry*. Portsmouth, NH: Boynton/Cook.

Qualley, D. (2016). Building a conceptual topography of the transfer terrain. In C. A. Anson & J. Moore (Eds.), *Critical transitions: Writ-

ing and the question of transfer (pp. 69–106). Fort Collins, CO: The WAC Clearinghouse and University Press of Colorado. Retrieved from http://wac.colostate.edu/books/ansonmoore/

Reid, E. S. (2013). What is TA education? In R. Malenczyk (Ed.), *A rhetoric for writing program administrators* (pp. 197–210). Anderson, SC: Parlor Press.

Reid, E. S., Estrem, H., & Belcheir, M. (2012). The effects of writing pedagogy education on graduate teaching assistants' approaches to teaching composition. *WPA: Writing Program Administration, 36*(1), 32–73. Retrieved from http://scholarworks.boisestate.edu/english_facpubs/266

Ricketts, A. (2010). Threshold concepts: "Loaded" knowledge or critical education? In J. H. F. Meyer, R. Land, & C. Baillie (Eds.), *Threshold concepts and transformational learning* (pp. 45–60). Rotterdam: Sense Publishers.

Rogoff, B. (1994). Developing understanding of the idea of communities of learners. *Mind, Culture, and Activity, 1*(4), 209–29.

Roozen, K. (2008). Journalism, poetry, stand-up comedy, and academic literacy: Mapping the interplay of curricular and extracurricular literate activities. *Journal of Basic Writing 27*(1), 5–34.

Roozen, K. (2010). Tracing trajectories of practice: Repurposing in one student's developing disciplinary writing processes. *Written Communication, 27*(3), 318–54. https://doi.org/10.1177/0741088310373529

Roozen, K. (2015). Writing is a social and rhetorical activity. In L. Adler-Kassner & E. Wardle (Eds.), *Naming what we know: Threshold concepts of writing studies* (pp. 17–19). Logan: Utah State University Press.

Rose, S. (2015). All writers have more to learn. In L. Adler-Kassner & E. Wardle (Eds.), *Naming what we know: Threshold concepts of writing studies* (pp. 59–61). Logan: Utah State University Press.

Rousculp, T. (2014). *Rhetoric of respect: Recognizing change at a community writing center*. Urbana, IL: Conference on College Composition and Communication, National Council of Teachers of English.

Russell, D. R. (2002). *Writing in the academic disciplines: A curricular history* (2nd ed.). Carbondale: Southern Illinois University Press.

Rutz, C. (2004). WAC and beyond: An interview with Chris Anson. *WAC Journal, 15*, 7–17.

Rutz, C., & Grawe, N. D. (2009). Pairing WAC and quantitative reasoning through portfolio assessment and faculty development. [Special issue on Writing Across the Curriculum and Assessment]. *Across the Disciplines, 6*. Retrieved from http://wac.colostate.edu/atd/assessment/rutz_grawe.cfm

Rutz, C., & Wilhoit, S. (2013). What is faculty development? In R. Malenczyk (Ed.), *A rhetoric for writing program administrators* (pp. 185–96). Anderson, SC: Parlor Press.

Salomon, G., & Perkins, D. N. (1989). Rocky roads to transfer: Rethinking mechanisms of a neglected phenomenon. *Educational Psychologist, 24*(2), 113–42.

Sapir, J. D. (1977). The anatomy of metaphor. In J. D. Sapir & J. C. Crocker (Eds.), *The social use of metaphor: Essays on the anthropology of rhetoric* (pp. 3–32). Philadelphia: University of Pennsylvania Press.

Schiffrin, D. (1987). *Discourse markers*. Cambridge: Cambridge University Press.

Schön, D. A. (1987). *Educating the reflective practitioner*. San Francisco: Jossey-Bass.

Schroeder, C. M. (2011a). Faculty developers as institutional developers: The missing prong of organizational development. In C. M. Schroeder & Associates, *Coming in from the margins: Faculty development's emerging organizational development role in institutional change* (pp. 17–46). Sterling, VA: Stylus.

Schroeder, C. M. (2011b). Identifying the factors that enable an organizational development role. In C. M. Schroeder & Associates, *Coming in from the margins: Faculty development's emerging organizational development role in institutional change* (pp. 111–42). Sterling, VA: Stylus.

Scott, T., & Inoue, A. B. (2015). Assessing writing shapes contexts and instruction. In L. Adler-Kassner & E. Wardle (Eds.), *Naming what we know: Threshold concepts of writing studies* (pp. 29–31). Logan: Utah State University Press.

Shuell, T. J. (1990). Teaching and learning as problem solving. *Theory Into Practice, 29*(2), 102–8.

Soliday, M. (2011). *Everyday genres: Writing assignments across the disciplines*. Carbondale: Southern Illinois University Press.

Sorcinelli, M. D. (2007). Faculty development: The challenge going forward. *Peer Review, 9*(4). Retrieved from https://www.aacu.org/publications-research/periodicals/faculty-development-challenge-going-forward

Sorcinelli, M. D., Austin, A. E., Eddy, P. L., & Beach, A. L. (2006). *Creating the future of faculty development: Learning from the past, understanding the present*. Bolton, MA: Anker.

Stenberg, S. J. (2005). *Professing and pedagogy: Learning the teaching of English*. Urbana, IL: National Council of Teachers of English.

Strober, M. H. (2011). *Interdisciplinary conversations: Challenging habits of thought*. Stanford, CA: Stanford University Press.

Sutton-Smith, B. (1997). *The ambiguity of play*. Cambridge, MA: Harvard University Press.

Tanis, D. J. (2012). *Exploring play/playfulness and learning in the adult and higher education classroom* (Unpublished doctoral dissertation). The Pennsylvania State University, State College.

Tarabochia, S. L. (2013). Negotiating expertise: A pedagogical framework for cross-curricular literacy work. *WPA: Writing Program Administration*, *36*(2), 117–41.

Tarabochia, S. (2016a). Gender in conversation: A case study of faculty talk about teaching writing. Presented at the International Writing Across the Curriculum Conference, Ann Arbor, MI. Retrieved from https://iwac2016.org/session-g/

Tarabochia, S. L. (2016b). Investigating the ontology of WAC/WID relationships: A gender-based analysis of cross-disciplinary collaboration among faculty. *WAC Journal*, *27*, 52–73.

Taylor, E. W. (2000). Analyzing research on transformative learning theory. In J. Mezirow (Ed.), *Learning as transformation: Critical perspectives on a theory in progress* (pp. 285–328). San Francisco: Jossey-Bass.

Taylor, K. (2000). Teaching with developmental intention. In J. Mezirow (Ed.), *Learning as transformation: Critical perspectives on a theory in progress* (pp. 151–80). San Francisco: Jossey-Bass.

Thaiss, C., & Porter, T. (2010). The state of WAC/WID in 2010: Methods and results of the U.S. survey of the International WAC/WID Mapping Project. *College Composition and Communication*, *61*(3), 534–70.

Thompson, J. L. (2009). Building collective communication competence in interdisciplinary research teams. *Journal of Applied Communication Research*, *37*(3), 278–97.

Timmermans, J. A. (2010). Changing our minds: The developmental potential of threshold concepts. In J. Meyer, R. Land, & C. Baillie (Eds.), *Threshold concepts and transformational learning* (pp. 3–19). Rotterdam: Sense Publishers.

Tisdell, E. J. (2003). *Exploring spirituality and culture in adult and higher education*. San Francisco: Jossey-Bass.

Tobin, K. (1990). Changing metaphors and beliefs: A master switch for teaching? *Theory Into Practice*, *29*(2), 122–27.

Toohey, K., & Waterstone, B. (2004). Negotiating expertise in an action research community. In B. Norton & K. Toohey (Eds.), *Critical pedagogies and language learning* (pp. 291–310). Cambridge: Cambridge University Press.

Tracy, K. (1995). Action-implicative discourse analysis. *Journal of Language and Social Psychology*, *14*(1–2), 195–215. https://doi:10.1177/0261927X95141011

Tracy, K. (1997). *Colloquium: Dilemmas of academic discourse.* Norwood, NJ: Ablex.
Tracy, K. (2002). *Everyday talk: Building and reflecting identities.* New York: Guilford Press.
Tracy, K. (2005). Reconstructing communicative practices: Action-implicative discourse analysis. In K. L. Fitch & R. E. Sanders (Eds.), *Handbook of language and social interaction* (pp. 301–19). Mahwah, NJ: Lawrence Erlbaum Associates.
Tracy, K. (2008). Action-implicative discourse analysis theory. In L. A. Baxter & D. O. Braithwaite (Eds.), *Engaging theories in interpersonal communication: Multiple perspectives* (pp. 149–60). Thousand Oaks, CA: SAGE Publications.
Trubek, A. (2005). Chickens, eggs, and the composition practicum. In S. I. Dobrin (Ed.), *Don't call it that: The composition practicum* (pp. 160–82). Urbana, IL: National Council of Teachers of English.
Tuitt, F. (2010). Working with underrepresented faculty. In K. J. Gillespie & D. L. Robertson & Associates (Eds.), *A guide to faculty development* (2nd ed., pp. 225–42). San Francisco: Jossey-Bass.
Tuomi-Gröhn, T., & Engeström, Y. (2003). Conceptualizing transfer: From standard notions to developmental perspectives. In T. Tuomi-Gröhn & Y. Engeström (Eds.), *Between school and work: New perspectives on transfer and boundary-crossing* (pp. 19–38). Boston: Pergamon.
Tuomi-Gröhn, T., Engeström, Y., & Young, M. (2003). From transfer to boundary-crossing between school and work as a tool for developing vocational education: An introduction. In T. Tuomi-Gröhn & Y. Engeström (Eds.), *Between school and work: New perspectives on transfer and boundary-crossing* (pp. 1–15). Boston: Pergamon.
University of Minnesota WEC Home Page. (n.d.). Retrieved from http://wec.umn.edu/
Van Manen, M. (1991). *The tact of teaching: The meaning of pedagogical thoughtfulness.* Albany, NY: State University of New York Press.
Van Manen, M. (2015). *Pedagogical tact: Knowing what to do when you don't know what to do.* Walnut Creek, CA: Left Coast Press, Inc.
Verbais, C. (2008). Incorporating play and toys into the writing center. In K. Dvorak & S. Bruce (Eds.), *Creative approaches to writing center work* (pp. 135–46). Cresskill, NJ: Hampton Press.
Villanueva, V. (2001). The politics of literacy across the curriculum. In S. H. McLeod, E. Miraglia, M. Soven, & C. Thaiss (Eds.), *WAC for the new millennium: Strategies for continuing writing-across-the-curriculum programs* (pp. 165–78). Urbana, IL: National Council of Teachers of English.

Vrchota, D. A. (2015). Cross-curricular consulting: How WAC experts can practice adult learning theory to build relationships with disciplinary faculty. *WAC Journal, 26*, 56–75.
Vygotsky, L. S. (1978). *Mind in society: The development of higher psychological processes*. M. Cole (Ed.). Cambridge, MA: Harvard University Press.
Waite, S. (2009). Becoming the loon: Performance pedagogy and female masculinity. *Writing on the Edge, 19*(2), 53–68.
Waldo, M. L. (1996). Inquiry as a non-invasive approach to cross-curricular writing consultancy. *Language and Learning Across the Disciplines, 1*(3), 6–22.
Walvoord, B. E., Hunt, L. L., Dowling, H. F. J., & McMahon, J. D. (1997). *In the long run: A study of faculty in three writing-across-the-curriculum programs*. Urbana, IL: National Council of Teachers of English.
Wardle, E. (2007). Understanding transfer from FYC: Preliminary results of a longitudinal study. *WPA: Writing Program Administration, 31*(1/2), 65–85.
Wardle, E. (2012). Creative repurposing for expansive learning: Considering "problem-exploring" and "answer-getting" dispositions in individuals and fields. *Composition Forum, 26*. Retrieved from http://compositionforum.com/issue/26/creative-repurposing.php
Wardle, E. (2013). What is transfer? In R. Malenczyk (Ed.), *A rhetoric for writing program administrators* (pp. 143–55). Anderson, SC: Parlor Press.
Wardle, E., & Downs, D. (Eds.). (2014). *Writing about writing: A college reader* (2nd ed.). Boston: Bedford/St. Martin's.
Welch, N. (1999). Playing with reality: Writing centers after the mirror stage. *College Composition and Communication, 51*(1), 51–69. https://doi.org/10.2307/358959
Willard-Traub, M. K. (2008). Writing program administration and faculty professional development: Which faculty? What development? *Pedagogy, 8*(3), 433–45.
Yancey, K. B. (1998). *Reflection in the writing classroom*. Logan: Utah State University Press.
Yancey, K. B. (2015). Learning to write effectively requires different kinds of practice, time, and effort. In L. Adler-Kassner & E. Wardle (Eds.), *Naming what we know: Threshold concepts of writing studies* (pp. 64–65). Logan: Utah State University Press.
Yancey, K. B., Robertson, L., & Taczak, K. (2014). *Writing across contexts: Transfer, composition, and sites of writing*. Logan: Utah State University Press.

Young, V. A., & Condon, F. (2013). Introduction: Why anti-racist activism? Why now? *Across the Disciplines*, *10*(3). Retrieved from http://wac.colostate.edu/atd/race/intro.cfm

Zakrajsek, T. D. (2010). Important skills and knowledge. In K. J. Gillespie & D. L. Robertson (Eds.), *A guide to faculty development* (2nd ed., pp. 83–98). San Francisco: Jossey-Bass.

Zhang, P., St. Amand, J., Quaynor, J., Haltiwanger, T., Chambers, E., Canino, G., & Ozias, M. (2013). "Going there": Peer writing consultants' perspectives on the new racism and peer writing pedagogies. *Across the Disciplines*, *10*(3). Retrieved from http://wac.colostate.edu/atd/race/oziasetal.cfm

INDEX

Ackerman, D., 109, 110, 140
Action-implicative discourse analysis theory (AIDA), 6, 22
Addison, J., 1
Adler-Kassner, L., 55, 76, 77, 101, 105
Anderson, P., 2
Andrade, A., 137
Andrus, J., 170
Anson, C. M., 2, 77, 128, 171
Apter, M., 110, 126
Artze-Vega, I., 156, 161, 166
Atwell, N., 101, 148
Austin, A. E., 157

Baillie, C., 76, 77, 78, 80, 98, 108
Barnett, R., 89, 98, 140, 141
Bartlett, L. E., 151, 152
Bazerman, C., 1, 4, 70, 88, 103, 131
Beach, A. L., 98, 157
Beach, K., 65
Bean, J. C., 160
Belanger, K., 1, 110, 111, 127
Belcheir, M., 55, 167
Belenky, M. F., 75
Berger, J. G., 89, 90, 98, 134, 150, 171
Bergmann, L. S., 70, 89, 106
Berlin, J. A., 8, 35
Bernstein, D. J., 157
Bethel, L., 1
Billig, M., 29
Bingham, C., 11, 167
Black, L. J., 5, 21

Boquet, E. H., 111, 142, 163, 165
Bowdon, M., 156, 161, 166
Bowman, J. R., 110, 135
Boyd, R. D., 79
Branch, K., 179
Bransford, J. D., 97, 142
Brennan, S., 55
Bridging dispositions, 139–40
Brooke, C., 87, 92, 131
Brown, A. L., 97, 131
Brown, S., 26, 109, 120–21, 131
Bruce, S., 111, 163
Bruner, J. S., 109
Bunnell, S. L., 157

Cameron, L., 114
Canino, G., 164
Carr, A., 87, 92
Carrithers, D., 160
Carroll, M., 111, 163, 165
Carter, M., 2, 54
Caswell, N. I., 156
Chambers, E., 164
Change, 25–26, 69–107, 175, 176, 177
  approaches to, 69–71
  assumptions about, 71–72
  discursive practice for pursuing, 175, 176, 177
  faculty as learners and, 73–106
  modeling, 104
  openness to, 101–3
  orienting to, 25–26
  threshold theory and, 76–106

transformative learning and, 69, 73–75
troublesomeness and, 78–98
Chavkin, T., 1
Clark, I. L., 76
Clary-Lemon, J., 170
Cocking, R. R., 97, 142
Collaborative research, 2
Collaborative teaching, 2
Collins, H., 53, 54, 56, 57, 66
Communication Across the Curriculum (CAC), 2
Comprone, J. J., 29, 70
Conceptually difficult knowledge, 87–90
Condon, W., 1, 2, 4, 72, 98, 99, 111, 163, 164, 165
Cox, M., 100
Craig, R. T., 22
Cranton, P., 73, 74, 75, 86, 142
Cross-curricular literacy (CCL) work, 1–28, 110–12, 145–73, 177
 cross-disciplinary faculty interactions in, 1–6, 151–54
 discourse-based studies of, 168–70
 expertise in. *See* Expertise
 methodology for, 6–28. *See also* Methodology for pedagogical ethic
 need for, 1
 pedagogical ethic for, 4, 145–73
 as pedagogical performance, 72–73, 151–54, 177
 role of change in. *See* Change
 value of play in, 110–12
Cross-disciplinary faculty, 49–67, 103–5, 155–57, 161–68
 applications of pedagogical ethic for, 155–57
 educating, 161–68
 inviting participation of, 52–67
 making learning visible for, 103–5
 urging acquiescence of, 49–52
Csikszentmihalyi, M., 26, 110

Dannels, D., 2
Data analysis, 22–28
Data collection, 21–22
Deep learning, connections of play to, 109–13
Deignen, A., 114
Denny, H., 162, 165
DeSanto, D., 2
Distributive consultancy model, 2
Dobrin, S. I., 168
Donis, K., 137
Dowling, H. F. J., 3, 71, 72, 99, 107, 170
Downs, D., 56, 87
Driscoll, D. L., 137, 142, 143
Dryer, D. B., 91, 131
Duckworth, E. R., 110, 142, 143
Dvorak, K., 111, 163

Earenfight, T., 160
Eddy, P. L., 157
Elbow, P., 7
Embedded writing fellows, 2
Embracing play (activity), 26–28
Emmons, K., 156, 161, 166
Entwistle, N., 140
Eodice, M., 2, 111, 142, 156, 159, 161, 163, 165, 166
Epistemic pedagogy, 8–9
Eriksson, A., 1
Estrem, H., 55, 76, 167
Evans, R., 53, 54, 56, 57, 66
Everyday life, orienting, 44–47
Expertise, 24–25, 29–68, 175, 177
 claiming, 29, 30–47
 dilemma of, 29–30
 discursive practice for negotiating, 175, 176, 177
 epistemological principles of, 37, 38–30
 everyday life and, 44–47
 expert networks and, 31–35
 expert techne and, 35–40
 framing as fitting response, 40–44

inviting participation and, 47–48, 52–67
methodological dimensions of, 36–37, 39
negotiating, 24–25, 29–30, 39–40, 66–67, 175
plotting, 53–56
pluralistic, 54
primary source knowledge and, 57–58
realist theory of, 53
rhetorical view of, 29, 30–31
sharing, 29, 47–67
urging acquiescence and, 47–48, 49–52
Expert networks, associating with, 31–40
pedagogical potential of, 35–40
Expert techne, establishing, 35–40
defined, 35–36

Faculty, 1–6, 73–75, 151–54, 158–61, 170–72
applications of pedagogical ethic for, 158–61
cross-disciplinary interactions among, 1–6, 151–54
as learners, 73–75
transformative learning of, need for studies of, 170–72
Faculty development, 2, 73–75
Farris, C., 70
Felix, S., 171
Finkelstein, N., 98
Fishman S. M., 71
Fitting response, 40–44
Flaherty, C., 158
"Foreign" or "alien" knowledge, 90–93
Fouquette, D., 1
Frivolity, rhetoric of, 124
Fulwiler, T., 29, 161

Gallagher, C. W., 7, 8, 9, 10, 11, 145
Garufis, J., 1
Gayle, B. M., 86

Geller, A. E., 2, 7, 111, 159, 163, 165, 169
Genre theory, 3
George, D., 1, 110, 111, 127
Gere, A. R., 4
Gilly, M. S., 75, 107
Globalization, in higher education, 1
Godbee, B., 21, 164, 165, 170
Gonzales, P., 66
Goodman, R., 171
Grabill, J. T., 131
Graduate student education, 165–68
Grawe, N. D., 2
Gray, P. M., 8
Grimm, N., 165
Grutsch McKinney, J., 156
Guiding ethic. *See* Pedagogical ethic
Gustafsson, M., 1

Habits of mind, 2, 145, 146–47
interdisciplinary, 2
reflexive, 146–47
Hall, R. M., 2, 164
Haltiwanger, T., 164
Haring-Smith, T., 2
Harrington, S., 2
Hart, C., 114
Hartelius, E. J., 24, 29, 30, 34, 35–36, 37, 40, 44, 47, 48, 49, 52, 59, 60, 66
Henderson, C., 98
Hernandez, A., 76
Hess, S. K., 156, 161, 166
Hillocks, G., 36, 92
Hofer, B. K., 137
Horton, M., 179
Huber, M. T., 72
Huckin, T., 170
Hughes, B., 162, 163, 164
Huizinga, J., 109
Hunt, L. L., 3, 71, 72, 99, 107, 170

Imaginary, rhetoric of the, 114–15
Inert knowledge, 83–87
Inoue, A. B., 88, 104

International Writing Across the Curriculum (IWAC) conference, 13
Iverson, E. R., 2, 72, 98, 99

Jablonski, J., 1, 3, 4, 11, 22, 29, 69, 70, 71, 112, 168, 179
Jackson, R., 156
Jacobs, C., 1, 3, 111, 127
Jacoby, S., 66
Johnson, M., 113, 114, 129
Jolly, A., 109
Jones, R., 29, 70
Jung, J., 151

Kameen, P., 7, 11, 25
Kane, P., 110
Kaufer, D., 1, 3
Kegan, R., 79, 171
Kerr, J. H., 110
Kinchin, I. M., 80
Kistler, R., 160
Knowledge, troublesome, 80–98
 conceptually difficult, 87–90
 "foreign" or "alien," 90–93
 inert, 83–87
 ritual, 80–83
 tacit, 94–98
Kolb, A. Y., 86
Kolb, D. A., 86
Koshnick, D., 76
Kuriloff, P. C., 1, 2

Lahey, L., 171
Lakoff, G., 113, 114, 129
Lamonica, C. C., 156, 161, 166
Land, R., 76, 77, 78, 79, 80, 94, 98, 99, 108
Langley, L., 86
Latta, M. M., 26, 110, 115
Learner's stance, maintaining, 148–50, 176
 discursive practice for, 176
Learning, connections of play to, 109–13

Learning transfer, 136–43
 debates about, 136
 dispositions conducive to, 137–43
 high-road, 137–38
 implications of play for, 136–43
LeCourt, D., 4, 71, 179
Lee, A., 7, 11, 28, 173
Leki, I., 100
Lerner, N., 96, 159
Lieberman, J. N., 110, 112
Lillis, T., 1
Liminality, 77–106
 play and, 108–9. *See also* Play
 postliminal stage of, 98–106
 preliminal stage of, 78–80
 stages of, 80–98
 troublesome types of knowledge and, 80–98
Liminal space, embracing play and, 108
Little, J., 1
Lord, B., 7
Low, G., 114
Lynch, P., 173

MacArthur, F., 114, 130
MacKenzie, I., 2
Magnotto, J. N., 2
Mahala, D., 4, 29, 70, 71
Majewski, J., 76
Malinowitz, H., 4
Manduca, C. A., 2, 72, 98, 99
Marshall, H. H., 114, 115, 129
Maslen, R., 114
Matchmaking, 62–64
Maule, J., 114
McCarthy, L. P., 1, 2, 3, 71
McConlogue, T., 1
McCune, V., 140, 159, 161
McGee, S. J., 1
McKinney, J. G., 156, 166
McLeod, S. H., 4, 70, 112
McMahon, J. D., 3, 71, 72, 99, 107, 170
McNair, L., 1, 110, 111, 127

Melamed, E., 89, 110, 112, 115
Melzer, D., 3, 168–69
Metaphor, as form of play, 114–20, 129–31
Methodology for pedagogical ethic, 6–28
   activities for, 24–28
   data analysis for, 22–28
   data collection for, 21–22
   methods for, 12–14
   institutions involved in study, 13–14
   participant overview for, 14–20
   theoretical framework for, 7–12
Meyer, J. H. F., 76, 77, 78, 79, 80, 94, 98, 99, 108
Mezirow, J., 73, 74, 75, 76, 86, 142, 145
Miller, sj., 141
Mitchell, S., 1
Moore, J., 76, 128
Mortenson, P., 7
Mullin, J. A., 2
Munby, H., 114, 129
Musolff, A., 114
Myers, J. G., 79

Napoleone, A. R., 179
Negotiating expertise, 24–25, 29–30, 39–40, 66–67, 175, 176, 177
Nelms, G., 156, 161, 166
Noddings, N., 47, 154, 167
Norgaard, R., 29
Nowacek, R. S., 21, 83, 145, 162, 163, 164, 169

Oncins-Martinez, J. L., 114, 130
Orienting to change (activity), 25–26
Ozias, M., 164, 165

Paretti, M. C., 1, 3, 4, 110, 111, 127, 168
Participation, inviting, 47–48, 52–67
   matchmaking technique for, 62–64
   pronoun use in, 60–62

Peake, K., 1
Pedagogical ethic, 4, 6–28, 145–73, 175, 176, 177
   applications for all faculty, 158–61
   applications for cross-disciplinary consultants, 155–57
   CCL conversations as pedagogical performance, 151–54, 175, 176, 177
   commitment to reflexive practice, 146–48, 175–76
   directions for future research, 168–72
   educating future cross-disciplinary consultants, 161–68
   implications for graduate student education, 165–68
   implications for writing center consultant training, 162–65
   maintaining learner's stance, 148–50, 176, 177
   methodology for, 6–28
Pedagogical performance, CCL conversations as, 72–73, 151–54, 177
Pedagogy, 7–12
   characteristics of, 8–12
   defined, 7
   epistemic, 8–9
   reflexive, 9–10
   relational, 10–12
Perkins, D., 77, 80, 81, 83, 87, 89, 91, 93, 94, 95, 98, 136, 137, 138, 139, 140
Piaget, J., 109
Piquer-Piriz, A. M., 114
Play, 26–28, 108–44, 147–48, 150, 153, 176, 177
   as adult phenomenon, 109–10
   cognitive functions of, 127–32
   connections to deep learning, 109–13
   discursive practice for embracing, 175–77
   forms of, 113–27

functions of, 127–43
   implications for learning transfer, 136–43
   lack of WAC/WID research on, 112–13
   learner's stance and, 150
   metaphor as, 113, 114–20, 129–31
   pedagogical performance and, 153
   properties of, 109
   reflexive practice and, 147–48
   relational functions of, 127, 128, 132–43
   silliness as, 113, 124–27
   storytelling as, 113, 120–24, 131–32, 133–35
   value in CCL work, 110–12
   worries about, 112–13
   in writing center scholarship, 111–12
Poe, M., 13, 164
Polanyi, M., 94
Popular understanding, 56
Porter, T., 1
Powell, K. M., 1
Practical grounded theory (PGT), 22
Preiss, R., 86
Primary source knowledge, 57–58
Prior, P., 83
Problem-exploring disposition, 138–39
Pronoun use, in inviting participation, 60–62
Pugh, M., 5

Qualley, D. J., 7, 9, 10, 26, 54, 55, 65, 74, 102, 141, 145, 148
Quaynor, J., 164

Rai, L., 1
Räisänen, C., 1
Randall, N., 86
Reflexive pedagogy, 9–10
Reflexive practice, 146–48, 175–76
   commitment to, 146–48
   discursive practice for, 175–76
   play and, 147–48
Reid, E. S., 55, 166, 167
Relational pedagogy, 10–12
Rhetoric of frivolity, 124
Rhetoric of the imaginary, 114–15
Ricketts, A., 99, 100, 101, 102, 104, 105, 106
Ritual knowledge, 80–83
Robertson, L., 22, 145, 171
Rogoff, B., 148
Roozen, K., 83, 88, 96, 103, 131
Rose, S., 87, 91, 100, 128
Rousculp, T., 165
Russell, T., 114, 129, 179
Rutz, C., 1, 2, 4

Salomon, G., 137, 138, 139, 140
Sanchez-Garcia, M., 114
Sapir, J. D., 131
Schiffrin, D., 113
Schön, D. A., 105, 146, 173
Schroeder, C. M., 157
Scott, T., 88, 104
Self-efficacy, 142–43
Shared experience, drawing on, 45
Shipka, J., 83
Sidorkin, A. M., 11, 167
Silliness, as form of play, 124–27, 133–35
   building relationships through, 133–35
Silver, N., 5
Situational frame, 7
Smith, J., 78
Soliday, M., 1, 3, 29, 169
Sorcinelli, M. D., 156, 159
Souvaine, E., 171
St. Amand, J., 164
Stanton, A. V., 75
Stanley, N., 114
Stenberg, A.-C., 1
Stenberg, S., 7, 8, 10, 11, 145
Storytelling, as form of play, 120–24, 131–32
   relationship building through, 123

Stout, B. R., 2
Stratton, P., 114
Strober, M. H., 2, 24, 160, 161, 172
Sutton-Smith, B., 114, 124
Swilky, J., 4, 29, 70, 71
Swofford, S. C., 5
Sylva, K., 109
Szysmanski, N., 160

Tacit knowledge, 94–98
Taczak, K., 22, 145, 160, 171
Tang, J. K., 164, 165
Tanis, D. J., 26, 110, 115, 120, 126, 131, 142
Tarabochia, S. L., 13, 22, 24, 170, 179
Taylor, E. W., 75
Taylor, K., 75
Textual analysis, 3
Thaiss, C., 1
Thompson, J. L., 24
Threshold theory, 76–106
  stages of liminality and. *See* Liminality, stages of
  troublesomeness and, 78–98
Timmermans, J. A., 79
Tinberg, H., 131
Tisdell, E. J., 75
Tishman, S., 136, 137
Tobin, K., 114, 130
Todd, Z., 114
Toohey, K., 60, 65, 66, 67
Tracy, K., 5, 6, 11, 13, 22, 23, 27, 120, 145
Transformative learning, 69, 73–75, 79–80, 98–106, 170–72. *See also* Change
  adult learning and, 73–74
  of faculty, need for studies of, 170–72
  multidirectional, 98–106
  nature and purposes of, 75
  as recursive process, 79–80
Troublesomeness, constructivist responses to, 78–98

Trubek, A., 167
Van Manen, M., 83, 106, 173, 180
Vaughan, C., 26, 109, 120–21, 131
Verbais, C., 111–12
Villanueva, V., 4, 13
Vrchota, D. A., 74
Vygotsky, L. S., 109

Waldo, M. L., 4
Walvoord, B. E., 1, 2, 3, 71, 72, 99, 107, 170
Wardle, E., 56, 76, 77, 83, 101, 105, 139, 147
Waterstone, B., 60, 65, 66, 67
Welch, N., 130
Wells, J., 137, 142, 143
Willett, G., 2
Willingness to learn, 137, 140–41
Willingness to offer, 140
Winberg, C., 1
Workshops, 2
Wright, J., 1
Writing Across the Curriculum (WAC)/Writing in the Disciplines (WID), 1–6, 31–47, 52–67, 71–72
  assessment methods of, 71–72
  conversations about, 1–2
  everyday life and, 44–47
  expert networks and, 31–35
  expert techne and, 35–40
  faculty development models for, 2
  fitting response and, 40–44
  historical overview of, 3–4
  inviting participation of disciplinary faculty in, 52–67
  need for, 1
  research in, 3–4
  traditional approaches to, 3–4
Writing centers, 111–12, 156, 162–65
  pedagogical ethic for, 156
  play in scholarship of, 111–12
  training of consultants in, 162–65
Writing Enriched Curriculum

Program (University of Minnesota), 2, 111
Writing in the Disciplines (WID). *See* Writing Across the Curriculum (WAC)/Writing in the Disciplines (WID)

Yancey, K. B., 22, 87, 145, 160, 171
Young, R., 1, 3, 164

Zakrajsek, T. D., 157, 166
Zhang, P., 164

AUTHOR

Sandra L. Tarabochia is an assistant professor in the Department of English at the University of Oklahoma where she teaches courses in composition, rhetoric, and literacy. Her work has appeared in *WPA: Writing Program Administration*, *Across the Disciplines*, and *WAC Journal*. She is a core researcher in the Writing Through the Lifespan Collaboration, and her current study of faculty writers was awarded a 2016–2017 CCCC Emergent Research/er Grant. Her research lives in the intersections of teaching, learning, and writing.

BOOKS IN THE CCCC STUDIES IN WRITING & RHETORIC SERIES

Reframing the Relational: A Pedagogical Ethic for Cross-Curricular Literacy Work
Sandra L. Tarabochia

Inside the Subject: A Theory of Identity for the Study of Writing
Raúl Sánchez

Genre of Power: Police Report Writers and Readers in the Justice System
Leslie Seawright

Assembling Composition
Edited by Kathleen Blake Yancey and Stephen J. McElroy

Public Pedagogy in Composition Studies
Ashley J. Holmes

From Boys to Men: Rhetorics of Emergent American Masculinity
Leigh Ann Jones

Freedom Writing: African American Civil Rights Literacy Activism, 1955–1967
Rhea Estelle Lathan

The Desire for Literacy: Writing in the Lives of Adult Learners
Lauren Rosenberg

On Multimodality: New Media in Composition Studies
Jonathan Alexander and Jacqueline Rhodes

Toward a New Rhetoric of Difference
Stephanie L. Kerschbaum

Rhetoric of Respect: Recognizing Change at a Community Writing Center
Tiffany Rousculp

After Pedagogy: The Experience of Teaching
Paul Lynch

Redesigning Composition for Multilingual Realities
Jay Jordan

Agency in the Age of Peer Production
Quentin D. Vieregge, Kyle D. Stedman, Taylor Joy Mitchell, and Joseph M. Moxley

Remixing Composition: A History of Multimodal Writing Pedagogy
Jason Palmeri

First Semester: Graduate Students, Teaching Writing, and the Challenge of Middle Ground
Jessica Restaino

Agents of Integration: Understanding Transfer as a Rhetorical Act
Rebecca S. Nowacek

Digital Griots: African American Rhetoric in a Multimedia Age
Adam J. Banks

The Managerial Unconscious in the History of Composition Studies
Donna Strickland

Everyday Genres: Writing Assignments across the Disciplines
Mary Soliday

The Community College Writer: Exceeding Expectations
Howard Tinberg and Jean-Paul Nadeau

A Taste for Language: Literacy, Class, and English Studies
James Ray Watkins

Before Shaughnessy: Basic Writing at Yale and Harvard, 1920–1960
Kelly Ritter

Writer's Block: The Cognitive Dimension
Mike Rose

Teaching/Writing in Thirdspaces: The Studio Approach
Rhonda C. Grego and Nancy S. Thompson

Rural Literacies
Kim Donehower, Charlotte Hogg, and Eileen E. Schell

Writing with Authority: Students' Roles as Writers in Cross-National Perspective
David Foster

Whistlin' and Crowin' Women of Appalachia: Literacy Practices since College
Katherine Kelleher Sohn

Sexuality and the Politics of Ethos in the Writing Classroom
Zan Meyer Gonçalves

African American Literacies Unleashed: Vernacular English and the Composition Classroom
Arnetha F. Ball and Ted Lardner

Revisionary Rhetoric, Feminist Pedagogy, and Multigenre Texts
Julie Jung

Archives of Instruction: Nineteenth-Century Rhetorics, Readers, and Composition Books in the United States
Jean Ferguson Carr, Stephen L. Carr, and Lucille M. Schultz

Response to Reform: Composition and the Professionalization of Teaching
Margaret J. Marshall

Multiliteracies for a Digital Age
Stuart A. Selber

Personally Speaking: Experience as Evidence in Academic Discourse
Candace Spigelman

Self-Development and College Writing
Nick Tingle

Minor Re/Visions: Asian American Literacy Narratives as a Rhetoric of Citizenship
Morris Young

A Communion of Friendship: Literacy, Spiritual Practice, and Women in Recovery
Beth Daniell

Embodied Literacies: Imageword and a Poetics of Teaching
Kristie S. Fleckenstein

Language Diversity in the Classroom: From Intention to Practice
Edited by Geneva Smitherman and Victor Villanueva

Rehearsing New Roles: How College Students Develop as Writers
Lee Ann Carroll

Across Property Lines: Textual Ownership in Writing Groups
Candace Spigelman

Mutuality in the Rhetoric and Composition Classroom
David L. Wallace and Helen Rothschild Ewald

The Young Composers: Composition's Beginnings in Nineteenth-Century Schools
Lucille M. Schultz

Technology and Literacy in the Twenty-First Century: The Importance of Paying Attention
Cynthia L. Selfe

Women Writing the Academy: Audience, Authority, and Transformation
Gesa E. Kirsch

Gender Influences: Reading Student Texts
Donnalee Rubin

Something Old, Something New: College Writing Teachers and Classroom Change
Wendy Bishop

Dialogue, Dialectic, and Conversation: A Social Perspective on the Function of Writing
Gregory Clark

Audience Expectations and Teacher Demands
Robert Brooke and John Hendricks

Toward a Grammar of Passages
Richard M. Coe

Rhetoric and Reality: Writing Instruction in American Colleges, 1900–1985
James A. Berlin

Writing Groups: History, Theory, and Implications
Anne Ruggles Gere

Teaching Writing as a Second Language
Alice S. Horning

Invention as a Social Act
Karen Burke LeFevre

The Variables of Composition: Process and Product in a Business Setting
Glenn J. Broadhead and Richard C. Freed

Writing Instruction in Nineteenth-Century American Colleges
James A. Berlin

Computers & Composing: How the New Technologies Are Changing Writing
Jeanne W. Halpern and Sarah Liggett

A New Perspective on Cohesion in Expository Paragraphs
Robin Bell Markels

Evaluating College Writing Programs
Stephen P. Witte and Lester Faigley

This book was typeset in Garamond and Frutiger by Barbara Frazier.
Typefaces used on the cover include Adobe Garamond and Formata.
The book was printed on 55-lb. Natural Offset paper
by King Printing Company, Inc.